CHANGING OUR MINDS:
Lesbian Feminism and Psychology

Celia Kitzinger & Rachel Perkins

Published by Onlywomen Press, Limited,
Radical Feminist Lesbian Publishers,
71 Great Russell St., London WC1B 3BN

Typeset by Columns, Reading, Berkshire, UK.
Printed and bound by Biddles, Great Britain.

ISBN 0906500–49–4 hardback
ISBN 0906500–47–8 paperback

British Library/Cataloguing-in-Publication Data. A catalogue
record for this book is available from the British Library.

Celia Kitzinger is a lecturer in the Department of Social Sciences at Loughborough University. Her previous books incluc *The Social Construction of Lesbianism* (Sage, 1987) and (with Su Wilkinson) *Heterosexuality* (Sage, 1993).
Rachel Perkins is a Consultant Clinical Psychologist at Springfield University Hospital, London. She has a particular interest in women and lesbians with serious ongoing mental health problems.

CONTENTS

ACKNOWLEDGEMENTS

Many lesbians and feminists have contributed to the arguments of this book. In particular, we are grateful to Naomi Weisstein and Phyllis Chesler, for their pioneering critiques of heteropatriarchal psychology, and to those many lesbian and feminist scholars who have written in opposition to purportedly "feminist" psychological practice and who have sought to develop ethical and political theory: especially Marilyn Frye, Sarah Hoagland, Sheila Jeffreys, Julia Penelope, and Janice Raymond. The anti-therapy articles and book reviews by Louise Armstrong, Pauline Bart, Caryatis Cardea, Joyce Cunningham, Anna Lee, Bonnie Mann, and Joan Ward were also very valuable to us.

Personal conversations with Marny Hall and JoAnn Loulan, and written exchanges with Laura Brown; Paula Caplan; Fox (Jeanette Silviera); Bev Jo, Linda Strega and Ruston; Renate Klein; Julia Penelope; Janet Powell; and Katherine Sender also sharpened our thinking. The members of the London Lesbian Anti-Psychology Group 'Psyching Us Out', (coordinated by Celia Kitzinger and Karen Ancill), also proved useful in developing our ideas, and we are grateful to everyone who took part. We also want to thank the many women and lesbians who prefer not to be named but who talked with us about both their good and their bad experiences of therapy.

Special thanks to Jenny Kitzinger, Sheila Kitzinger, and Sue Wilkinson all of whom read through various drafts of different chapters and made useful suggestions. In particular, Sue Wilkinson, as founding editor of the international journal, *Feminism and Psychology*, has created one of the few academic fora in which ideas such as those advanced in this book can be published and publicly debated.

Rachel would particularly like to thank Margot Jane Lidstone for the fifteen years of love, friendship and passionate argument we shared until Margot was killed in a cycling accident on 5th May, 1992. She had an enormous influence on my ideas. Thank you also to all those who propped me up and enabled me to cope, both in the period following Margot's death, and during the preceding depressive illness that left me unable to look after myself. I owe a great deal to Miriam Burke, Niki Duckworth, Julie Hollyman, Martha King, Sylvia King, Celia Kitzinger and Lilian Mohin; to my sisters Helen Needham and Katie George (especially Helen, who also had to put up with the piles of paper all over our flat); and to my parents, Marjorie and Paul Needham. I am also indebted to all those women and lesbians who have talked to me about their experiences of madness, and who have shaped my ideas about social disability; and to Jacky Bishop, Celia Kitzinger and Lilian Mohin who have helped and encouraged me to develop these ideas.

Celia would particularly like to thank Jacky Bishop, Sylvia King, Jenny Kitzinger, and Rachel Perkins for proving that lesbian community is more than an empty promise; Sheila Kitzinger, for being a wonderful mother and friend; Anna Livia, for her letters from America and her anti-psychology humour; and, most of all, and for far too much to list here, Sue Wilkinson, who continues to surprise me.

Finally, we are also both grateful to our editors, Karla Jay in New York, and Lilian Mohin in London, for their enthusiasm for this project.

We have developed the ideas expressed in this book in other publications as follows:
Chapter 1:
Kitzinger, Celia (1992), "The 'Real' Lesbian Feminist Therapist: Who is She?", *Feminism & Psychology* 2(2): 262–264.
Perkins, Rachel (1992), "Waiting for the Revolution – or Working for It? A Reply to Laura Brown and Katherine Sender", *Feminism & Psychology* 2(2): 258–261.

Chapter 2:

Kitzinger, Celia (1991), "Feminism, Psychology, and the Paradox of Power", *Feminism & Psychology* 1(1): 111–129.

Kitzinger, Celia (1987), "Heteropatriarchal Language: The Case Against 'Homophobia'", *Gossip: A Journal of Lesbian Feminist Ethics* 5: 15–20. Reprinted in Lilian Mohin (1993) (Ed), *An Intimacy of Equals: Lesbian Feminist Ethics*, London: Onlywomen.

Kitzinger, Celia (1993), Update on Homophobia in Lilian Mohin (1993) (Ed), *An Intimacy of Equals: Lesbian Feminist Ethics*, London: Onlywomen.

Chapter 3:

Perkins, Rachel (1991), "Therapy for Lesbians? The Case Against", *Feminism & Psychology* 1(3): 131–139.

Kitzinger, Celia (1991), "Mujeres, Psicologia e Ideologia", in Maria Jose Aubet (Ed), *Panel Discussions, IV Fira Internacional Del Llibre Reminista, Barcelona 19–23 de Juny de 1990*. Barcelona: Ajuntament de Barcelona.

Chapter 4:

Kitzinger, Celia (1992), "The Individuated Self" in Glynis Breakwell (Ed), *The Social Psychology of the Self Concept*, London: Academic Press.

Kitzinger, Celia (1993), The Psychologisation of Lesbian relationships: The case against 'merger' in Lilian Mohin (Ed), *An Intimacy of Equals: Lesbian Feminist Ethics*, London: Onlywomen.

Chapter 5:

Perkins, Rachel (1991), "Women with Long-Term Mental Health Problems: Issues of Power and Powerlessness", *Feminism & Psychology* 1(1): 131–139.

Perkins, Rachel and Sarah Dilks (1992), "Worlds Apart: Working with Severely Socially Disabled People", *Journal of Mental Health* 1(1): 3–17.

Perkins, Rachel (1992), "Working with Socially Disabled Clients: A Feminist Perspective", in Jane Ussher and Paula Nicolson (Eds), *Gender Issues in Clinical Psychology*, London: Routledge.

Perkins, Rachel and Celia Kitzinger (1993), "Lesbians Against Psychology: Madness, Social Disability and Access", *Lesbian Ethics* (in press).

Perkins, Rachel (1993), "Worlds Apart" in Lilian Mohin

(Ed), *An Intimacy of Equals: Lesbian Feminist Ethics*, London: Onlywomen.

Chapter 6:

Kitzinger, Celia (1993), "Depoliticising the Personal: A Feminist Slogan in Feminist Therapy", *Women's Studies International Forum* (in press).

We are grateful to Sheba Feminist Publishers for permission to quote from Audre Lorde (1980) *The Cancer Journals*, London: Sheba.

FEMINISM or PSYCHOLOGY

This is a book about why, as lesbians and as feminists, we think psychology is a bad thing. We wrote it for all lesbians and feminists who have ever used, or thought about using, psychological services, or who know another lesbian who does. If you have ever been in therapy, counselling or twelve-step programs, or know any lesbians or feminists who have, then this book is for you. We hope that it will also be read by psychologists and therapists (of all theoretical persuasions) who are willing to take a critical look at their theory and practice.

Many lesbians and feminists, while recognising the grosser abuses of psychology, are themselves involved in psychological or psychotherapeutic activities which they find personally valuable. Such readers will find arguments which we hope will lead them to reconsider and reevaluate this involvement. Many lesbians and feminists express a general discomfort about certain psychological approaches, without necessarily being able to articulate quite why. Some simply feel a shudder of distaste when they hear phrases like "healing your inner child" or "getting in touch with your real self". Others are dismayed by the proliferation of disorders from which women are now supposed to suffer, from codependency to lack of self-esteem. For these readers, we hope that the book will offer a clearer understanding of the problems of psychology.

Other lesbians and feminists have very specific concerns. Some are especially worried about abuses and exclusions in therapy: therapists who charge very high prices, or who have sex with their clients, for example. Many lesbians who talked to us wanted this book to focus on particular kinds

1

of psychology they thought were especially bad: "new-age psychology" (those books and audiocassettes of affirmations for self-renewal, positive visualisations for recovering adult children, and subliminal messages for sex and love addicts); academic psychology (particularly the post-modernist, deconstructionist variant); psychiatry; the codependency movement; twelve-step programs. We are concerned about all of these individual psychologies, but are pleased to find that they have already been criticised elsewhere. A special issue of *Lesbian Ethics* (1985) described instances of abusive lesbian therapists and the dangers of "new age" neofeminist psychologies have been analysed (eg Francis, 1991; Sethna, 1992; Wilkinson and Kitzinger, 1993). Feminist "reinterpretations" of Freud have been trenchantly criticised by Stevi Jackson (1983) and we ourselves have written critically about post-modernist academic psychology (Kitzinger, 1990a). Various self-advocacy groups comprised of mental health system survivors have produced articulate condemnations of psychiatric practice (eg Chamberlin, 1990); object relations theory has been dismissed as inadequate for feminists (Gardiner, 1987; cf Burack, 1992); twelve-step and codependency programs have been dissected by lesbian political scientist Betty Tallen (1990a, 1990b) (see also Kaminer, 1992); and Susan Faludi (1991) does an admirable job of analysing the role of groups for "women who love too much" in implementing the "backlash". All these analyses have been important in developing our thinking and forming our own ideas about the relationship between psychology and lesbian feminism. But in this book we have deliberately chosen not to attempt an analysis of each different type of psychology in turn, but rather to focus on what they have in common. We use the term "psychology" to cover the whole range of different theories about individual minds and behaviours; "therapy" is one application of "psychology" and it is one of those on which we focus most extensively in this book.

This is not a book about the different kinds of therapy available, nor do we make any attempt to argue that some are better, or more "feminist" than others. Unlike other critiques by lesbians and feminists, ours does not attack any one particular brand of psychology. Our aim is to draw attention to the political problems inherent in *the very idea* of "feminist therapy" or "feminist psychology". In responding to our arguments, some feminists have expressed "incredulity that Celia and Rachel ... had not taken into account ... the myriad *differences* between therapists, therapies and therapy consumers" (Anonymous, 1992, our emphasis). Another critic, commenting on an earlier exposition of our ideas (Perkins, 1991), says that "the lumping together of, for example, psychoanalytic and cognitive perspectives, renders the enormous differences between them insignificant, to a point at which the discussion of 'therapies' becomes meaningless" (Sender, 1992). We disagree. The reasons for our disagreement can perhaps be made most clearly if we draw a parallel. There are myriad differences between the dead animals people call "meat": but ethical vegetarians are not expected to compare and contrast the different methods of stockkeeping, transporting and killing various species of animals in defending their vegetarianism. Instead, the similarities between different species of dead animal are taken for granted, and debate focuses on the extent to which eating them is, or is not, compatible with feminism. Of course, some people may point out that the production of some kinds of meat (eg veal) involves particular cruelty and suffering (which is true), but as far as vegetarians are concerned that doesn't make the eating of other kinds of dead animal any more acceptable. In the same way, we are focussing in this book on the extent to which psychology is, or is not, compatible with feminism and although some kinds of psychology (eg Freudian) may be worse than others, that doesn't make other psychologies any more acceptable to us. We know a great deal about the "myriad differences" between various brands of psychology (our combined sixteen years in full-time higher education studying psychology taught us little else), but we see discussion of them in this context as diversionary. In the same way that the ethical vegetarian is unlikely to be drawn into detailed discussion about the differences between pork and beef, we choose not to engage with the differences between (for example) psychoanalysis and

3

cognitive therapy. Whatever the relative merits of one therapy over another, it is critical to address the central issue of whether a compatibility can be achieved between psychological therapy and feminist politics. Of course it matters *how* therapy is done – the perspective and approach taken; but it also matters *whether* therapy is done. Our central focus is on the relationship between (generic) psychology and (lesbian feminist) politics.

Unlike other critiques, which focus primarily on what is wrong with the psychology *men* do (eg Schofield, 1964; North, 1972; Chesler, 1972; Gross, 1978), we focus here on the psychology *women* do – in particular, the psychology practised by women who describe what they are doing as "feminist" and as "lesbian". This is not because we think they are worse than men. On the contrary, they are in many ways much better. Unlike other psychologists, some of whom still believe that lesbianism is a sickness, lesbian/ feminist psychologists are clear that it is not; and while many other psychologists have very little understanding of lesbian lives, lesbian/feminist psychologists often have first hand experience of the problems which lead lesbians into therapy – the trauma of coming out, problems in lesbian couple relationships, the difficulties of living as lesbian in an oppressive world. We focus on lesbian/feminist psychology not because we think it is worse than any other kind, but because this is the form of psychology that is now most influential for many lesbians in the English-speaking world. According to Diane Hamer (1990), an Australian lesbian feminist living in London, "more and more of us are going into therapy and it is almost becoming unfashionable not to be in it". In the United States of America, three out of every four lesbians has been "in therapy" at some point in her life (cf Lyn, 1991), often with a lesbian or feminist therapist, and popular psychology books by lesbians are best-sellers: Marny Hall's (1985) *The Lavender Couch*, a consumer's guide to psychotherapy for lesbians and gay men, was among the first trickles of what is now a swelling flood of lesbian/feminist authored psychology books which are making their way onto many of our bookshelves.

The development of lesbian and feminist psychologies marks a major shift. Twenty or so years ago, at the beginning of second-wave feminism, it was common for feminists and lesbians strenuously to oppose psychology as a discipline. Now, many feminists and lesbians enthusiastically embrace psychological models of understanding. We have "changed our minds" about psychology. Once feminists characterised it as "a pseudo-scientific buttress for patriarchal ideology and patriarchal social organisation" (Weisstein, 1970), "a myth to keep women in their place" (Hanisch, 1971). Writing back in 1970, Barbara Leon, a member of Redstockings, described how "the field of psychology has always been used to substitute personal explanations of problems for political ones, and to disguise real material oppression as emotional disturbance". In 1972, the groundbreaking book, *Women and Madness*, by Phyllis Chesler described and documented the extent of women's oppression at the hands of psychology and psychiatry.

Today, feminist writers are increasingly resorting to psychological explanations of political phenomena. This is true even of feminists who once spoke in very different terms. External structures of male supremacy are ignored, as feminists argue that responsibility for our subjugation lies, in the words of Ros Coward's book title, with "our treacherous hearts". "In society in general", says Ros Coward, "women have enough opportunity, experience, and dare I say it, power to demand great changes. But they have not done so ... The reasons for this passivity lie ... in aspects of the male and female psyche ... (Coward, 1992: 13). For Gloria Steinem (1992), too, it is now "Revolution From Within" which preoccupies. Her book of this title sold nearly 17,000 copies in hardback within the first three months of publication, and was number one on *The New York Times Book Review*'s best-seller list. Feeling better about oneself, raising one's self-esteem, loving one's inner child, surviving one's toxic family .... – all these self-improvement goals have taken over from the political goals of radical lesbian and feminist politics. These psychological approaches teach us to privatise, individualise and pathologise our problems as women and as lesbians, rather than to understand these difficulties as shared consequences of oppression. Whatever it pretends, psychology is never "apolitical". It always serves to obscure larger social and political issues (sexism, heterosexism, racism, classism), converting them into individual pathologies by an insistent focus on the personal.

Once, feminists and lesbians set ourselves up in clear opposition to psychology. Now, it seems, psychology is part of what passes for feminism. And so invidiously has it insinuated itself into feminist thinking, that many now speak in psychological language and use psychological concepts without any awareness that they are doing so. Psychological diagnoses are taking the place of political debate. Psychology's influence extends well beyond those in therapy and self-help groups: many lesbians and feminists now think about themselves in purely *psychological* terms. Psychology has replaced feminism as a way of understanding the world.

As feminists, we oppose psychological explanations. In this book we show how these translate political issues into private, individual concerns. We show how lesbian/feminist psychology is dangerous for lesbians because it is antifeminist. For that reason, although we are both lesbians, both feminists, and both fully qualified psychologists, we do not call ourselves "lesbian/feminist psychologists", nor do we believe that we can practice a psychology compatible with our lesbian/feminist goals.

"If it works, don't knock it"?

We've heard enough lesbians say "it saved my life" to feel almost guilty about challenging psychology. Many lesbians have told us that it was only with the help of therapy that they became able to leave an abusive relationship, to rid themselves of incapacitating fears and anxieties, or to stop alcohol or drug abuse. Through psychological intervention (self-help books, counselling, therapy) lesbians say they have become happier, more fulfilled, better able to cope with the demands of everyday life. Anything that saves women's lives, anything that makes women happier, *must* be feminist; mustn't it?

Well, no. First of all, it's possible to patch women up and enable them to make changes in their lives without ever addressing the underlying political issues that cause these personal problems in the first place. Psychology and feminism offer different and competing explanations for the same difficulties in our lives. Feminism tells us our problems are caused by oppression; psychology tells us they're all in the mind – at least, the important ones are, the ones we can do something about in therapy. "I used to bitch at my husband to do housework and nothing happened", a woman from Minnesota told Harriet Lerner (1990); "Now I'm in an intensive treatment program for codependency and I'm asserting myself very strongly. My husband is more helpful because he knows I'm codependent and he supports my recovery". For this woman, the psychological explanation ("I'm codependent and need to recover") was *more successful* than the feminist explanation 'women's work as unpaid domestic labour for men', (Mainardi, 1970) in creating change: with an idea of herself as sick, she was able to make him do housework. As Carol Tavris (1992) says, "women get much more sympathy and support when they define their problems in medical or psychological terms than in political terms". The codependency explanation masks what feminists see as the real cause of our problems – male supremacy. Instead we are told that the cause lies in our own "codependency". This is not feminism.

Second, although it's clear that today many women and lesbians are finding in psychology a source of support and meaning for their lives, this too is not feminism. Historically, women "have sought refuge in such institutions as the Catholic church or the military. But does that mean that these are institutions that should be fully embraced by feminists, let alone lesbians?" (Tallen, 1990a). Psychology, like a convent or the army, is "home" for many lesbians, but it is not a feminist institution, or one which feminists can support. As Anna Lee (1986) says:

> "Many wimmin have been strengthened by many things which we would probably not consider intrinsically good. It does not matter if one womon is helped, unless it helps wimmin free ourselves from the institutions which hold us down and keep us weak. . . In the black community, the availability of alcohol and

7

> heroin increases as black people increase our struggle
> against racism. Those who survive these addictions
> often become incredibly strong... I believe few would
> argue that alcohol or heroin are intrinsically good.
> Therapy must also stand on some intrinsic good,
> instead of parading a token womom who has become
> strong to prove its value."

We also need to think about what lesbians get out of
therapy when they say it helps them, and whether those
benefits can be provided in other ways. Often what's
important is having someone who will listen, someone
who won't dismiss your feelings, someone who will attend
to you, and bear witness to your experiences. Sometimes
the therapist is the only person who isn't frightened by a
lesbian's anger, despair or self-hatred. In the chapters on
"therapeutic lifestyles" (Chapter 3) and "mad lesbians"
(Chapter 5), we explore why and how, as feminists, we
need to become able to attend to each other in this way.
The fact that lesbians in distress have nowhere to turn for a
consistent source of support such as that which therapy
offers, is an indictment of our lesbian and feminist
communities.

Third, in fairness, we should listen not only to the voices
of those who say they have been helped by psychology, but
also to those who have found it of no use to them, or who
have found it damaging. Many people have tried self-help
books without success, and indeed, psychologists know
that these are not very helpful. Gerald Rosen is a
psychologist who wrote a book called *Don't be Afraid*
(1976). According to the blurb on the back cover, "In as
little as six to eight weeks, without the expense of
professional counseling, and in the privacy of your own
home, you can learn to master those situations that now
make you nervous or afraid". Unfortunately, if you read the
research on which this book is based (published in the
highly prestigious professional journal, the *Journal of
Consulting and Clinical Psychology*, Rosen et al, 1976), it
is quite clear that many readers of the book will be
disappointed: the *best* results Rosen achieved showed that
only half his readers will be successful, and in one of his
studies, *not one* person lost their fear of snakes! Gerald

Rosen now recognises, and is concerned about the "exaggerated claims" made for self-help books (including his own). He suggests that, when these fail, people should be encouraged to seek professional help instead.

And if they do, is the success rate any better? After reviewing research on how therapists relate to their clients, one leading researcher concluded that only one in four therapists is competent to practice (Meehl, cited in Gross, 1978: 43); another claims that two out of three counsellors are "ineffective or harmful", and psychiatrist Joel Kovel states: "It is impossible to avoid the observation that ineptitude is more the rule than the exception in the world of therapy" (both cited in Zilbergeld, 1983: 190). There are literally thousands of studies in the professional journals addressing the question, "does therapy work?". The results are not impressive. There is a lot of evidence that the people it works best for, are those who do not really need it in the first place. Consider, for example, this description, by a leading psychotherapist, of the "ideal" patient – the kind most likely to be helped by therapy:

> "Patients considered good prognostic risks tend to be young, physically attractive, well-educated, members of the upper-middle class, possessing a high degree of ego-strength, some anxiety impelling them to seek help, no seriously disabling neurotic symptoms, relative absence of deep characterological distortions or strong secondary gains, a willingness to talk about their difficulties, an ability to communicate well, some skill in the social-vocational area, a value system relatively congruent with that of the therapist, and a certain psychological-mindedness that makes them see their problems as emotional rather than physical."
> (Strupp, 1973)

The client most likely to feel that she has been helped conforms to the YAVIS model (Schofield, 1964): that is, she is young, attractive, verbal, intelligent and successful. Moreover, if these clients do "improve" (whatever we mean by that) with therapy, it's hard to know whether it's due to the therapy, or whether they'd just have got better over time anyway, with or without the therapy. Numerous different studies have shown that people kept on waiting lists for a few months after seeking therapeutic help do just as well as people who get to see a therapist immediately (Gross, 1978: 18–26). Moreover, for decades, psychologists have known that their treatments are likely to make some patients *worse*. In 1976 Suzanne Hadley and Hans Strupp at Vanderbilt University surveyed 150 experienced therapists and researchers and reported, "there is a real problem of negative effects". So-called "deterioration effects" (Bergin, 1967; Matarazzo, 1967) are very common: about 10% of patients in therapy get *worse*, compared with people who have similar symptoms but who are not getting any kind of therapy (Spitzer, 1980; Gross, 1978: 41).

Nonetheless, virtually every lesbian/feminist psychotherapist is firmly convinced that the vast majority of *her* patients are helped by therapy, and many lesbians have told us that, if you shop around, you can find a therapist who's right for you, and a therapy that works. We have listened to many lengthy catalogues of disappointments and failures endured before lesbians find "a therapy that works". At this point, we need to examine what, as feminists, we mean by "a therapy that works". The "solutions" we come up with when we frame our problems in psychological language tend to be different from those which emerge if we think in political terms. Often, psychological language leads to psychological "solutions" which may mask the underlying problems. For example, commenting on the use of the psychologised word "stress", Carol Tavris (1990) argues we should dump the word altogether:

> "If a friend says to you, 'Gee, I've been under a lot of stress lately', you could say, 'What a shame; have you tried relaxing, jogging, watching funny movies or taking naps?' But if your friend says, 'Gee, I have a problem; I'm about to be evicted because I can't come up with the rent,' you wouldn't dream of advising a nap, because it would be wildly inappropriate."

We need to be careful about allowing pychological thinking to obscure the causes of our problems, and the full range of different solutions to them.

As psychologists, we are sceptical of the idea that we have any special skills to help people. When therapy "works" in the sense of making people feel better (as it sometimes does), we need to ask why and how this is achieved, and whether there are other ways of achieving it. We need also to ask what the costs of therapy "working" might be. For example, nuclear power stations "work" in the sense that they produce electricity, but many of us would wish to balance this effectiveness against the costs of the production of millions of tons of highly toxic nuclear waste. We may well consider that, despite the short-term benefits accrued by the production of electricity, the costs are too high and that there are other ways of generating at least some of the electricity we need. In the same way, lesbian/feminist therapies may "work" in that they help individual women to survive and feel better. But the costs of this effectiveness to our lesbian politics and lesbian communities (including the individual lesbian members of those communities) must also be counted.

Thinking about the costs of something that (may) make you feel good is not always easy. In her analysis of the recovery movement, Wendy Kaminer (1992) points to people's unwillingness to think about psychology in any terms other than the way it makes them feel. Personal testimony – descriptions of feelings – has become a substitute for thinking. This book asks you to consider not only how therapy makes us *feel* but also the costs of psychology to our lesbian/feminist communities. It describes the high price paid by all of us, including those who have never been in therapy, for our acceptance of psychological ways of thinking.

How Did We Get Here? Our Personal and Political Journeys

We first met on October 26th, 1989, at a meeting of an informal group of lesbian psychologists, the London Lesbian Psychologists and Psychotherapists Discussion Group, shortly after it was formed. A small group of lesbian psychologists started the group after a presentation Celia gave on "Lesbian Theory" at the British Psychological Society Annual London Conference, and invited Celia to speak to the group on "The Perils and Paradoxes of being a

Lesbian Psychologist". In the discussion period afterwards, Rachel was a vocal participant; we argued, challenged each other, got excited by the possibilities of further discussions, arranged to meet for a meal, and became friends. We soon recognised our different but compatible skills and experience, and became involved in joint teaching, conference presentations, political activism, and, finally, began to write together. This book is a product of that collaboration.

In writing this book, we draw on our own experiences as lesbians, as feminists, and as psychologists. By the time we met we had already arrived separately at a realisation that psychology was, at best, problematic for feminism as a political movement: our collaboration enabled us to articulate our criticisms more clearly and comprehensively. Despite many commonalities between us, there are also, of course, differences and disagreements. In combining our individual views and experiences into the authorial "we", our identities as two separate authors is sometimes obscured. So here, at the beginning of our book, we want to chart our separate journeys, describing the different routes by which we arrived together at the starting point for developing our critique of lesbian/feminist psychology.

Celia

When I was seventeen, I was expelled from school for suspected lesbianism. I had developed a close and passionate relationship with a young woman teacher at the school, who later became my lover, but when I was summoned by the headmaster and castigated for spending "too much time" with her, and for not socialising with the boys, I had very little idea what I was being accused of. It was my mother who first made it explicit. Sweeping into the headmaster's office, cape swirling, eyes blazing, she demanded: "Are you accusing my daughter of lesbianism?" In response to his incoherent stammering and blushing, she affirmed that "what my daughter does in bed is nobody's business but her own".

I was lucky with my parents, both of them writers and activists. My mother, Sheila, who campaigns for women's rights in pregnancy and childbirth, has described how:

"My husband, Uwe, and I have always shared fundamental values – values which may, just possibly,
have had something to do with the fact that three of
our five daughters are lesbian feminists, and that we
both admire their strength and idealism. He knew
what it was it be a Jew as a child in Nazi Germany. We
first encountered each other (briefly) at a meeting
exploring the problems and challenges of building a
better society. We were anti-racist, anti-sexist, anti-
discrimination of any kind... We called for world
government, full employment, international understanding, world peace... We married in the Quaker
Meeting House at Oxford, and in doing so, we
committed ourselves not only to each other, but to
work for political and social change as equals, 'flying
wing to wing'." (Kitzinger, S. 1992: 440)
I grew up in a house full of political argument and
discussion: questions of right and wrong, both in personal
morality and in international politics, were fervently
discussed. As children we were all encouraged to be
independent and critical thinkers, to challenge taken-for-
granted understandings, to question and to take stands
where we believed we were in the right, "speaking truth to
power". Although our sex education began at an early age
and included all the details about menstruation. intercourse, conception, pregnancy and birth, I knew nothing
about lesbianism: "it just didn't occur to me that any of you
would be lesbian", Sheila told me, years later.

So when, at the age of seventeen, I began my first sexual
relationship with a woman, I was, despite my liberal
upbringing, desperately confused and unhappy. Searching
for information about my "perversion", and too frightened
to ask anyone, I read every psychology book I could find. It
was the early 1970s, and virtually all the books I consulted
told me I was sick. Lesbians were described as jealous,
insecure and unhappy, the sick products of disturbed
upbringings, suffering from unresolved castration anxiety,
or oedipal conflicts, pursuing other women in a futile
attempt to substitute a clitoris for a nipple as a result of
their unresolved weaning problems. I remember particularly two thin blue paperbacks which I read (concealed

13

inside a large glossy book on Byzantine art), behind a pillar in the public library: Donald West's (1968) *Homosexuality* and Anthony Storr's (1964) *Sexual Deviation*. Both books include sections on treatment, prevention and cure. Both paint a sorry picture of lesbian life. "No one in his right mind would opt for the life of a sexual deviant" says West, "to be an object of ridicule and contempt, denied the fulfilments of ordinary family life and cut off from the mainstream of human interests." According to Anthony Storr, "to be a woman who is loved by a man, and who has children by him, is the first and most important aim of feminine existence." Books like these made it very hard for me to identify myself as a lesbian: despite my sexual relationship, I stubbornly refused to believe that these theories applied to me or had any relevance to my own life; I held on to the belief that I *wasn't* a lesbian, that I *couldn't* be a lesbian – partly because there were very very few of them (and those that did exist were prisoners, prostitutes, or members of obscure tribes in New Guinea) and partly because I didn't want to dress up in a suit or bowler hat or smoke a pipe. Expulsion from school, exposure to such negative and stereotyped images of lesbians, and feelings of extreme isolation, led to a suicide attempt and subsequent hospitalisation. Three months in a mental hospital diagnosed as "immature" and "jealous of adult sexuality" contributed to my developing sense of psychology and psychiatry as dangerous and oppressive to lesbians.

Fired with the arrogance of youth, and the idealism instilled in me by my upbringing, I decided that what was needed was for lesbian psychologists to speak out about their experience and reform the discipline. So, I struggled through my exams (having left a second school under a cloud of disapproval, working in a bookstore during the day, and studying at night), obtained a place at Oxford University, and chose to study Experimental Psychology. There, much to my naive surprise, I soon discovered that lesbianism didn't feature on the syllabus – although I did learn a lot about rats. I also began to meet other lesbians and feminists, finished my degree as an out "lesbian feminist", and worked in a voluntary counselling organisation for lesbians and gay men for a couple of years before returning (in 1980) to do my doctoral research on lesbianism.

By that time, psychology had begun to change. The political campaigns of the early 1970s (cf Jay and Young, 1975) had borne fruit, and although *some* psychologists still stereotyped lesbianism as pathology, this was no longer the commonly accepted view of mainstream Western psychology. Instead, most psychologists saw lesbians as women who happen to prefer loving, sexual relationships with women. Modern psychology described lesbians as (generally) happy, healthy human beings, no different from heterosexual women except for their choice of sexual partner. Lesbianism was no more than "another way of loving"; we're just like heterosexual women except for whom we go to bed with. This new psychology said that people who are prejudiced against us are sick (suffering from "homophobia") and that lesbians need therapy – not to convert us into heterosexuals, but to help us become comfortable with our lesbian identities in a homophobic world. Although I might have welcomed this approach seven or eight years earlier, when I was just coming out as lesbian, my feminism had now taken me far beyond a point at which these were acceptable views. My Ph.D. thesis, and the book based on it (*The Social Construction of Lesbianism*, 1987) argues that this type of psychology destroys our politics, dilutes our values, and makes the task of building lesbian communities much more difficult. Those arguments are developed (with Rachel's help) much more fully in this book.

After completing my doctoral research, I found myself virtually the only 'out' lesbian involved in academic British psychology, and apparently unemployable. Lesbian academics in the USA have described being fired, not being rehired, and failing to gain tenure because of their insistence on putting lesbianism into the university curiculum (McDaniel, 1982): the situation in the UK was still more depressing. For a new lesbian Ph.D., in a reactionary discipline, prospects were bleak. I was unable to obtain an academic post for over a year, and was then grateful to be able to find short-term jobs in less prestigious departments (education, nursing studies) or in polytechnics with very heavy teaching loads. During these years I suffered two periods of clinical depression, for which antidepressants were prescribed, and, during the same years, sought counselling from three or four different sources (including lesbian/feminist) for difficulties in my long-term couple relationship.

In sum, I have been at the receiving end of both traditional psychiatry and its alternatives. I have first hand, painful experience of the effect of psychology's hetero-sexism on my own life and career prospects, and have failed to find in lesbian/feminist therapies a workable alternative, either as consumer or as service provider. Part of why such therapies failed to "work" for me was because they negated my political views. Non-judgmentalism, uncritical acceptance of everyone's "right to her own opinion", and the bland "validation" of everyone's dis-parate experience, does not seem either possible or desirable from a feminist perspective. Feminism is, after all, about choosing to prioritise certain values in our lives and trying to live according to those. Feminism is a *moral* framework; it involves making judgments about right and wrong, good and bad.

People often ask me how I can continue to work as a "psychologist" given my radical critique of the discipline. Today, I am employed, as an out lesbian, to teach social psychology and women's studies within a university social sciences department. I accept the label "psychologist" in so far as it means that I possess all the relevant occupational qualifications. I do not experience any contradiction between my job as a psychology lecturer and my radical lesbian feminist politics, because I do not teach "straight" psychology, nor do I teach "lesbian/feminist" psychology. Instead, I encourage students to approach psychology from a critical "sociology of science" viewpoint: here is a body of so-called knowledge; how is it constructed and by whom?; what rules determine (within different branches of psychology) what counts as "true" knowledge (scientific experiment? intuition? clinical judgment?); what social factors determine the adoption of some theories as "true"? what kinds of rhetoric do psychologists use to persuade us they are right? I do not see myself as teaching "psychology"; instead I am teaching "about psychology", and that is an important lesson to teach. I believe it is essential for students – especially feminist students – to learn "about" psychology so that they become able to challenge it, and to counter its detrimental effects on all our lives.

Rachel

My parents first met in their university debating society. Born in 1926, the year of the general strike, both came from socialist working class families who saw education as a means of change. Despite the privations, evacuations and conscientious objections of the war years, they managed to fund themselves to go to university, married soon after, and I am the eldest of their three daughters. I always describe myself as having had no "childhood". From as far back as I can remember, we were treated as little adults, expected to take part in long family debates, to consider the rights and wrongs of any situation, and to take responsibility for our actions. Family mealtimes were invariably accompanied by vigorous debates, and guests were often shocked at the volume and passion of these discussions which often left at least one of us in tears of righteous indignation.

My sixteenth year, in 1971, was eventful. I set up and became president of a Student's Union at my College of Further Education, joined the Trotskyist "International Socialists" (now the Socialist Workers Party), became involved in the Women's Liberation Movement (via Women's Voice and Working Women's Charter groups), and had my first sexual relationship with a woman. Two years later, after a woman lover left me for a man, I went to university still passionately involved in politics, but having decided that I was going to be heterosexual.

During my university years, I was involved in the campaigns of the day: abortion rights, day care for children, wages for outworkers in the pottery industry. I got married, which made me deeply unhappy, and got a degree in psychology and economics. By 1978, I was an out lesbian, involved in a variety of campaigns against male violence (anti-pornography and "reclaim the night"). My socialist feminist years ended with my expulsion from the International Socialists, as a member of the "left faction", and I moved from a Working Women's Charter Group to a Consciousness Raising Group – a decision much derided by my male left-wing colleagues who continually told me that direct action and banner-waving were the only valid form of politics, and that "the working class was not ready for lesbians". I had finally discovered lesbian/feminist politics! I was in a lesbian discussion group, and a university women's liberation group, and I was doing a Ph.D. on "The Nature and Origins of Boredom". During this period, I also met the lesbian with whom I was to share the next fifteen years of my life, initially as a lover and subsequently as my closest friend and confidante, Margot Jane Lidstone.

Both my lesbian/feminist, and my earlier socialist feminist, politics lead me to grave suspicions of psychology. Both ingrained in me the principle that "the personal is political" – a notion entirely at odds with the psychology I studied. Despite these suspicions, I began my clinical psychology training after finishing my doctorate, in 1980. I cannot now remember all the reasons for doing this, but I was feeling a growing concern about feminist theories of madness. The accepted wisdom seemed to be that madness was an invention designed to discredit those who deviated from patriarchal norms. I knew the arguments well and expounded them in many forums, yet I had niggling doubts.

My cousin is autistic, so I had grown up watching the progress of someone who doesn't fit in being derided and excluded, and the battles of the family to ensure him access to school and work. At my secondary school, two of the fifteen children in my class grew up to become lesbian: myself, and a girl who was then my close friend. We used to play in the lacrosse team together, but when I left school in 1971 I lost contact with her. Some years later, I found out that her life had been dramatically transformed by the illness they call "schizophrenia" (we quote some of her experiences later in this book, in Chapter 5). I tried to talk about madness (serious disabilities of thought and feeling), and my concerns about lesbian/feminist therapy, in feminist circles, but soon found that these ideas met with anger and hostility. I was accused of destroying a lesbian psychology discussion group, and called "oppressive" for denying lesbians the feminist therapy they need (although, clearly, I have no special powers to prevent anyone from engaging in therapy). I have been accused of collaborating with heteropatriarchal psychiatry in arguing the need to theorise severe disabilities of thought and feeling more adequately. It was therefore a great delight to me when I met and began to work with Celia, who welcomed discussion of these issues.

I have always been "out" as a lesbian within clinical psychology, and have never seen my clinical practice as an attempt to change, through therapy, people whose strange beliefs and behaviours render them unacceptable. Although I am a trained therapist, who has been involved in the training of other therapists and counsellors, I have used these opportunities critically to review the political implications of psychotherapy (Perkins, 1991a, 1992b). In my work for the British National Health Service I do not do therapy. I am involved in setting up community based alternatives to the old long-stay psychiatric institutions in which so many have been incarcerated for so long – trying to ensure that no-one has to call such an institution 'home'. As lecturer, researcher, trainer and practitioner I am engaged in ensuring that those who have hitherto been, or would otherwise be, incarcerated, have the help and support they need to live outside hospital. Ensuring, for example, that they have the benefits to which they are entitled, somewhere to live and help to do ordinary day to day tasks such as shopping, cooking, getting out and about – the rights that any other citizen might expect. The lack of a relationship between this and the psychology I learned as a trainee has not gone unnoticed by my colleagues: as my last 'Head of Department' said to me "What you do isn't psychology, Rachel, it could be done by any intelligent person".

One of our concerns about psychology, a concern which runs throughout this book, is the way in which feminist political discussion is increasingly replaced by psychological diagnosis. That is, when one lesbian presents an argument or opinion with which another lesbian is in disagreement, she is likely to be told that her beliefs mirror her personal pathology. Instead of responding to the argument as such, the hidden psychological "causes" of her belief are probed. Our own anti-psychology arguments are often psychologised in this way. For example, therapist Marny Hall (in Hall et al, 1992), has expained our "self-righteous moral fervour" in terms of underlying "needs" to armour ourselves. Whereas we claim to hold certain beliefs on the basis of rational thought and consideration of alternatives, Marny Hall suggests that we adhere to these beliefs because, in some psychological sense, we "have" to. Psychologising involves a refusal to engage in a discussion of the explicit politics presented, and a reflection instead on the psychological characteristics of the presenter.

Opponents of psychology, ourselves included, are often subjected to two contradictory psychologisations. One is the accusation that we are especially "together" and "sorted out" lesbians, more mentally healthy than most, specially protected from and untouched by the stresses, strains and life tragedies of ordinary folk. Our criticisms of therapy are then dismissed as irrelevant to the lives of "ordinary" lesbians: imagining that we have superhuman psychological strengths and abilities ourselves, other lesbians sometimes accuse us of failing to appreciate the neediness and desperation of our lesbian sisters. The second psychologisation is in direct contradiction to this. We are told that our anger about therapy, and our hostility to psychology, is evidence of our own deep-seated denials and repressions. We are supposed to be rigidly "in defence" against the awful realisation of our own personal inadequacies: we need therapy to sort ourselves out! For example, when Beth Freemann wrote a critical article about Alcoholics Anonymous which appeared in *off our backs* she was accused of having written it only because of her own "unexamined addiction" (cited in Tallen, 1990); and feminist therapist Joanna Ryan (1988: 106) claimed that the belief that to be in therapy is "self-indulgent" is simply "a projection on to therapy of the parts of ourselves we feel to be most unacceptable." In the process of developing our anti-psychology arguments, we have often been subjected to psychological diagnoses like these. They are made, we think, not because people are actually interested in whether or not we are mentally "healthy", but as a way of discounting our arguments. When critics speculate as to our psychological (mal)functioning, as purportedly revealed in our political arguments, they refuse to engage with those arguments in feminist terms.

We hope that our autobiographical accounts can be read as revealing not only our privileges (especially in terms of our family backgrounds), but also our ordinary human and lesbian suffering. Our privileges have not shielded us from attempted suicide, hospitalisation in a psychiatric institution, anti-lesbian discrimination, marriage, and normal human misery. More recently, during the course of writing this book, we have both confronted major losses: for Celia, the break-up of a seventeen-year lesbian couple relationship; for Rachel, the death of her closest friend of fifteen years. Most saliently in terms of the arguments of this book, we have also both had to cope with the emotional, practical, and political implications of Rachel's personal experience of madness.

Rachel

For 12 years I have been a "service provider" and most of this book was written from that perspective. Recently my world was turned upside down by madness. I experienced a severe depressive illness that left me unable to work, read, drive, or even look after myself properly, for over four months. I stopped menstruating, lost my appetite, was unable to sleep, and found myself unable to think clearly. My thoughts slowed down to the extent that I was unable to follow what people said to me, unable to concentrate on anything for more than a very short time, and was overwhelmed with a sense of hopelessness that seemed enormously alien to me. I was appalled and frightened by my lack of control. I often thought about killing myself, and was only prevented from doing so by the belief that I was ill and would get better. After six weeks of being unable to work, my dearest friend, Margot, who was staying in my home and looking after me at the time, was killed in a cycling accident.

21

I can now look at my previous writing about disabilities of thought and feeling through the eyes of someone who has had a glimpse of what these mean. The awful experience of a depressive illness has allowed me to elaborate some of my ideas (see Perkins and Bishop, forthcoming). I did not realise how frightening it is to be so out of control. I watched myself behaving in ways that seemed alien to me, seeing the anger and pain I generated in those around me, but was powerless to stop. For months I was appalling company, all too often engendering in my friends the same sense of frustration and hopelessness that I felt myself. Throughout this period I have refused any form of "therapy", although I have found useful the antidepressant drugs prescribed by a psychiatrist. It is my friends who have helped and supported me, looking after me in shifts. Without them, I would have been admitted to a psychiatric hospital.

I used to talk rather apologetically about lesbian community – as if it were a good idea that didn't really exist. People told me that my stand against therapy was all very well, but in the absence of lesbian community, it was a necessary resort (Brown, 1992; Sender, 1992). My experience has shown me that I am indeed part of a lesbian community. Others have looked after me, have refused to be scared off by my distress and disturbance, have completed work I was no longer capable of doing, and have helped me to function and contribute where I could. I do not pretend that my experience is in any way "typical", but there is nothing special about me, or the depressive illness I have suffered. I was fortunate to receive such help from my lesbian community, and undoubtedly, others are less fortunate. Yet my experience of providing help to others, and of receiving it myself, confirms my belief that our communities *can* accommodate the reality of madness without recourse to psychology.

In sum, it is possible to dismiss our arguments by psychologising them away in a variety of ways. We have been "mad", depressed, disturbed, unhappy, crisis-ridden and hospitalised – and therefore our crazy ramblings should not be taken seriously. Alternatively (or in addition), we are privileged middle-class, relatively affluent, professionals – and therefore our elitist arguments should not be taken seriously. We think it is diversionary (and not very interesting) to focus on whether we, as authors, are more or less psychologically wounded than are other lesbian/feminists. While our personal experience has, of course, been influential in forming our ideas, we hope that readers will resist speculations as to our psychological motives, unconscious desires, and repressed inner children, and will engage instead with the substantive content of our arguments. We would welcome *political* discussion and debate of all the issues we raise here.

The Lesbian/Feminist Therapist: Who is She?

We focus in this book on criticising lesbian/feminist psychology, and, in particular, therapy. We use the terms "lesbian therapy" and "feminist therapy" to mean those therapies provided by psychologists or psychotherapists who publicly identify themselves as "lesbians" and/or "feminists" and who describe themselves as offering psychological help or therapy which is rooted in lesbian and/or feminist understandings of the world.

We recognise that, depending on the criteria one applies, some "lesbian/feminist therapists" are in fact *not* lesbian, *not* feminist and *not* therapists. A few feminist therapists explicitly state that they are not themselves lesbian and write of how much they have learned from their lesbian clients (eg Siegel, 1985). Many therapists working with lesbians identify themselves as bisexual. For example, Tina Tessina, a licensed therapist in Long Beach, California who has written a book about lesbian and gay male relationships, says she is "bisexual" (Tessina, 1989: 5), and reading through the "notes on contributors" in the Boston Lesbian Psychologies Collective (1987) book, it is a little surprising to find how few identify themselves as lesbians. Sex therapist Margaret Nichols, who has two chapters in the collection on sex therapy with lesbian couples, describes herself as "bisexual with a gay consciousness"; Lucida Orwoll is "active in the Boston Bisexual Movement"; and Karla Jackson Brewer "lives in New York

23

City with her husband Gary". According to sex therapist JoAnn Loulan (1984), "sometimes, those of us who have seen ourselves as lesbians become sexually involved with men. . . For some lesbians sex with men is a wonderful adjunct to their on-going sexual relating to women". Although it is not clear that JoAnn Loulan intends to include herself amongst those for whom "sex with men is a wonderful adjunct to their on-going sexual relating to women" (and comments she has made elsewhere might suggest that she does not), this remark certainly supports Linda Strega and Bev Jo's (1986) radical criticism of JoAnn Loulan's book:

> "We object to someone who, by our and many other Lesbians' definition, is *not* a Lesbian putting out a book with the title 'Lesbian Sex' in which very definite statements are made about what Lesbians do. (Interestingly, 'Sapphistry: The Book of Lesbian Sexuality' is not by a Lesbian either, but is by a woman who is also sexual with men: Pat Califia.)"

Overall, it is clear that not all "lesbian/feminist therapists" are themselves lesbian.

Neither, according to some critics, are they all feminists. Again, as with the term "lesbian", we run into definitional problems: who gets to define who is to count as a "real" feminist? We *could* argue that, by definition, anyone who practices psychotherapy is not a feminist (no "real" feminist would engage in such an individualising and privatising exercise), but we don't think this is very helpful. Rather, we explore (in the next section) how, in the attempt to render feminism and therapy compatible, therapists (and clients) are forced to redefine feminist goals.

There is no one "feminist therapy", but rather a huge range of models which have been used within a "lesbian" and/or "feminist" framework. Lesbian/feminist therapists borrow male theories, with minor adaptations along with way. Often they make no attempt to disguise the "borrowing". Sex therapist Margaret Nichols, in the book *Lesbian Psychologies* (1987a) calls one of her chapters, "Doing Sex Therapy with Lesbians: Bending A Heterosexual Paradigm to Fit a Gay Lifestyle". In the Women's

Therapy Centre book, *Living with the Sphinx*, feminist therapist Sheila Ernst attempts "A feminist re-reading of [Donald] Winnicott". Lesbian psychotherapist Marny Hall (1985: 53) has produced a "Consumer's Guide to Psychotherapy for Lesbians and Gay Men", in which she presents a chart outlining what's available: every single one of the approaches she lists was invented by a man: client-centered therapy (Carl Rogers), Gestalt therapy (Fritz Perls), Transactional Analysis (Eric Berne), Rational-Emotive therapy (Albert Ellis), psychoanalysis (Carl Jung or Sigmund Freud), cognitive therapy (Aaron Beck), behaviour modification (John Watson). One approach Marny Hall doesn't mention, which is also very popular, especially in the various writings of the London Women's Therapy Centre, and in the collection produced by the Boston Lesbian Psychologies Collective (1987) is object relations theory, invented by Douglas Fairbairn.

Discussions amongst lesbians and feminists often revolve around which type of therapy is "best" or "most feminist". It is not our intention to engage in such discussion here. Many lesbians and feminists have published critiques of particular kinds of psychology: cognitive therapy (Perkins, 1991a), Rogerian therapy (Waterhouse, 1993), twelve step programs (Tallen, 1990a), "codependency" treatments (Tallen, 1990b; Gomberg, 1989, Brown, 1990b) and so on. Many (though not all) of these critiques are written by therapists promoting their own brand of therapy in preference to that they criticise. "Bad" or "unfeminist" therapies are used for contrast effect to sell "truly feminist therapy". Even when this is not the intention of the author, readers of such critiques often draw such conclusions for themselves. So, for example, when we have talked about the dangers of cognitive therapy, our audience has often been persuaded by our arguments, but then gone on to extol twelve step programs. When we have spoken of the anti-feminism of twelve step programs, those of our audience who agree have then argued in favour of co-counselling groups. Psychology has spawned so many different therapies that critiques of any one of them leave the vast bulk unscathed. The sheer diversity of therapies available is used to deflect criticism. Criticising one therapy from the perspective of another ensures that all debate is contained within the terms that therapy itself lays down. In focussing on the relative merits and demerits of different therapies, it is easy to miss the features they have in common. Our aim is to step outside the frame of psychology, and to address these issues politically. While individual criticisms made in this chapter apply more clearly to some brands of therapy than to others, no therapies are exempt. Our aim is to address the underlying principles shared by *all* therapies and to show that these are dangerous and damaging for lesbian politics.

Finally, some critics attack "lesbian/feminist therapists" for not being real *therapists* – that is for not having the appropriate academic and professional qualifications. Some of this criticism comes from male psychologists anxious to defend the status of the discipline. Some of it comes from other lesbians, albeit with some scepticism about the value of such qualifications in the first place.

"To call yourself a 'therapist' in New York State . . . you have to have certain degrees in psychology. Several of the therapists here have degrees all right, but in English, art, history, etc. . . Don't get me wrong: I'm not for qualifications in the legal or educational sense of the word. Twenty years of Freud and Jung will probably just rot your brain. However, I like to know what I'm getting. . . . If she's a doctor, but a doctor of botany, I should know that because I'm not a plant. If she's on welfare for insanity, as is one counselor I know of, I should know that. Only with adequate information can you make a rational choice. You may still want to choose the woman judged insane by the State because that may mean she's the sanest person around, but you should know what you are paying for." (Jay, 1975: 207–8)

In fact, the lesbian/feminist therapists we cite are usually well-endowed with the proper degrees and professional qualifications. The contributors to the Boston Lesbian Psychologies Collective book (1987), for example, hold among them at least eight Ph.D.s in psychology, ten "masters" in relevant disciplines, and have taught psychology at such institutions as the University of Washington, the

University of Maine, CUNY, Rutgers University, and Smith College. Even the much less academic "pop-psychology" books are often written by authors with impeccable credentials: Marny Hall (1985), Tina Tessina (1989), Merilee Clunis and Dorsey Green (1988), are all licensed therapists with Ph.D.s in psychology, and Lynne Namka (1989) has an Ed.D. and is a certified psychologist. (The different labels with which lesbian/feminist mental health practitioners describe themselves ["therapists", "psychotherapists", "psychologists", "clinical psychologists", "counsellors", "analysts" etc] reflect in part the nature of their professional qualifications, and in part their therapeutic orientation. For further information about the meaning of all these degrees and qualifications in the USA, see Hall, 1985: 86–89; in the UK, the British Psychological Society has produced an explanatory leaflet.)

In any event, the fact that some lesbian/feminist therapists have *not* been awarded certificates from hetero-patriarchal institutions is not the problem. As Laura Brown (1984) describes, *achieving* such awards is itself part of the problem:

> "For myself, as for other lesbian feminist therapists, professional training carried a somewhat schizophrenogenic [*sic*] air. I was simultaneously becoming expert in a perspective that had traditionally devalued women, and planning to return, once trained, to a community where valuing women was the highest ethical statement that could be made."

There is no guarantee that lesbians' ability or willingness to achieve such qualifications makes them more suitable as therapists for other lesbians. We are not asking for better qualified therapists. We are asking for an end to therapy altogether.

When we (and others) have criticised lesbian/feminist therapy, one common response is that lesbian/feminist therapy would be just fine, if only the women who practised it were *genuine* lesbians, *genuine* feminists and/ or *genuine* therapists. The problem, people tell us, is all these charlatans in our midst. The feminist therapists who aren't really lesbian ... the lesbian/feminists who aren't properly qualified to be therapists ... the lesbian therapists whose feminism is deeply suspect. We think this argument is an attempt to silence criticism – to cling to the false hope that a "lesbian/feminist therapy" is indeed possible.

For example, feminist psychologist Paula Caplan (1992), offers a carefully muted criticism of therapy in which she claims that "one part of what all of this is about is fake feminist therapists giving genuinely feminist therapists a bad name". Similarly bent upon rescuing the chimera of a "truly lesbian/feminist therapy" Laura Brown responded to our critique (Perkins, 1991a) by suggesting that the therapists criticised are not truly feminist but are "liberal and well-meaning therapists who do not have a feminist political analysis or who hold a reformist perspective on feminism" (Brown, 1992). They engage, she says, in "distortions of feminist therapy". Like Paula Caplan, Laura Brown invokes the spectre of "fake feminist therapists":

> "Because the term 'feminist therapy' has not been precisely defined, either in North America or else-where, there is a good deal of fuzziness around what we mean when we speak of such practice; often women therapists who support the general ideals of reformist feminism will describe themselves as feminist therapists although they lack an integration of feminist analysis into their work." (Brown, 1992).

We wonder who she means. The article to which she is responding cites that leading figure in feminist cognitive behaviour therapy for lesbians, Christine Padesky. Surely Laura Brown doesn't mean to accuse her of being a well-meaning reformist liberal? Not only does Christine Padesky clearly identify herself as a feminist therapist, she also trains other feminist therapists. One of her recent training seminars was called "Cognitive Therapy As Feminist Therapy: Combining Empirical Effectiveness with Political Correctness", and aimed to teach therapists "egalitarian methods for empowering women by teaching skills to overcome depression, panic attacks etc. . . [and] methods to enhance affirmative psychotherapy for lesbians." It seems unlikely that Laura Brown is refering to the Boston Lesbian Psychologies Collective when she writes of "distortions of feminist therapy", as she is a contributor to their book, *Lesbian Psychologies*. It seems equally unlikely that she means to accuse the therapists working at the London Women's Therapy Centre of not being "genuine" feminists, as they work outside the National Health Service and not for "an agency of a growingly heterosexist conservative government". We are at a loss to know which "feminist therapists" she wishes to disqualify.

In sum, the therapists we refer to describe themselves as "feminist therapists" and/or are widely accepted as such by their clients and readers. Arguments about who is and isn't a "genuine" feminist simply distract attention from our criticism of the whole notion of "feminist therapy".

Focussing our Critique

This book is not a critique of heteropatriarchal psychology. Nor is it (primarily) a critique of *heterosexual* feminist psychology, although some of the feminist psychologists we quote are – as far as we know – heterosexual. We have included reference to the theories and therapeutic practice of heterosexual feminists only when we see their work as having been influential for lesbians. This means we have not included some of the easiest targets for radical feminist criticism: heterosexual feminist psychologists who do therapy with heterosexual couples to help them sustain their heterosexual relationships, for example (see DeHardt, 1992), or those who help women sexually abused as girls to learn to "trust" and have sex with men (see Kitzinger, J, 1992). Many lesbians are suspicious of heterosexual feminist psychology such as this, and we are pleased that it is increasingly coming under attack. Here, however, we have drawn on heterosexual feminist psychology only when it appears to us that many lesbian/feminists have incorporated it into their own thinking – as for example with the work (in the UK) of the London Women's Therapy Centre. On the whole, however, our focus is on that psychology which describes itself as both feminist *and* lesbian. In general, we use the descriptor "lesbian/feminist psychology", meaning psychology which claims to be, or is widely accepted as, either lesbian, or feminist, or both, and which appears to us to have been influential on lesbian/ feminist communities.

Most of the psychologists we cite are North American: this is because most of the world's mental health practitioners inhabit that small portion of the globe. North America is the capital of psychology, with more professional therapists than librarians, firefighters or mail carriers, and twice as many therapists as dentists or pharmacists. Writing in 1983, Bernie Zilbergeld said:

"Of the estimated 90,000 psychiatrists in the world, a third are Americans. Half of the 4,000 members of the International Psychoanalytic Association practice here. It is said that New York City has more psychoanalysts than any European country. And far more than half of all clinical psychologists in the world are Americans."

These figures are out of date only in that the total numbers have dramatically increased over the last ten years; but it is still true that psychology is a rampantly North American product. Moreover, only in North America has lesbian/feminist psychology established a secure footing for itself, and only there do both the "psychology of women" *and* "lesbian/gay psychology" have formal recognition within a national professional body. Lesbian/feminist psychology as it exists in other countries is heavily dependent on imports.

In the UK, despite the London Women's Therapy Centre, and various earlier groupings of women in psychology, the "psychology of women" only achieved professional recognition in 1987 (Wilkinson, 1990), and the contribution of UK lesbian/feminist psychologists to the total output of lesbian/feminist psychology remains relatively small. Perhaps because psychology has not (yet) entirely transformed British lesbian/feminist politics, we are, as British feminists, in a better position to see its dangers. North American lesbian/feminists are often so immersed in psychology that rejection of it seems, sometimes, literally unthinkable. But the rest of the world is catching up. Opening *City Limits* (a London listings magazine) this month, we find, in the lesbian and gay section, adverts for: "Lesbian Rebirthing Group", "Lesbian Alcoholics Anonymous", "Sexual Compulsives Anonymous" and a "Lesbian Codependents Anonymous Group. . . Twelve steps to recovery from relationship problems with a lover, family, friends or work" (all in Jan

23–30, 1992 issue). For a Californian reader, the fact that only four such groups are advertised this week for the whole of London might come as a shock; as British readers, we still have the luxury of being surprised by the existence of as many as four. But such groups are proliferating month by month.

This is not a book about how to make lesbian/feminist psychology *better*. We are not interested in reforming psychology, or in demarcating the differences between "good" and "bad" lesbian/feminist psychologies, or in distinguishing between "real" lesbian/feminist therapists and the charlatans. We acknowledge that, in criticising the very idea of lesbian/feminist psychology, we have lumped under that heading people who would probably rather not be bracketed together; many of them have expressed misgivings about each other. For example, Laura Brown (1990b) criticises codependency groups (but promotes individual psychotherapy) and Luise Eichenbaum (1987) criticises self-help guides ("they assume that the reader can't think for his or herself") but writes her own best-selling psychology books from an object relations perspective. We are addressing a fundamental question about the relationship between lesbian/feminist psychology and lesbian/feminist politics, and it is the similarities between different psychological approaches (rather than the differences) which most engage us. We are concerned with therapy as a cultural phenomenon, not as a set of clinical techniques.

Finally, we are not denying that lesbian/feminists suffer, or the good intentions of (most of) those who seek to relieve that suffering. We are not saying that therapists or those who seek therapy are bad people. We know that many lesbians experience terrible emotional pain and we are deeply concerned that labeling it "mental illness" (or "erotophobia", "merger", "codependency" or whatever other label is fashionable) simply makes the underlying problems more difficult to address. As lesbian feminists, we want to acknowledge the existence of problems in living but to do so from within a political rather than a therapeutic framework. We also think such problems need to be addressed here and now: they are not simply going to disappear "after the revolution".

In this book we criticise aspects of the work of a huge range of prominent self-identified lesbian and feminist therapists in the USA and in the UK, as well as that of many others whose work is influential in lesbian communities. It is indeed possible to argue that not all of them are lesbians, not all are feminists, not all are properly qualified therapists. Nonetheless, their work is what passes for lesbian/feminist psychology in the English speaking world. Instead of simply asserting the notion of a "truly" lesbian/ feminist therapy, we should pay more critical attention to the lesbian/feminist therapy currently in vogue. This is the work which is deeply influential on lesbian theory and lesbian politics today. It may not be "really" lesbian, "really" feminist or "really" therapy, but its effects on our lives are real enough.

WATCHING OUR LANGUAGE

A bizarre new language is steadily invading our lesbian communities. Words and phrases like "codependent", "self-parenting", "merger", "processing", "being centered" and "being in recovery" are now part of many lesbians' vocabularies. Lesbians speak to each other about "healing the child within", "getting in touch with our needs", "discovering our erotic archetypes", or "dealing with our own stuff so as not to dump it on others". Instead of having opinions, we "have energy around some issues", instead of agreeing with someone's views we "feel comfortable" with them and instead of disagreeing we "can't relate to that".

These words and concepts have now become an accepted part of lesbian and feminist culture. Unlike words like "sexism" or "sexual harassment", which were new words invented by women and lesbians to describe our experience of the world, this new way of speaking comes directly from male-led cults of humanistic and existential psychology and new age thinking.

Writing in the journal *Lesbian Ethics*, Caryatis Cardea (1985) comments that, when psychology first started to insinuate itself into lesbian and feminist language, "those of us not involved in – or even familiar with – therapy felt as though the earth were shifting beneath our feet... Language and vocabulary skidded away from us; words skirted around the edges of clear meanings". Psychobabble is increasingly replacing political language. In this chapter we explore some of this psychological vocabulary, and discuss its political implications.

As Caryatis Cardea points out, it's difficult to work out what many of these psychological words mean. Certain psychological words seem to have acquired a positive flavour without any clear meaning being attached to them. Many lesbians nod approvingly at the idea of "growth" or "development", without asking awkward questions like growth and development of what, in what direction, and for what purpose? "Circles" and "spirals" are clearly a "good thing", while anything "linear", "hierarchical" or "polarised" is bad and must be "transformed", through "personal growth" into an "integrated" or "balanced" "whole". Hyphenated self-words are very popular – self-discovery, self-fulfilment, self-validation – and many lesbians use these terms as though their meanings, and their desirability as goals, were transparently obvious. It is becoming harder and harder to ask what we think are serious and important questions about what is meant by the "self", why it is considered necessary to discover, fulfill, and validate it, and how we theorise the relationship between "self" and "society".

The literature on psychology and therapy often reads as though all these current buzz words have been thrown together to create, for those who believe in it, a warm, reassurring patter. For the rest of us, it is often literally unintelligible. For example, courses at the Skyros Personal Development Centre claim to teach us how to "integrate disowned aspects of oneself through here-and-now awareness" or to "encourage a balanced free flow of energy". A flier advertising something called "The Serpent Institute" promises that by enrolling in its therapeutic program we will gain "the sense of co-presence with people" – which presumably means "meet others" – and explains that its program has "an emphasis on encouraging stuck energies to flow and putting people in touch with their natural physical rhythms" – which sounds like a cure for constipation. "The Crapola Test" measures how much shit you're willing to put up with from other people, and Lynne Namka (1989: 7) encourages her readers to answer honestly with the exhortation, "Ask your Inner Wisdom to assist you" (p 37). "Doormats", she says, "have a low crapola index", but she promises cure: "You can drop out of Doormat School and go to the University of Standing on Your Own Two Feet" (p 7). If you don't like the scholastic metaphor, how about joining a "Women's Healing Circle" instead, where you can "reclaim the loving power of the Goddess, bloom forth in the eternal dance of cosmic circle's renewal"? Or work with Sage Freechild, a professional counsellor and bodywork therapist, who specializes in creative visualisation and guided meditation and wants to help clients to "reach a centered place... Through the integration of physical, mental, and spiritual energies, clients are empowered to make clearer choices based on full awareness" (advertising flier). A poster advertising a "Woman in Power" seminar, facilitated by a "spiritual psychologist, healer, and founder of the Inner Light Center of Sedona who playfully and lovingly assists people in moving from fear into their power and full potential" announces that the seminar will enable participants to

"– Expand Your Limits
– Remove Unconscious Blocks
– Rewrite the Script of Your Life to Recreate a New You
– Learn to Receive Love, Money and Inner Peace
– Understand Unconscious Hopes and Fears Which Govern Your Relationships
– Learn the Truth About Your Personal Laws"

In this literature, and increasingly in lesbian groups, it is seen as an unquestionably good thing to expand personal limits, remove unconscious blocks, integrate energies, reclaim true selves, get in touch with inner children, and reach centered places. To refuse those goals is almost heretical. The existence of the psychological apparatus of unconscious blocks, centred places and so on is taken as given. When we've said to other lesbians that we don't think we have an "unconscious" to discover, or inner children to relate to, they often react with incredulity – as though we've denied having lungs. As Stevi Jackson (1983) points out, in criticizing the mystificatory language of much psychoanalytic writing as "arrogant and condescending", it is constantly implied that if we reject Freud it is because we are too stupid to see the Great Truths that he has uncovered.

The words we use to talk about lesbian experience define lesbian politics. Language does much more than simply provide a convenient label or tag for the world. The

35

labels we choose reflect and constitute our politics. To call us "lesbians" is to make one kind of political statement; to call us "gay women", or "female homosexuals" is to make a different kind of political statement. The phrase "father-daughter rape" carries one set of political implications; words like "intergenerational sex" or "paedophilia" carry others. Language *matters*. The power of naming is, as Mary Daly (1978) has shown, to define the quality and value of that which is named, and to deny reality to that which is not named.

For example, as British lesbians we are very unclear about the meaning of the word "process" in its psychological manifestation. It hasn't caught on over here yet. Anna Livia, a British lesbian feminist writer who recently emigrated to California, has tried to explain it to us. Reflecting, in her autobiographical fiction, on the use of psychological language, she says "since I've been in the Bay Area I have lived in a benign state of perpetual bafflement. I have begun to suspect that I prefer being baffled to understanding what is going on":

> "Benign bafflement notwithstanding, I have caught on that not only waste but people are to be recycled. Rebirthed. Their inner children re-released, like so many Osmond classics, to whinge and moan once more, just when we thought they'd safely grown out of it. Every bad thing that ever happened to them is regurgitated and rechewed like the cud of a battery cow – didn't their mummies tell them not to pick their sores? It's called processing. A friend of mine tells me he is processing almost continually these days.
>
> 'That's nice,' I say, 'You must be very busy. I hope it pays well.'
>
> 'Aw,' he says, 'I don't do paid work. I wouldn't have time.'
>
> You have to discover your addiction; the women who love too much, too little, too often or too soon; the ones who always pick the same bad apples thinking they will change, thinking they can change themselves, thinking they can change the world. We used to think we could change the world, we used to say that those who controlled the process controlled the product. Funny how words change." (Livia, 1992)

Louise Armstrong (1991) points to a similar linguistic shift, with the conversion of the noun "incest", into the verb "incested", as in "I was incested when I was 5". "This struck me when I first heard it as truly horrific", she says. "Doesn't it sound like a rite of passage? I was baptized? I was confirmed? But – it occasioned no remark." (Armstrong, 1991). As lesbian/feminists we need to be aware of the power of language in naming our experience.

Psychological language is a way of naming our experience and describing our reality. As such, it has political implications. However meaningless it sometimes sounds, psychology reflects and perpetuates a particular way of looking at the world, a specific theory about lesbian experience under heteropatriarchy. It is a theory which starts from an understanding of experience as individual and personal. When someone is unhappy, psychology therefore seeks individual and internal solutions, which locate the "cause" of the unhappiness inside individual lesbians. Many new words have been invented to describe the various things that are wrong with us. We are no longer sick simply because we are lesbian; instead we suffer from unconscious blocks, unexpanded limits, internalised homophobia, merger, codependency and so on. Whatever the causes of this individual pathology (sometimes it's our mothers' fault, sometimes "society's", sometimes our own), it is now our job to "deal with" it. Lesbians are supposed to become conscious of our defects and pursue self-improvement. The various self-improvement programs on offer (modern-day variants of "I must, I must improve my bust") are marketed as leading not (necessarily) to a better figure, or a higher-paid job, or the lover of our dreams – those are goals to which we might be relatively impervious. Instead self-improvement is sold to us as offering what we have sought, and so far failed to achieve, in our political movements. Psychology claims to be able to offer us "liberation", "power", "rights", and "freedom of choice" – everything we've always wanted, with personal happiness thrown in as well! In attempting to make these claims plausible (it is, after all, a little difficult to see how lesbians talking to cushions – or even to therapists – can bring heteropatriarchy to its knees), psychology has redefined the meanings of these political terms. In their therapeutic reformulations, "power", "liberation" and "freedom of choice" refer to individual, internal, psychic phenomena instead of social and political transformation.

These shifts in the meanings of words are much more significant than whether or not particular psychological programmes "work". For at the centre of these changes are new concepts of right and wrong, power, freedom, choice, oppression, the personal and the political. Through the invention of new words and the re-definition of old words, our social and political consciousness as lesbians and as feminists is being profoundly affected. Psychological language has enormous implications for how lesbians think about ourselves, personally, socially and politically, and for how we act.

Psychology has used three different strategies to inflitrate our vocabulary. It has co-opted and redefined existing political words; it has invented new depoliticised terms of its own; and it has tried to ban words from our vocabulary. We want to discuss examples of each of these. First, in order to look at the political implications of psychological language, we have selected out five words which psychology uses, but which have their origins in political theory: power, choice, freedom, liberation, and revolution. How has psychology changed the meanings of these words and what problems arise in developing lesbian theory when it is unclear, much of the time, whether other lesbians in our communities are using the words in their "political" or in their "psychological" sense? Second, as an example of a new concept invented by psychology, we have focused on a word which, although it emerged directly from psychology, has now become incorporated into many lesbians' political theory; "homophobia" (and "lesbophobia"). What is the effect of drawing on a psychological concept in building our politics? Third, we look at some of the words which psychology has tried to ban from our vocabulary – words like "right" and "wrong", "should", and "ought". What is lost when we surrender to psychology's demand that we purge our language of these terms? We want to show how the influence of psychology is to depoliticise, individualise, and privatise our language, and hence to inhibit the development of clear political goals and strategies.

The effects of psychological language are much more far-reaching than we discuss in this chaper. Therapy prescribes not just *what* is said, but how we are to say it: we must speak "from our gut feelings"; we must not "intellectualise"; we must "own our statements"; we must preface our remarks with the phrases "I think. . .", "I feel. . . .", "It seems to me. . .". What we say to each other is often censored or rephrased in terms of the pet psychological theory imposed upon experience by the therapist. Psychological books, and other forms of psychological practice (co-counselling, group therapy, therapy workshops, etc) teach us how to speak with each other in a way that increasingly resembles the therapist's interaction with her clients. Many therapeutic programmes are explicitly designed to alter the way we talk to each other – to make us more assertive, more open about our "needs" and so on. The numbing use of clichés, platitudes and meaningless phrases, slung together as though they represented hard-won insights is devastating lesbian conversation. Emotions are categorised and dismissed as what Mary Daly (1984) has called "plastic passions", and the emphasis on tell-it-all openness, characteristic of the therapy hour, means that conversations between us too often degenerate into spurious confession and undigested personal disclosure (Raymond, 1986: 155–60). These problems are all explored in other chapters, particularly the chapter on "Therapeutic Lifestyles" and the chapter on relationships, "Loving Ourselves, Loving Each Other: Lesbians in Community". In this chapter we are focussing simply on psychological vocabulary, and exploring the damage done to our political agenda when we accept psychology's vocabulary.

"Power"

When men exercise power, what they are often demonstrating is their control over women. Male power is vested in the state which witholds free contraception, abortion, or child-care facilities to women, or in governments which outlaw lesbians, endorse police harassment, refuse public acknowledgement of our relationships with one another, and sack us from our jobs. But male power extends beyond the formal powers of states and governments. As Mary Daly has documented, it is also expressed through male religion and myth, in the practice of Indian Suttee, Chinese footbinding, African genital mutilation, European witchburnings and American gynecology. Adrienne Rich has shown how male power is manifested through the institutions of compulsory heterosexuality and compulsory motherhood. Kathleen Barry and Andrea Dworkin have shown how male power operates through the widespread use of pornography, rape, and sexual terrorism. Male power means domination, oppression, coercion. It means men's control over women, men's right of access to women, men's ability to make a wide range of relatively unfettered choices about their lives, men's control of 99% of the world's material resources. That is the kind of power that men have. It is real, concrete, and it affects our daily lives as women and lesbians.

Lesbians know that, even under male domination, we are not completely powerless. We have power over those weaker than us – children and animals. We may have power over other lesbians who are oppressed in ways which we are not – because of their race, ethnicity, class, or disability. A lesbian can exercise power, of a sort, over men when she uses "feminine wiles" to get her own way. Lesbians, as a group, have the power to protest, to picket, to march, to chain ourselves to railings or abseil into the House of Commons. We have the power of sabotage. We have the power to withdraw consent from male versions of reality, to refuse their definitions of us, to separate ourselves from them, and to construct our own alternative versions. Those are real powers. But we do not have the kind of power men have, to the same extent that men have it. Women's power, and lesbians' power, exist only within the framework of male domination and the institution of compulsory heterosexuality. White ruling class male power makes the rules; lesbians (sometimes) have the power to break, evade, or protest against them. Those powers are not symmetrical.

Psychology claims to offer women and lesbians power. Real power. Power as good as men's power, but a special "female" version. Equal but different. This power has nothing to do with governments or states, laws or institutions. It lies inside us. "Power", in the psychological reformulation of the term, means getting in touch with our authentic, natural female self, the inner child, a free spirit supposedly untouched by social oppression, which can spontaneously generate its own actions and free choices. Power, according to this psychological definition, means reclaiming an essential inner self. We already have "power": what psychology does is enable us to claim it as our own. As Laura Brown, lesbian psychologist, puts it:

"... part of what I do with the people I work with in therapy is to point out to them that they are already powerful in ways that the culture does not define as being powerful." (quoted in Malina, 1987)

According to Louise Hay (1984a), author of the best selling, *Heal Your Body*:

"No person, no place and no thing has any power over you, for you are the only thinker in your own mind. You are the creative power, and you are the authority in your life."

All that is necessary is to get in touch with this inner power. Psychologist Lynne Namka describes how to do this:

"Stand and bring your personal power to one place by closing your eyes and breathing deeply. Plant your feet firmly on the ground and feel your connection with the earth. Visualize deep, deep roots going from your feet into the earth to give stability. As you stand with this wide base of potency, focus on the strength that is within. Breathe deeply, knowing you are in touch with the power of the universe. Allow personal, loving power to circle through you, flowing in the top of your head, passing through your body and going into the earth where it recycles to the universe. Visualize yourself impervious to being knocked over by using this position of strength.... State the following affirmations as you pull the power of the universe through you by deep breathing. State the

41

following words out loud in your Power Voice. Practice saying them in a loud voice until you really believe what you are saying:
– I am a woman/man of power
– I center myself drawing on that internal strength from within
– I stand tall and proud of my ability to draw from my own strength
– I acknowledge the deep resources of my Inner Wisdom from which I draw
– I empower myself and others through my loving actions
– I celebrate my ability to love myself and others
– I am a woman/man of true personal power."
(Namka, 1989: 59)

"Power", then, is reformulated as an awareness, an affirmation, a belief that you already have power, albeit power that the culture does not recognise. All that is necessary is to pursue psychological programs which enable us to "feel more comfortable about being powerful" (Chaplin and Noack, 1988: 226). Browsing through the bookstall at the Association for Women in Psychology annual conference in Arizona (March, 1990), one of us (CK) jotted down the following titles: they give a flavour of the task faced by women who want this type of "power" and make very clear where that power is located: *Journey into Me*; *The Journey Within*; *Healing the Child Within*; *A Gift to Myself*; *How to Accept Yourself*; *How to Live Your Own Life*. "Power" lies within, and is identified as, the compulsive pursuit of a true, essential, authentic "self". (For a more detailed analysis see Kitzinger, 1991a.)

At its most extreme, psychology claims that we have total power over our own lives, because we create our own reality. Louise Hay (1984b) again:

"It is my belief that we are each one hundred percent responsible for every experience in our lives – the best and the worst. We all create our experiences by the thoughts we think and the words we speak. The universe totally supports us in every thought we choose to think and believe. ... Whatever is happening 'out there' is only a mirror of our own inner thinking. I am not condoning their behaviour, but it is our beliefs that attract people that will treat us that way. If you find yourself saying 'Everyone always does such and such to me' – criticises me, is never there for me, uses me like a doormat, abuses me – then this is *your* pattern. There is some thought in you that attracts this behaviour. It is you that must change the belief that creates the experience. *When you no longer think that way, they will go and do that to somebody else.*" (Our emphasis!)

If women are so powerful, then it is your own fault if you got raped, or battered, or if you have not received love, money, and inner peace. According to Louise Hay, "all illness is self-created". Cancer is "the outer effect of a mental pattern of deep resentment that is held for a long time until it literally eats away at the body". Arthritis is caused by feeling permanently critical of others, and AIDS is a result of sexual guilt. These are not simply extremist or fringe psychologies. The *British Medical Journal* and many mainstream professional psychology journals have run articles about the psychological causes of illness, and "the cancer personality". If we have caused our own illness, we alone can cure it:

"Say to yourself over and over every time you think of your illness, 'I am willing to release the pattern in me that has created this condition'. The minute you say it, you are stepping out of the victim role. You are no longer helpless. You are acknowledging your own power." (Hay, 1984b)

When you fail to cure yourself of cancer or AIDS it is because you were unable to let go of old patterns of thinking, unable to acknowledge your own power. You are to blame – it's all your own fault!

Another example of victim-blaming appeared recently in *New Woman* magazine. Again, it is argued that women have power, and that if bad things happen to us, we're to blame for letting them happen. Drawing upon psychological research allegedly proving that rapists, when shown videos of women in crowds or dangerous situations, tend to pick out the same women as potential victims, a (woman) journalist argues that there is "a victim look": if you get raped, it's your own fault for projecting the wrong image and for having the wrong kind of beliefs about power. Power, she says, is internal – a belief in yourself, not something you exert in the world outside – and women who attract rapists lack the proper mental set: "a victim is someone who feels she doesn't have power" (Morris, 1990).

The goal of much lesbian and feminist psychology is to "empower" women – and the word "empowerment" is a great deal more common than the word "power". According to Donna Hawxhurst and Susan Rodekohr (cited in Kramarae and Treichler, 1985: 137), empowerment means "acting as agents or advocates to the process of redefining, experiencing and realizing one's own power". "Empowerment", then, means redefining the word "power" in such a way that we get to feel we've got some of it. It attempts to create in women a certain state of mind (feeling powerful, competent, worthy of esteem, able to make free choices and influence their world), *while leaving structural conditions unchanged*. One feminist therapist states explicitly that her purpose is to help women to find ways of "enacting one's wholeness within the context of society as it is" (Heriot, 1985: 27).

When psychologists focus on "empowerment" and represent power as an internal individualistic possession, they permit and encourage precisely these kinds of victim blaming accounts. Jenny Kitzinger has analysed the political implications of the child sexual abuse prevention programmes that focus on "empowering" children by telling them they have the right to say "no". In such programmes, children are told to "speak up, say no", are taught that "you're in charge" and learn catchy jingles like "my body's nobody's body but mine". Power is seen in individualistic terms as something that can be "claimed" or "given away" by a five year old. The reality, of course, is that children are *not* "in charge", that girls can say "no" and still be abused, battered and raped, and that men very often see children's bodies as *their* rightful property. The slogans and jingles proclaiming children's power conceal this reality. A follow-up study found that, after one such prevention programme, children were *more* likely to believe that if they were abused it was their own fault. Giving children an illusory belief in their own power results in guilt and self-blame when they find themselves unable to put this "power" into operation. Victimization is seen as evidence of collusion (Kitzinger, J. 1990).

We need to be clear that women and lesbians do *not* have the powers psychologists fantasise about. When we think about the meaning of "power" in relation to rape and sexual assault we need to recognise the notion that we brought it upon ourselves by not saying "no" confidently enough, or by projecting a "victim look", for the fantasy it is. Rather, we are victims of male sexual violence and this happens to us despite the choices we make and against our will. Acknowledging our own lack of power may lead us to feel humiliated and despairing. As Dale Spender has said:

> "My entry to the women's movement has led to feelings of vulnerability, despair and shock. That cannot be denied. For identifying with women, instead of men, means taking on, in part, the notion of one's powerlessness, victimization, and lack of resources. In my own head, for example, I was much less exposed to the danger of rape when I believed that the women who were raped contributed to it in some way, for after all there was no way *I* would provoke or initiate such an attack. Recognising now that *all* women are potentially rape victims, that most rapists are known to their victims, that the object of rape is domination, I no longer have that (false) security that it won't happen to me." (Spender, 1984: 211)

Women's powerlessness is a *reality*. As lesbians we must, in the words of (heterosexual) feminist Leah Fritz (1979: 237), "eschew false pride. For a slave to be a victim, to *admit* she is a victim, is not ignominious".

Lesbian separatists Bev Jo, Linda Strega and Ruston (1990: 15) use the term "victim" to describe girls raped by men in their families. " 'Survivor' ", they say, "is a U.S. psychotherapy term that glosses over the fact that many females *don't* survive the attack – they're either killed as girls or kill themselves later". They go on to explore the implications of both terms:

> "If there's nothing shameful about being victimized,

why not say it? Considering that *no* girl is in any way to blame for being attacked, why not use 'victim'? After all, it has traditionally meant someone who was subjected to harm against their will... Identifying as family rape *victims* supports the victim, and those who love her, in their natural desire for justice and revenge. It helps us assert our power. If we're victims, then we have the right to bring our attackers to justice." (Jo et al,1990: 15)

Similarly, many lesbians with serious illnesses make a political decision to identify themselves as victims. Abandoning the psychologists' fantasies of personal power, they recognise that our illnesses are caused by germs, viruses, chemicals in our environment, industrial pollutants, toxic fumes, and medical malpractice. Not by the thoughts we have about ourselves. Nancy Johnson (1981), a lesbian with pervasive cancers in different sites of her body, describes herself as:

"... a victim of the government's irresponsible bombing experiments in the Nevada desert. Here I was a victim of fall-out when I was just a teenager and stood outside watching the beautiful yellow sky.

My sisters (I have five) began, now, to get cancer. My older sister and the one just younger than me. (Did we three stand under the same yellow sky, or did we drink the same contaminated milk or chew on a blade of grass thick with poisons: rolling on the lawn on hot summer nights after the big mushroom's death particles bathed our homes and gardens with 'safe-level fall-out'?)"

A lesbian understanding of "power" in relation to physical illness cannot mean resorting to victim-blaming fantasies of omnipotence over the course of our disease. Lesbian understandings of "power" have rather to mean developing a politics of illness, and laying claim to our lesbian experience of illness (see Wilkinson and Kitzinger, 1993a for a more detailed discussion). Audre Lorde, in her autobiographical account of breast cancer and mastectomy reflects on victimhood and self-blame, and its political alternative.

"Last week I read a letter from a doctor in a medical

magazine which said that no truly happy person ever gets cancer. Despite my knowing better, and despite my having dealt with this blame-the-victim thinking for years, for a moment this letter hit my guilt button. Had I really been guilty of the crime of not being happy in this best of all possible infernos? [. . .]

Was I wrong to be working so hard against the oppressions afflicting women and Black people? Was I in error to be speaking out against our silent passivity and the cynicism of a mechanized and inhuman civilization that is destroying our earth and those who live upon it? Was I really fighting the spread of radiation, racism, woman-slaughter, chemical invasion of our food, pollution of our environment, the abuse and psychic destruction of our young, merely to avoid dealing with my first and greatest responsibility – to be happy? [. . .]

The happiest person in this country cannot help breathing in smokers' cigarette fumes, auto exhaust, and airborne chemical dust, nor avoid drinking the water, and eating the food. The idea that happiness can insulate us against the results of our environmental madness is a rumor circulated by our enemies to destroy us. And what Woman of Color in america over the age of 15 does not live with the knowledge that our daily lives are stitched with violence and with hatred, and to naively ignore that reality can mean destruction? We are equally destroyed by false happiness and false breasts, and the passive acceptance of false values which corrupt our lives and distort our experience." (Lorde, 1980: 66–67)

Through consciousness raising or illness support groups, such as that described in *off our backs*, lesbians can gain strength enough to challenge male power.

"The group does not make illness go away, it does not bring back breasts or vision or the ability to walk without pain, but it tells me that in other Lesbians' lives the struggle goes on, and when I see their power and courage, I am close to the heart of everything that has given my life meaning – the lesbian spirit of defiance and creation." (Nestle, 1981)

Nancy Johnson was a member of this group and was supported by it in her class action suit against the U.S. government for condemning the people of Utah to years of cancer. That is what "stepping out of the victim role" really means.

Lesbians and feminists say that we want power. By "power", we mean economic power, the power to prevent male violence against women, power to speak and be heard, power to define our own experience of the world, on our own terms. Psychology redefines "power" as ours already, waiting to be tapped. "Power", in psychological language, is a sense of personal agency quite unrelated to the objective and material facts of our lives. Psychology has redefined "power" in privatised and individualised terms antithetical to radical lesbian politics.

"Choice"

In psychology, "choice", like power, is yours for the asking. You have unlimited choices in life, and can choose to do or be just whatever you want. "Everything we do in life is done by choice" (Hay, 1984). Jane Mara, a lesbian/feminist psychotherapist, and co-founder of the Women's Growth and Therapy Center Collective in Washington DC says:

> "We have a choice about our lives... We can choose to live in and collude with the patriarchy's creation of reality, thus strengthening and enforcing it, or we can choose to leave it behind and create a reality which nurtures and sustains us as wimmin, as lesbians individually and collectively. In recognizing this choice we learn that we are utterly responsible for our own lives." (Mara, 1985: 152)

It's as easy as that! We are utterly responsible for our own lives and can just "choose" to leave patriarchy behind. As one of Jane Mara's patients is quoted as saying (clients usually learn to talk just like their therapists), "Goodbye patriarchy, hello ME". As Lynne Namka (1989: 87) puts it, "Stop playing victim and victimizer. As you learn and grow, you can choose to leave a situation that is not good for you".

"Choice", in psychological terms, is a purely personal matter. You may, nonetheless, need psychological guidelines to help you discover the choices available to you, and to learn how to make positive, life-affirming choices. A book like, *Choicemaking: For Co-dependents, Adult Children and Spirituality Seekers* (Wegscheider-Cruse, 1988) may be just the thing. Another self-help therapy book suggests using the following exercises to help you make your "choices":

> "Standing, eyes shut, recall in detail a recent difficult situation in your life. Now take five minutes to dance out that situation *and a resolution to it....* Sit comfortably with eyes shut, then take several minutes to imagine your life in a year if you decide one way, then if you decide the other way." (Ernst and Goodison, 1981: 140, emphasis in original)

Thinking about the consequences of your decisions (as sugggested in this latter quotation) seems to us to be a very good idea – although there's nothing particularly "psychological" about it. What troubles us is the extent to which psychologists conceptualise these consequences as if they exist outside any social, cultural or political context. For example, the authors recommend using this second technique for making decisions such as "Shall I have a baby or not?" (p 167) on the grounds that "we often know a lot more unconsciously about what these decisions mean than we do consciously; by opening up to a visualisation of what effect a decision will have on our life, we can tap some of this inner knowledge" (p 167–8).

In this psychological version of "choice", a woman simply chooses what she wants for herself within the existing social order. Any understanding she may have of social matters serves only to aid her in obtaining private satisfaction. What is left out of this psychologised view of "choice" is any sense that decisions are made within a social and political context which weights options in systematic ways – some choices "cost" more than others, and no choice is ever really "free". Discussing lesbians' "choice" to have babies, for example, Sheila Shulman says:

> "I think those of us who are having children are doing so because that is what women are 'meant' to do, and

that not to do so will feel like being less than a woman. I think this is particularly true for lesbians, despite all the mystification about the 'creativity' of childbearing and motherhood. I still feel that the terrible question of what it is to be a real woman, a whole woman, squats powerfully in the centre of each of us. That is by no means a situation in which a free choice is possible." (Shulman, 1981)

Once we begin to explore the pressures on us to have children to "prove we're 'real' women", or the social demands that we *not* have children because, as lesbians, we're 'sick' or 'unnatural' (pressures still more intense for disabled lesbians, cf Pies, 1985), it becomes hard to sustain the idea that the choice whether or not to have a baby can be made simply by closing our eyes and visualising our future. When we opt for one decision or another, we have to do so with full awareness of the social and political context within which we are acting – and with the knowledge that choices like these are never "free".

When early second-wave feminists fought for a woman's "right to choose", this didn't mean women's right to overcome unconscious blocks and to get in touch with their inner needs. It meant actual material changes in the world – free contraception and abortion on demand. As black and third world women forced white European and North American feminists to become more aware of the oppression of women through compulsory sterilisation, the dumping of dangerous contraception, and enforced abortions, the concept of "choice" was expanded to mean, again, structural changes in the real world, including challenging drug companies and "population control" policies. "Choice" was not conceptualised as an individual, private phenomenon: it was public and political. Susan Himmelweit has addressed the question of what "choice" means for the oppressed with specific reference to reproductive rights:

"If we question whether the right to choose has been genuinely exercised when a woman chooses to abort a female foetus because of the greater value put on sons, should we not also do so when she aborts a foetus with Downs syndrome because society does not provide sufficient support to make raising a mentally handicapped child a choice she can contemplate? And what about the woman who chooses an abortion because her low woman's wage does not make single parenthood, even with a healthy child, economically feasible? Have any of these women really exercised a right to choose?" (Himmelweit, 1988: 41–42)

Reproductive decisions, like all others, are always made within a material and cultural context. Psychology encourages a relentless emphasis on the individual decision-maker and her "choice". Radical lesbian politics, while not denying that we experience the problem of making decisions, "choices", about our lives, emphasises the material and cultural context which constrains and controls those choices. As radical lesbians have pointed out, the everyday personal "choices" made by women in their "private" lives are irrevocably and inextricably connected to women's powerlessness under male supremacy. "When material conditions eliminate 99% of the options, it is not meaningful to call the 1% of things a woman can do 'choice' " (Douglas, 1987). Would we rather be oppressed by living with a man who rapes and beats us, or by living in poverty on the streets and sleeping in a cardboard box? Choose your oppression! We have no choice about living under patriarchy, and to insist on choice *within* that system, rather than opposing the system itself, disguises the nature of the problem we face – which is not that women don't have choices, but that women are systematically oppressed.

To take another example. So-called "lesbian" and "feminist" psychologies often treat lesbianism and hetero-sexuality as "choices" which any woman can make. One of Jane Mara's patients came out as lesbian, after two years in therapy, when she realised, "I had chosen the marriage, I had chosen not to listen to my own voice, to swallow my anger, to act out of fear." Realising that she had "chosen" heterosexuality, she was free to "choose" lesbianism in its place. Lesbian sex therapist, JoAnn Loulan (1990) defends the right of lesbians to "choose" sex with men. These facile accounts of "choice" omit from consideration any under-standing of the social structure of compulsory hetero-

51

sexuality within which such "choices" are made. Heterosexuality is not so much a 'free choice' as a coercive
institution, not a free expression of personal preference
but an institution of male domination. As Adrienne Rich
points out:

> ". . . to acknowledge that for women heterosexuality
> may not be a 'preference' at all but something that has
> had to be imposed, managed, propagandized, and
> maintained by force, is an immense step to take if you
> consider yourself freely and 'innately' heterosexual. . . .
> To take the step of questioning heterosexuality as a
> 'preference' or 'choice' for women – and to do the
> intellectual and emotional work that follows – will call
> for a special quality of courage in heterosexually
> identified feminists. . . ." (Rich, 1980)

Many radical lesbians have challenged the idea that women
do (or can) "freely choose" to be heterosexual: under
patriarchy, such choices are *not* free and "only the deluded
would have investment in pretending that lesbianism and
female heterosexuality are *comparable, equivalent choices*!!"
(Penelope, 1986). The badge proclaiming that "any woman
can be a lesbian" was in part an attempt to demonstrate the
incomparability of heterosexuality and lesbianism as
"choices". It challenged biological notions of causation,
and defied heteropatriarchal categories. By contrast, it is
hard to imagine what could possibly be gained by a badge
reading, "Any woman can be a heterosexual". We all *know*
that. Heterosexuality and lesbianism are NOT equivalent
options, and the processes governing the "choice" of one
or the other are radically different (cf. Wilkinson and
Kitzinger, 1993b). Ariane Brunet and Louise Turcotte
(1982: 455) extend this analysis further in showing how the
concept of lesbianism as a "choice" is used to defend the
institution of heterosexuality:

> "If we have been able to become Lesbians in a
> heterosystem, then our very existence can be used to
> validate their assertion that heterosexuality is *their*
> choice. If resistance to heterosexuality is possible,
> then hetero-feminists can justify their belief that they,
> too, have made a 'choice'. Whereas in the past
> Lesbians were 'bad' because we didn't 'choose'

heterosexuality, now we are 'good' because our lives are used to validate their 'choice'."

This same contrast between the psychological emphasis on individual freedom of choice, and radical lesbian insistence on an examination of the nature of power in determining "choice" recurs again and again. Lesbian sexual fantasy and activity, falls, for psychologists, within an area of private choice or preference: "whatever is right is what turns you on" (see our Chapter 4). Whereas radical lesbians have pointed out that "there is no such thing as 'pure' sexual pleasure. Sexual 'pleasure' cannot be separated from the emotions that accompany the exercise of power and the experience of powerlessness" (Leeds Revolutionary Feminist Group, 1981). The wearing of dresses, makeup, and jewellery, is represented by psychologists (eg Loulan, 1990) as a choice lesbians have – as though the wearing or not of feminine adornments are equal and equivalent choices. "Well, yes, of course," says Julia Penelope (1986), "one can 'choose' to embrace her oppression, one can 'choose' to display the external signs of her bondage, and, perhaps, one can even speak of her 'right' to remain in her oppressed state, but is that ALL feminism was about?". When we make such choices we are often making what Sarah Lucia Hoagland (1988: 50) calls "survival choices" – the "choice" of embracing femininity and male authority in order simply to "get by" and survive.

Psychologists place enormous value on "choice". A great many therapies are sold as offering clients the tools they need to make "freer", "better" or "more" choices about their lives. "Choice" is clearly considered a good thing to have. When psychology promotes the notion of "choice", it reflects and supports the central tenet of a liberal capitalist system. The rightwing British MP, John Selwyn Gummer comments approvingly that:

"Choice lies at the heart of being human. ... The government of the right is continually extending choice from the few to the many. Whether it is spreading power over schools to parents and governors, opening up trade unions to democracy, outlawing the professional closed shops, encouraging charities and voluntary bodies, offering choice in pensions or extending home ownership, competitive tendering or privatisation, the right is committed to the morality of individual choice." (Gummer, 1988)

Margaret Thatcher, too, was apt to eulogise about choice, and her interpretation of Christianity boiled down to:

"... a theological legitimation for the doctrine of the individual's *right to choose*. The word 'choice' is hammered into each Article, and by Article 3 the meaning of the Crucifixion itself turns out to be that Christ was exercising His right to choose.

That phrase! It has been used by Margaret Thatcher so often before, in contexts so far removed from the theological, that an unseemly bathos attaches itself to it here. Christ dying on the Cross joins those folk who have exercised their right to choose – to buy their own council homes, to send their children to private schools, to occupy 'paybeds' in NHS-funded hospitals." (Raban, 1989)

In preserving the illusion of choice, blame is inexorably attached to those people who make the "wrong" choices – who don't "choose" to buy their own homes, send their children to private schools, or have private health care plans.

Several important issues are lost in this eulogising of "choice" as a Good Thing in and of itself. The extension of "freedom of choice" in one area curtails the possibility of "free choice" in another. The widely available choice for middle-class Western women over the age of 35 to have amniocentisis and diagnose disability in utero, may mean that it is much harder to "choose" to bear a disabled child. Women who do so may be reminded that they could have avoided bearing the child and so have less "right" to demand help of the state (cf Rothman, 1986). The "choice" available to the wives of white wealthy Western men to have their infertility investigated and "cured" with in-vitro fertilisation or other forms of medical intervention, make the "choice" of accepting infertility much harder (Kitzinger, 1991b). The "choice" to have a car, when widely available, closes off all of our "choice" for a noise-free and pollution-free environment, and also the "choice" to travel (for most functional purposes) by horse, or (often) bicycle, or even public transport. (In particular, cars mean decreased mobility for women and children.) When one choice is made widely available, other choices are closed off. When we commit ourselves to *any* course of action (having a baby, buying a car, going back to university, leaving a marriage) we open up certain possibilities for ourselves, but we simultaneously close off other possibilities. In this way, as Susan Himmelweit points out, the extension of choice "has become a burden as well as a source of liberation – a loss as well as a gain" (Himmelweit, 1988: 45).

Not only are individuals' choices always made within an economic, cultural and political context, but that context is itself affected by the decisions of individuals. Our individual "choices" may have social and political effects which are undesirable in terms of effecting a lesbian feminist transformation of society. It is in that sense in which, however limited our choices are, we are still acting as moral beings. We have moral agency, even under oppression. Acknowledging the limits and constraints on "choice", lesbian philosopher Sarah Lucia Hoagland (1988) argues that we are inevitably moral agents when we make choices – not because we are "free" to make "free" choices (we are not), but because "moral agency simply is the ability to choose in limited situations". We have a moral responsibility to each other for the choices that we make. What is core to us, as radical lesbians, is not our "right to choose", but the moral quality of the (necessarily constrained) choices that we make.

Psychology pretends that we are able to make free choices about our lives – that once we have overcome the hidden blocks, and discovered our "true selves", we will be able to act according to our own unfettered and authentic desires. Establishing in individuals the ability to make these kinds of "choices" is generally the stated or implicit goal of psychological and therapeutic programs. A radical lesbian understanding of "choice", by contrast, emphasises that choices can never be free, that "desires" (sexual, maternal, social) are constructed within us by the forces which oppress us; we would do better to address those oppressive structures and institutions directly than to search within for illusory "pure" choices. A lesbian politics addresses itself to transforming the social and economic conditions within which our choices are made, rather than trying to extend the choices available to us under heteropatriarchy. In our daily experience of making choices, what is important is not that we feel "free to choose", but that we make those choices which help to counter our oppression and to create and build lesbian community.

"Freedom", "Liberation" and "Revolution"

Until the publication of Gloria Steinem's, *Revolution from Within* (1992) the words sounded slightly passé – reminiscent of the politics of the sixties or seventies. It's possible to read through recent lesbian and feminist books without ever coming across these terms. Sarah Lucia Hoagland's (1988) *Lesbian Ethics* has no entries in the index for "liberation" or "revolution" and only this for "freedom":
   " 'freedom', problems with concept, ..."
Dorchen Leidholdt and Janice Raymond's (1990) recent edited book, has this single entry:
   "Freedom, criticism of, 5"
Perhaps it's symptomatic of the times we live in that, searching indices for "liberation", what we kept finding was "libido".
   "Freedom" . . . "Liberation" . . . "Revolution". . . . These terms have an honourable history within feminism. "The Revolution" was the name of a women's rights newspaper founded by Susan B Anthony and Elizabeth Cady Stanton, and published weekly from 1868–1870. But, as bell hooks (1984:157) comments: "today hardly anyone speaks of feminist revolution". The widespread use of terms like "sexual liberation" and "men's liberation" have made many lesbians and feminists suspicious of the term. The so-called sexual "liberation" turned out to mean the liberation of men to fuck more women in a greater variety of ways. Men mocked and trivialised us with the diminutive "women's lib", and perpetrated the myth of the "liberated woman". Based on the notion that there are individual solutions to

political problems, so that women can liberate themselves in their personal lives, the term, when used by men and the media, generally refers to a woman who has achieved success on male terms, and/or who is perceived to be attractive and sexually available. The development of so-called "men's liberation" (cf Wetherell and Griffin, 1991 and 1992) suggested a false parallel between the oppression of women and the difficulties faced by men in a heteropatriarchal society. All these problems seem finally to have destroyed the usefulness of the term "liberation" for many lesbians and feminists.

And as for "freedom".... Adrienne Rich (1978) described as "the worst thing of all ... the failure to want our freedom passionately enough". Robin Morgan wanted a woman's revolution "like a lover", wanted "so much this freedom ... that I could die just with the passionate uttering of that desire" (Morgan, 1972). But "freedom", too, became associated with the male "sexual liberation" movement, in which "sexual freedom" meant the freedom to be fucked by men in a greater variety of ways (Jeffreys, 1990a). Male "freedom of speech", too, made the meaning of the term problematic for us, when it turned out to mean men's right to produce, distribute and read pornography (Dworkin, 1981).

It seems a long time since those early exhilarating days when "freedom", "liberation" and "revolution" (all words proudly displayed on our badges and banners) were just around the corner. We used to say we were "oppressed". Now we say we are suffering from "internalised homophobia" (see next section) or from "repression". The difference between "oppression" and "repression", is that oppression is what men did to us, and repression is what we do to ourselves. Oppression meant the imposition of unjust constraints on the freedom of individuals or groups. "Liberation" meant the removal of these oppressive constraints – and because the whole system was rotten to the core, it was going to take not reform, but "revolution". They were political terms, used to describe our political goals.

Some of the difficulties in using these terms have become clearer, and they are now often subject to careful analysis and criticism. "The concept of freedom is freedom to abuse", says Carol Ann Douglas (paraphrasing Catherine MacKinnon, 1987); "The powerful could experience the thrill of power and call its experience freedom. Feminists did not want this 'freedom' for themselves." Another lesbian writing in *The Dykes Digest* makes a similar point about the difficulties inherent in the word:

> "Freedom must be considered in the context of power relations. There exists no such 'thing' as 'universal freedom', in which everyone has an equal share and therefore an equal interest in protecting 'it'. Those who have power have freedom (to the extent that they can maintain their power) and the freedom of those who are oppressed by those in power is limited *by* that power – they are merely allowed by those in power to exercise certain 'rights'. Those who do not have power cannot enforce 'rights', these can be regulated or taken away depending on how those in power decide to exercise their freedom. Men own over 99% of *the* world's wealth – it is therefore not too difficult to see who wields the power, and whose freedom, whose freedom of speech, women are expected to protect. 'The Freedom' reserved for huMANs is achieved, and exists at the expense of WOMEN's freedom and necessarily precludes it."
> (Lauritzen, 1987)

Whatever our current, politically sophisticated, doubts about these words, they still carry, for many people, very positive connotations. Advertisers know it. That's why "freedom" has become associated with sanitary protection, "liberation" with the latest household gadget, and every invention is "revolutionary". Psychologists, too, know the power of these words. "Revolutionary" new therapies and self-help books offer readers "real liberation" and "true freedom".

As we might expect, in the language of psychology, "freedom" and "liberation" are psychic rather than political phenomena. "We have only one real shot at 'liberation'," says Colette Dowling (1981: 28), "and that is to liberate ourselves from within."

"I have learned that freedom and independence can't

be wrested from others – from the society at large, or from men – but can only be developed, painstakingly, from within." (Dowling, 1981: 214)

"Springing free" (a subheading in Dowling 1981: 213) is what you can do when you believe in yourself. In the therapeutic sub-culture, "self-disclosure becomes equated with liberation" (Raymond, 1986: 157).

Lesbians and feminists often enter therapy because they want to be "free". Tracey Payne (1984) says of her own experience in therapy;

"Looking back on it I see very little that I could not have got from close friends or a CR group, but at the time therapy also offered 'freedom'. In particular freedom from my past. I felt that if I kept 'shoveling shit' fast enough I could catch up and be free of it. . . ."

Many lesbians want freedom, earnestly desire liberation, are prepared to struggle toward revolution. These were originally political terms. They meant social and political transformation. As an increasingly jaded lesbian feminist movement abandons these terms – partly out of exhaustion, partly because men have turned them against us – psychology co-opts them. Lesbians are offered instead individual freedom, private liberation, and a revolution in their personal lives through Brand X therapy.

"Homophobia" and "Lesbophobia"

These words are different from the others we've looked at so far in this chapter. Whereas words like "choice", "freedom", "power", and "liberation" are political terms, with a political history, "homophobia" was invented by psychologists. And despite the critical analysis of "homophobia" published in the British journal of lesbian ethics, *Gossip*, (Kitzinger, 1987b) and recently reprinted in the Onlywomen ethics anthology (Mohin, 1993), many lesbians, feminists, and liberals continue to use the term without any awareness of its psychological origins.

The notion that some people might have a 'phobia' about homosexuals and lesbians first began to appear in psychological writing in the late 1960s and early 1970s. "Homophobia" is defined as "an irrational persistent fear or dread of homosexuals" (MacDonald, 1976) or "an irrational fear or intolerance of homosexuality" (Lehne, 1976). Someone who suffers from this fear is diagnosed as a "homophobe". The word "phobia" comes from the Greek for "fear" and is used within psychology to mean an irrational fear or dread, as in "claustrophobia", the irrational fear of being in small enclosed spaces. Within contemporary psychology the "sick" lesbian has been largely replaced with the "sick" homophobe. 'I would never consider a patient healthy unless he [sic] had over-come his prejudice against homosexuality' writes one psychoanalyst (Weinberg, 1973: 1), and homophobia has been described by other mental health professionals as a "severe disturbance" (Freedman, 1978: 320) and "a mental health issue of the first magnitude" (Marmor, 1980). Psychologists have described homophobes as authoritarian, dogmatic and sexually rigid individuals who are supposed to have low levels of "ego development" and suffer from a whole range of personal problems and difficulties with their relationships (MacDonald and Games, 1974; Weis and Dain, 1979; Hudson and Ricketts, 1980).

Before psychology invented "homophobia" we wrote about "lesbian oppression", "lesbian-hatred", "anti-les-bianism" or "heterosexism" (though see Lilian Mohin, 1987, who describes this last term as an "academic polysyllabic hoax designed to diminish our justifiable rage [and dull our pain]"). Terms like "anti-lesbianism" are now used less and less. "Homophobia" (or, sometimes, its female derivative, "lesbophobia") is used instead. This is a striking example of the invasion of a purely psychological term into our political vocabulary. Just as psychological redefinitions of "power", "choice", "liberation" and so on are damaging to us, so too the redefinition of our oppression in terms of "homophobia" is destructive of radical lesbian politics.

The word "homophobia" defines fear of lesbians as *irrational*. There are, according to the psychological definitions of "homophobia", no rational, sensible logical reasons for fearing lesbianism. This is completely at odds with radical lesbian politics. We cannot think of lesbianism as a challenge to heteropatriarchal structures and values, and simultaneously claim that there are no reasonable grounds for men (or heterosexually-identified women) to fear us. We cannot write, as Adrienne Rich (1980) has done, that "a militant and pluralistic feminist movement is potentially the greatest force in the world for a complete transformation of society", and simultaneously claim that fear of lesbianism is irrational. We cannot say, with Rita Mae Brown that "lesbianism is the greatest threat that exists to male supremacy", and simultaneously claim that men's fear of us is irrational. If lesbianism is a blow against the patriarchy, the bonding of women against male supremacy, then it is entirely *rational* for men to fear it. Contemporary psychology evades these political implications of lesbianism and presents us as essentially harmless. Fear of lesbians is just another phobia some people have. When we use a term that describes fear of lesbians as intrinsically irrational, we obscure the fact that there are good reasons for fearing lesbianism and we deny lesbianism its revolutionary potential.

Within psychology, there is only one alternative to "homophobia" – liberal humanism. (For a more detailed analysis of liberal humanistic approaches to lesbianism see Kitzinger, 1987a.) People who don't talk about lesbianism in liberal humanistic terms are automatically diagnosed as homophobic. Unless you see lesbianism as a harmless sexual preference, an alternative choice of lifestyle, an entirely normal and natural sexual orientation you are suffering from "homophobia". This is obvious from the tests psychologists have invented to diagnose homophobia. Most of these tests are collections of statements about lesbians or male homosexuals (often both!) to which the subject is asked to respond "Agree" or "Disagree". The "mentally healthy" (non-homophobic) person must say that homosexuals are basically just the same as heterosexuals, and that we do not constitute any threat to the social system. Here are some sample items from these tests, with the "right" ("non-homophobic") answers marked in.

Agree   Disagree

The basic difference between
homosexuals and other people is only
in their sexual behaviour. (cf
Dannecker, 1981)   x

61

	Agree	Disagree
Homosexuals are just like everyone else: they simply chose an alternative lifestyle. (Hansen, 1982)	x	
Female homosexuality is a choice of lifestyles. (Millham et al, 1976)	x	
Just as in other species, female homosexuality is a natural expression of sexuality in humans. (Millham et al, 1976)	x	
Female homosexuality is just as natural as heterosexuality. (Millham et al, 1976)	x	
Homosexuality endangers the institution of the family. (Larsen et al, 1980)		x
It would be beneficial to society to recognise homosexuality as normal. (Larsen et al, 1980)	x	
If homosexuality is allowed to increase it will destroy our society. (Price, 1982)		x

According to these tests, then, the 'non-homophobic' or unprejudiced person must say that there is no difference between lesbians and heterosexual women, that lesbianism is merely a sexual preference or choice of lifestyle, that it is normal and natural (even the birds and the bees do it), and that it does *not* threaten the nuclear family or society as we know it. This set of views constitutes the typical liberal humanistic approach and is profoundly opposed to the theory and practice of radical lesbianism.

Julia Penelope, responding to criticism of her use of the term "homophobia" (Kitzinger, 1987b), argues that:

"Lesbians might still want to talk about heterosexuals experiencing 'an irrational fear of lesbians', as a *subversive* tactic. But *only* if we're fully conscious that we're lying to heterosexuals and doing so purposefully for articulated political reasons. It's possible that we might use 'liberal guilt' to increase whatever marginal space we can manage for political manoeuvring and sabotage. There might be some usefulness in lulling individuals in the heteropatriarchy by *pretending* we aren't dangerous to them." (Penelope, 1987: 21)

We think there are many dangers with this strategy. Most heterosexuals know perfectly well how threatening we are to them, even if this knowledge is sometimes camouflaged with liberal guilt. In 1988, the British government passed a discriminatory law (Section 28 of the Local Government Act) designed to prevent the "promotion" of "homosexuality". In the months of campaigning against this, lesbians and gay men argued that we were "harmless", "just like heterosexuals", that we do not try to "promote" our way of life (nor *could* we because "sexual orientation" is fixed at a very young age), and we accused those who rejected these arguments of "homophobia". The law got passed anyway. Nobody believed us – and radical lesbians seriously questioned the political implications of telling lies like these, as well as linking our movement with that of gay men (Kitzinger, 1988; Alderson and Wistrich, 1988). When we say we are "harmless", often the only people we fool are ourselves. As Julia Penelope (1990: 99) herself has argued "a first step toward a real Lesbian community must be relearning honesty, a difficult project when all we know is lies." Yet, as she also says, one of the lies which many lesbians believe is precisely the lie of our similarity to heterosexuals, promoted in "homophobia" tests. "Too many Lesbians," she says, "believe they are 'just like everyone else,' ie 'like heterosexuals', or at least *wish* that were so". In promoting "homophobia", psychology has encouraged lesbians in that belief, which in turn leads to incomprehension and political impotence when – inspite of our "harmlessness" – they legislate against us, ban our books, sack us from our jobs, take our children away. There are often reasons for "lying to the enemy", but we have to choose our lies (and the ways in which we use them) with great care, and we must realise the extent to which our whole lives and communities are defined by those lies.

Another problem with the term "homophobia" is that

the word "phobia" is a psychological *diagnosis*; that is, someone suffering from homophobia is considered to have something wrong with them psychologically, some kind of personality disorder or immaturity, and to be in need of psychological or psychiatric help. There is a long history, within psychology, of labelling people as sick because they threaten to disrupt the established social order. Two often quoted examples are "drapetomania" and "dysaethesia aethiopis", diagnosed by the nineteenth-century physician Cartwright (reprinted, 1981). Both diseases are peculiar to slaves, the former manifested by their tendency to run away from the plantations, the latter (also known as "rascality") is caused by idleness and cured by whipping and hard physical labour. The Soviet diagnostic category, "reformist delusions" (cf Stone and Faberman, 1981) is clearly a method of discrediting people with certain political views; in Britain in the seventies, there was an illness called "state benefit neurosis", which was characterised by refusal to take poorly paid employ-ment when more money is available through state benefits – an illness diagnosed by Price (1972) and discussed by Pearson (1975) in terms of social inequalities.

While it may be convenient to label one's political enemies as mentally ill, to do so removes the argument from the political arena and relocates it within the domain of psychology, giving more power and prestige to an oppressive institution. This reinforces the power of psy-chology to label people as "sick" or "mentally healthy" at will. Yesterday it was lesbians who were "sick" for being lesbian, today it's homophobes who are "sick" for believing that we are sick for being lesbian. It also depoliticises our oppression, by suggesting that the oppression of lesbians comes from the personal inadequacy of particular individuals suffering from a diagnosable phobia. Psychol-ogy has systematically replaced *political* explanations (in terms of structural, economic and institutional oppression) with *individual* explanations (in terms of the dark workings of the psyche, the mysterious functioning of the subconscious). When we use the term "homophobia" (or "lesbophobia") we are buying into this whole psycho-logical scenario. We are imputing sickness to specific individuals who supposedly deviate from the rest of society in being prejudiced against lesbians. We are borrowing a term from a psychology which has always reserved for itself the right to decide who is and who is not sick, and for which a shift from classifying *homosexuals* as sick to classifying *homophobes* as sick, is far less threatening than any attempt to look at the issue in political terms. In focusing on private, individualised solutions to problems, our political understanding is diluted and hence our ability to make material changes in the real world.

Translating the oppression of lesbians into the pathology of individual oppressors has other dangerous implications too. First, if "homophobia" is an illness, individuals suffering from it should, presumably, be treated with compassion. The political goal of overthrowing hetero-patriarchy is translated into a call for the mass treatment of homophobia. In a classic attempt to use psychology against gay people, a defence lawyer in San Francisco argued that his client, a convicted murderer, had killed a gay man while suffering a sudden attack of "homophobia" or "homosexual panic" – this supposedly constituting a defence. (It failed – on this occasion.)

Second, if heterosexuals can suffer from "homophobia", lesbians can suffer from "heterophobia". (This is one of many false equivalences to which psychology succumbs, because of its refusal to understand the dynamics of social and political power.) "Heterophobia", like "homophobia", is an illness, but it's an illness suffered almost exclusively by lesbian separatists who don't like men, and have political objections to heterosexuality in women. It can be "cured" by a lesbian therapist. The notion of "heterophobia" has become almost as acceptable as "homophobia" in some circles. It crops up as an entry in the "Feminist Dictionary" edited by Cheris Kramarae and Paula Treichler (1985: 190–191), where it is defined as "Fear of and resistance to heterosexuals which sometimes surfaces in women's movements around the world. It relies on a 'sexual-fundamentalist reduction of curiosity and desire' (Robin Morgan, 1982: 145)". Following the publication of Marilyn Frye's (1990) article, "Do You Have to Be a Lesbian to Be a Feminist", several women wrote to *off our backs* accusing either Marilyn Frye, or *off our backs* more generally, of being "heterophobic" (eg Name Withheld, 1991; Koehner, 1991).

Third, and most important, "homophobia" turns out not to be restricted to heterosexuals after all. Lesbians suffer from it too. We have "internalised homophobia". Back in the seventies, lesbian psychologists said lesbians were *not* sick. They said we were just as mentally healthy as heterosexuals, if not more so, and they challenged the very categories of mental "sickness" and "health" as instrumental in our oppression. Now, lesbian psychologists say we *are* sick, and "internalised homophobia" is one of our major diseases. Lesbian therapists aren't alone in this. Julia Penelope, too, wants us to keep the word "lesbophobia" to describe our own self hatred:

> "We might want to continue to use the term *'Lesbophobia'*, 'an irrational fear of Lesbians', among ourselves, restricting its sphere of reference to the self-hatred, the fear of our Lesbian Selves, that we acquire from heteropatriarchal 'authorities' and internalize as a destructive program that keeps us in our place. I think we need a way to label that acquired self-hatred lest we forget to work at ridding our Selves and our communities of its insidious effects" (Penelope, 1987: 22)

Bev Jo, Linda Strega and Ruston (1990: 15) make the same point – that some lesbians are revolted by and terrified at their own and others' lesbianism. Yes, many lesbians fear their own lesbianism, hate their lovers for loving them, and act destructively in lesbian communities as a result. But do we really want to label this as a mental pathology? Do we really want to put ourselves in the position of handing over such lesbians to therapists for "cure"? Labels have implications, and the implication of labelling something a "phobia", a psychological disorder, is that we seek psychological solutions to it. We would recommend seeking, instead, political solutions – consciousness raising with other lesbians, reading radical lesbian theory (now appropriated by the lesbian psychology industry as "bibliotherapy"!), and carrying on political struggle to end the social conditions which create this self-hatred in the first place. We explore these ideas about "internalised homophobia" in more detail in the chapter on "Therapeutic Lifestyles".

Although most lesbians use the word "homophobia" without any awareness of its meaning and context in the academic psychological literature, we don't think it can be dislocated from that context. And we don't think it's a word that can be "reclaimed". Listening to lesbians using the term "homophobia" in everyday speech, and looking at the way the word is used in lesbian and feminist publications, we see very real dangers in reducing our oppression to the status of a little problem called "homophobia". "Homophobia" is one of a whole series of psychological terms we have borrowed, or had foisted upon us, so that we construct our own experience in the depoliticised, individualised terms of psychology.

"The Tyranny of 'Should' "

As part of her comedy routine, lesbian feminist Robin Tyler, addressed her audience with the question: "Who here thinks they are politically correct?". Two women in the front row pointed to each other. "Well, you can leave now. Because if you think you're right that means that you think the rest of us are wrong, and I've had enough of being told that. Our community seems to have its own Moral Majority" (*The Pink Paper*, October 13th, 1988).

As lesbians and feminists we have been critical of the moral frameworks available to us. Indeed, we have sometimes equated the very word "morality" with rigid prohibitions, ossified codes of conduct, judgemental puritanism and sanctimonious bigotry. Used against women, "morality" has often had sexual connotations: an impure woman, a fallen woman, a woman who has left the straight and narrow, a woman of loose morals or easy virtue. In recent calls for a return to "victorian values" or "moral re-armament", the word "morality" has functioned as a euphemism for banning abortion, hounding lesbians and gay men, and keeping women locked into marriages through the sentimental romanticising of the sanctity of "family life".

But morality is not the exclusive property of the political right. As lesbians we, too, have developed moral frameworks for thinking about our lives. When we say that rape or other forms of violence against women are "wrong", that they "should" be stopped, we are making moral judgements. At least two lesbian journals, *Lesbian Ethics* (in the USA) and *Gossip: A Journal of Lesbian Feminist Ethics* (in the UK) have been devoted to attempts to articulate radical lesbian concepts of what is "right" and "wrong" for us. Lesbian morality has been discussed by (amongst others) Nancy Berzon (1984), Sarah Lucia Hoagland (1988), Sue Cartledge (1983), Claudia Card (1990) and in a series of articles in 1978 in *The Lesbian Tide*.

In order to develop lesbian morality, we need to be able to use words like "right" and "wrong"; and we need to be able to talk about what we think we (or indeed others) "should" do, how we "ought" to behave within our communities. We need to be able to make moral judgements.

But psychologists are very sceptical of moral terms. The phrase "the tyranny of 'should'" is used by psychoanalyst Karen Horney (1942), and she, like many other psychologists, wants us to overcome this "tyranny", to drop words like "should" from our vocabulary. For a long time psychologists have said that, as psychologists, they can (and must) avoid using words like "ought", "should", "right" and "wrong". This is because psychology thinks of itself as "value-free". Some psychologists think they are practising an "objective science". Others say that, by taking each person's values as given, by allowing each client to define their own moral position, they avoid the necessity of making moral judgements. This is particularly the case with humanist psychologists and it is also very common amongst lesbian and feminist psychologists. They admit that sometimes it can be very difficult to eschew moral judgements, but they do try hard. For example, Dorsey Green and Merillee Clunis describe their therapeutic work with women whose choose to stay married to men while conducting secret sexual relationships with women, remaining closeted, and deceiving their husbands. They comment that, "it may be particularly difficult for openly

lesbian therapists to avoid making judgements about
married lesbian lifestyles" (Green and Clunis, 1989: 48).
Dorsey Green and Merillee Clunis are clearly concerned
about these women's use of "heterosexual privilege" (p 45)
and worry about the extent to which "married lesbians may
seem an uncomfortable contradiction in terms" (p 48). "Is
it enough," they wonder, "to invite a married lesbian to
look at the consequences of her staying closeted?" But as
good psychologists, they do their best to "avoid making
judgements" (p 48) and get on with the therapy. We don't
think this is good enough. As lesbians and as feminists, we
think we should actively challenge women in this position
and explore with them the ways in which they can come
out as lesbians.

Psychology not only refuses to take an explicit moral
stand, it also actively distrusts morality in its clients.
Consumers of psychology are asked to put aside moral
considerations. The question "is this right or wrong?"
becomes "is this going to work for me?" "Oughts" or
"shoulds" are rejected as intrusive manifestations of
coercive authoritarianism. In the self-help book, *In Our
Own Hands* "shoulds" and "shouldn'ts" are described as
"pressures which have alienated us from our feelings."

> "Many of these pressures can be summed up under
> the word 'should'. Since childhood we have been told
> 'You should be clean' or 'You should work hard' or
> 'You should behave yourself'. It is very helpful to
> become aware of the 'shoulds' we have heard during
> our life because often we are still carrying them round
> as a voice in our heads. When we are familiar with
> them we can start to recognise when they affect or
> inhibit us in the present and begin to lessen their grip
> on us." (Ernst & Goodison, 1981: 53)

Nowhere in this section of their book is there any mention
of the value of some of the "shoulds" and "shouldn'ts" we
might have learnt as children – values which we might
want to carry through into adulthood rather than "lessen
their grip on us". (Because most of us learned important
"shoulds" and "shouldn'ts" from our mothers, this is also
an example of mother-blaming – a frequent problem in
psychology.) Moreover, there is no mention of "shoulds"

and "shouldn'ts" we have consciously worked out as adults as part of our consciousness raising and in developing political theory. According to psychology *all* "should"s and "shouldn't"s are equally *bad* – and all to be discarded altogether.

Other psychologists make the same point. Sheila Ernst and Marie Maguire, editors of *Living with the Sphinx: Papers from the Women's Therapy Centre* (1987) comment approvingly on one chapter exploring women's feelings "about an issue which is usually discussed in terms of rights and wrongs, oughts and should nots". Pam Trevithick, who ran "Lesbian Workshops" at the London Women's Therapy Centre says she was worried about "whether our workshops would be seen by some lesbians as a way of 'depoliticising' lesbians, or diverting them/us from developing solutions to our oppression" (1988: 106). She continues: "In answer to this, I would say that it's important to extend the choices open to us as lesbians, not to confine them to political dogmas of 'shoulds' and 'oughts'". Lynne Namka (1989: 53) says that "for the sake of better mental health, give up the 'shoulds' for others and learn how to change your unrealistic expectations." She also tries to jolly us out of using "should"s for ourselves:

> "Look at the humour of your always trying to live up to your rule. Visualize yourself going through the day obsessively and rigidly following that 'should' rule. . . Visualise yourself worn out and frustrated in trying to follow the unrealistic dictates of your rule. How could you change the 'should' so that it would be easier for you? Remember, all of life is choice and you have learned to think this way, so you can unlearn it."
> (Namka, 1989: 67)

Louise Hay is more authoritarian in her approach; she simply *orders* us to remove the word "should" from our vocabulary.

> "Even using the word 'should' limits us, and removing it from your vocabulary will make a great difference in your life. . . . Let's take the word 'should' and discard it forever, never to be heard of again. 'Should' is a word that makes a prisoner of us. Everytime we use 'should' we are either making ourselves wrong, or someone

else wrong... Replace the word 'should' with the word 'could'. 'Could' lets you know that you have choice, and choice is freedom." (Hay, 1984b)
Psychology, then, not only changes the meanings of existing words, and infiltrates new words into our vocabularies. It also prohibits the use of certain words, demanding that we expunge them from our political language; words like "right" and "wrong", "should" and "ought" are banned as suspect and inauthentic manifestations of personal pathology. Not only is language censored by psychology, but the making of moral judgements at all is also forbidden. Words like "moralistic", "prescriptive", or "politically correct" (a term which has now become an insult) are used to dismiss the opinions of those speaking from principled positions. This is especially true of those speaking as radical lesbians or separatists. There is even a group therapy exercise described in *In Our Own Hands* (1981) called "Exercise in Not Judging" (p 16). In therapy the worst thing you can do is to make a moral judgement – that's called "being judgemental".

Notice, too, how often morality is banned in the name of the psychologised concepts of "choice" and "freedom": "remember all of life is choice..." (Namka, above), or, "Replace the word 'should' with the word 'could'. 'Could' lets you know that you have choice, and choice is freedom" (Hay, above). Of course, we *do* have more choices (and therefore more "freedom") if our choices are not constrained by moral considerations. The question we have to ask ourselves is, is this the kind of "freedom" we want?

The two of us had a conversation with two lesbian therapists, JoAnn Loulan and Marny Hall, about some of these issues. Here is an extract from that discussion. (The full transcript, in which the four of us discuss many other issues relevant to the themes of this book, can be found in the journal *Feminism and Psychology* Vol 2(1), 1992.)

"MH: But right and wrong is a patriarchal dualism. We have to get out of that too. It's dualism. It's heaven and hell, it's sin and redemption.
CK: Men oppressing women is *wrong*, apartheid in South Africa is *wrong*, millions starving to death while others live in affluence is *wrong*. Struggling against

oppression is *right*. Treating each other with respect is *right*. Trying to build community is *right*. What do you find unacceptable about those statements?

MH: I think they get us sooner or later in cul-de-sacs.

JL: Yes, that's the problem.

MH: Because eventually I think we trash each other because we think something's right and something's wrong.

CK: Do you mean we make judgements about each others' behaviour?

JL: That's trashing each other. How is that different from trashing each other?

CK: Utterly different. I have done things Rachel thinks are wrong. Rachel has said to me, 'That is wrong'. We have discussed it. Sometimes I have agreed with her, sometimes not, but I rely on her to do that, to help me make moral judgements, and I do the same for her.

JL: Don't you think eventually that takes you down the road to trashing each other?

RP: No, I think it makes it possible to develop our moral positions.

CK: And to develop a lesbian ethics.... That's one of the things I think is eroded by psychology – any attempt to build concepts of right and wrong, a lesbian ethics. That's all eroded by a psychological framework which says, 'whatever turns you on is okay', or 'different strokes for different folks'. Within a psychological framework it becomes virtually impossible to talk of right or wrong without your morality being described as some sort of psychological hangup.

MH: I don't know how to get out of it, I really don't, but I'm so suspicious of dualistic thinking. I do think that's the gravest legacy of patriarchy. Whenever you get into dualistic thinking, you *know* you're in the territory of patriarchy.

RP: In that case, it's interesting how the patriarchy tries to get us *out* of dualistic thinking on occasion, isn't it. Take for instance the patriarchal construct that there's this nice continuum of sexuality between heterosexuals and lesbians. The patriarchy is *desperate* for there *not* to be lesbians who are lesbians and heterosexuals who are heterosexuals.

JL: You're thinking of the Kinsey scale, right?

CK: Absolutely. And what that did was prevent lesbians organising as lesbians, because we were 'all bisexual really'. The patriarchy was really into destroying the dualistic categories 'lesbian' and 'heterosexual' that they'd created in the first place.

JL: I don't think we can get away from concepts of right and wrong. *You* may have this ideal that wouldn't it be great if we could, but *I* think everybody makes judgements about everything.

RP: No, that's *not* what we're saying. I *don't* share that ideal.

CK: We *should* be making judgements. We *need* to make moral judgements.

RP: And need to be doing it more."

(Hall, Kitzinger, Loulan and Perkins, 1992)

Part of what we were trying to communicate to JoAnn and Marny was our sense of the need to extend and develop our concepts of right and wrong. We don't think that "gut feelings" constitute an adequate criterion for ethical choice. Nor can we see each lesbian as an arbitrary centre of volition whose only duty is to discover "her true self" and act accordingly. "Gut feelings" and "real selves" are constructed in the context of a heteropatriarchal society. Once we have thrown off the last vestige of external influence, and reached some illusory pure, contentless freedom, there are no moral values left – only a set of wants, desires and impulses constructed in us by the society in which we live. When psychology treats each "self" as an independent moral universe, so that the "right" act in any situation is simply the one which yields the individual the most good feelings about herself, we abandon the possibility of developing a collective sense of lesbian ethics and lesbian values. Politics degenerates into a struggle, not for social change, but for self-realisation.

Speaking Politically

Psychology is rooted in modern liberal individualism, and places the individual at the centre of the moral and political universe. Contemporary psychology manifests an intense concern with the individual self in pursuit of private goals of freedom, choice and liberation. "Empowerment" is offered as a substitute for "power", "oppression" is reduced to the individual pathology of the oppressors, and liberation becomes a psychic rather than a political phenomenon.

Psychological vocabulary is pervasive in our articulation of lesbian politics. Psychology has invaded our speech partly by co-opting existing political words, reinterpreting them within its own individualised and privatised frame of reference; partly by infiltrating new terms of its own which replace political words (as "homophobia" has become the acceptable term for talking about our "oppression"); and partly by demanding that we expunge certain words from our vocabulary. The result is psychology's colonisation of our political terrain.

In order to build a strong and radical lesbian politics, in order clearly to debate and articulate our political goals and strategies, we need to be able to tell the difference between political language and psychobabble. We need to speak politically, not psychologically.

THERAPEUTIC LIFESTYLES

Therapy pervades our lesbian communities. More and more lesbians are in individual therapy or therapy workshops, reading DIY therapy manuals, know other lesbians in therapy, are training to be therapists. Over the last couple of decades there has been an upsurge of therapy amongst the Western middle classes and leftist liberal communities in general, but as therapist JoAnn Loulan (1990: 73) points out, "nowhere did therapy become so universal as in the lesbian community". A national survey in the United States found that three out of every four lesbians had been in therapy at some point in their lives (Bradford and Ryan, 1987; cited in Lyn, 1991). This is a new phenomenon. Even in the height of psychology's woman- and lesbian-hating diatribes in the fifties and sixties, comparatively few lesbians ever entered therapy. The development of "feminist" and "lesbian" psychologies and therapies means that more of us are now willing voluntarily to submit ourselves to psychological interventions. Lesbian/feminist therapy is a booming business.

The vast majority of therapists advertising in the lesbian and feminist press do not aim to treat lesbians with severe mental illnesses – so-called "schizophrenia" or "manic-depression", for example. They hope and expect to attract "ordinary" lesbians without long-term mental illnesses, but in need of help to get them through a crisis in their lives, or wanting to explore and develop themselves. Few private therapists in the UK will even see someone who carries a label from the psychiatric system, and someone who is too distressed to hold down a job would be unlikely to be able to pay for psychotherapy in any case (Laws, 1991). Some lesbian and feminist therapists (in both the USA and the UK) state explicitly that their workshops or therapy programs are not suitable for severely disturbed women. Consequently, our focus in this chapter is on therapy for "able-minded" lesbians only. We discuss issues related to therapy for lesbians with severe disabilities of thought or feeling in Chapter 5.

The kinds of problems that prompt most lesbians to go into therapy are the ordinary everyday miseries of life. One lesbian health group recommends going into therapy if you feel lonely, isolated, alienated or over-burdened with responsibilities, if you experience on-going unhappiness, feel constantly exhausted or anxious, want to become more assertive, or to learn to show softness and gentleness; or if you feel numb or out of touch with feelings. "Basically," they say (O'Donnell et al, 1979), "the time to go is when you want to make a life change and would like someone to be there with you, to really listen to you in a focused way, and to act as a guide". Lesbian clinical psychologist Bronwyn Anthony (1982) says that about half her clients first consulted her for difficulties in their relationships with their lovers and about a third came to her "because of difficulties in working through the grieving process necessary to letting go of a former relationship". Others came for anxiety (especially related to coming out) and for advice about their careers. These are the sorts of everyday experiences for which many lesbians now enter therapy. Ordinary feelings, painful reactions to the normal vicissitudes of life – despair, anger, grief, frustration – have now become "problems" in need of psychological treatment. Emotions like these are made to appear not only undesirable, but unnecessary, "curable". Increasingly it seems that suffering is equated with poor mental health, and we have given up the right to be both mentally healthy and desperately unhappy at the same time. This is what we mean when we talk about "therapeutic lifestyles": therapy entered into to deal with the normal, ordinary, everyday problems of living.

In this chapter we ask why so many lesbians are seeking out therapy, and we discuss the effect of the therapy industry on lesbian ethics and lesbian politics. We argue that therapeutic lifestyles are a very bad thing for radical lesbian politics, no matter how honourable the intentions of therapists and how real the distress of their clients.

Privatising Pain: From Consciousness Raising to Therapy

The oppression of lesbians causes suffering. Anti-lesbianism can mean rejection by a mother, daughter, or sister. It can mean losing our jobs, or our children. It can mean being mocked, ridiculed, or physically assaulted. All these experiences cause immense pain and distress to individual lesbians. Most of us feel, to varying degrees at different times, angry, hurt, rejected, and lonely because we do not fit into heterosexual society. Sometimes this is enough to make us hate ourselves – and other lesbians.

Some very serious problems in our lives are caused – directly or indirectly – by heteropatriarchal oppression. Drug and alcohol abuse, self-starvation, depression and anxiety attacks can all have their roots in the lesbian-hating world in which we live. Physical illnesses, too, can be the result of damage caused to our bodies by a male-dominated world; and our individual struggles to come to terms with these illnesses are made more difficult by the brutality we often experience at the hands of the medical profession. The trauma of rape, including memories of childhood rape, is another serious problem for which many lesbians seek out therapeutic help.

Often, too, lesbians seek out therapy because it seems the only way to deal with the anguish of a mother's death, the ending of a sexual relationship, or problems in their relationships with lovers and friends. Lesbians go into therapy because they feel generally miserable, unable to cope, isolated, or anxious. All these problems are exacerbated by the lesbian-hating world in which we live, but they are problems in any world.

These were the sorts of problems we used to take to consciousness-raising groups. At the beginning of the second wave of feminism, consciousness-raising (CR) was the place to speak out about our pain (as well as our joy).

This was never supposed to be therapy, or to fulfil therapeutic "needs". Irene Peslikis (1970: 81), a founding member of Redstockings, described the idea that women's liberation is therapy as a "resistance to consciousness":

"This ... implies that you and others can find individual solutions to problems, for this is the function of therapy. Furthermore the statement expresses anti-woman sentiment by implying that when women get together to study and analyze their own experience, it means they are sick, but when Chinese peasants or Guatemalan guerrillas get together and use the identical method they are revolutionary."

Kathie Sarachild (1978: 148) makes the same point.

"The purpose of hearing people's feelings and experience was not therapy, was not to give someone a chance to get something off her chest... It was to hear what she had to say. The importance of listening to a woman's feelings was collectively to analyze the situation of women, not to analyse *her*. The idea was not to change women, was not to make 'internal changes' except in the sense of knowing more. It was and is the conditions women face, it's male supremacy, we want to change."

In consciousness-raising, then, personal pain – along with other personal experiences – was discussed, analysed, and used to build political theory. Consciousness-raising didn't necessarily take the pain away – but it did put it to good use. Consciousness-raising is the practice of making the personal political.

Sometimes, of course, consciousness-raising can and does alter the way we feel. In exploring our body image, our relationships with our mothers, our sexuality with other lesbians, our understanding and experience of all of these can change. But change in the way we feel is not the be-all and end-all of CR. We cannot always assume that our distress and misery will be magically done away with. CR is not intended to be a psychological aspirin or a mental anaesthetic. Feeling miserable some of the time is inevitable, not only because we live in an oppressive anti-lesbian world, but also because nasty things are an integral part of life. Even "after the revolution", our lovers and friends will die, leaving us feeling bereft and alone; people will let us down and behave in ways we do not like; we will suffer from physical ailments and personal anxieties. Perhaps it was the mistaken hope that we would all feel better that led many to turn away from consciousness-raising to therapy.

Right from the beginning there were those who expected CR to be therapy. Small wonder when, according to Kathie Sarachild (1978: 168), popular feminist magazines like *Ms* depicted it that way: "everything they'd ever written about consciousness-raising described it like group therapy, self-improvement, change your personality. The power of positive thinking line – if women change their personalities, they'll have power". Karla Jay (1975) describes the early drift into therapy as a result of the unrealistic expectations of many women involved in early second-wave feminism:

> "The entire movement, in fact, seemed to be burdened by those women who came into the movement to find a cure for their problems, or to find mediators for their relationships. Yes, a primary function of the movement is to support our sisters in every way possible, but it seemed increasingly difficult to make political progress, to formulate actions, and even simply to think when everyone was screaming, 'Give me, save me, fill this need, fill that need!' In other words, women were draining strength from the movement instead of bringing strength *to* it. Instead of asking what they could do for the movement or to liberate other sisters, they were interested only in what would be done for them – and immediately."
> (Jay, 1975: 206–7)

Many lesbian/feminist therapists describe therapy as the natural successor to consciousness-raising groups. According to Luise Eichenbaum and Susie Orbach (1982) emotions "operate on an unconscious level" (p 74) so that "deeply rooted" (p 74) feelings were often not addressed in consciousness-raising groups – they remained "hidden beneath the surface". Consciousness-raising then, was a failure. Therapy is the answer:

> "... the therapist provides the safety net so that the

79

feelings can come out rather than stay hidden under the surface and remain threatening as they do so often in women's relationships with each other." (Eichenbaum and Orbach, 1982: 74)

Sue Krzowski (1988), another London Women's Therapy Centre therapist, says that therapy enables us to "explore things at a deeper level than in consciousness-raising groups", (Krzowski, 1988: 189) because therapy workshops "function at a feeling level and do not simply look at things intellectually" (p 190). Some lesbian/feminist therapists are explictly hostile to consciousness-raising, and see it as psychologically damaging for lesbians. According to psychotherapists published by the Boston Lesbian Psychologies Collective, consciousness-raising (and radical political action) causes lesbians to become dangerously "homophobic":

> "Consciousness-raising and political action groups have had major impact in identifying social and institutional forms of homophobia... [But] more deeply internalized forms of homophobia, those without clear political sources, are rarely reached by these external activities. These untouched forms are often left unnamed, denied, or deemed unacceptable. When feelings are not afforded room for conscious expression, they are repressed and acted out instead. Consequently, when consciousness-raising or radical politics make the homophobia unacceptable, the internal forms become more subtle and insidious." (Margolies et al, 1987: 234)

According to this argument, consciousness-raising causes "homophobia". But again, therapy is the answer:

> "The particular focuses and freedoms of therapy offer greater access to internalized homophobia, with few restrictions on expression... The therapeutic milieu and the relationship between client and therapist afford a unique opportunity to search below the social surface of homophobia." (Margolies et al, 1987: 234)

Feminist psychoanalyst, Ruth-Jean Eisenbud (1986: 278) describes how a young woman (who had sought out therapy in part to deal with her sexual frustration in her marriage) came to the session one day with a question that had arisen in her consciousness-raising group: was Eisenbud basing her therapy on Freudian theory, and did she believe in penis envy? Eisenbud was at first reluctant to answer this question and referred it back to her patient: "What did she think? After all, we had already worked for eight months." The patient persisted and, under pressure, Eisenbud admitted (a modified) "yes" in response to both questions, at which point, "the patient froze, and when she could speak again, she said we could not work together ever again. She rose and left." Ruth-Jean Eisenbud interprets this question as indicative of her patient's psychological failure to individuate herself from other women in her consciousness-raising group, and of "a transference need for symbiotic merging". Commenting that this can "seriously threaten the analytic alliance and even inflict critical narcissistic injury", she goes on to lament the problems posed by her patients' involvements in consciousness-raising groups:

"During the 1970s, with women's consciousness-raising groups breaking new ground, women patients seemed not to come alone to the office. Like adolescents, each was invisibly accompanied by her group. Unless the analyst would in effect become a dues-paying [*sic*] member of the group, she was considered an enemy; as in class war, there were no neutrals there." (Eisenbud, 1986: 278)

Again, the same message. Consciousness-raising is bad for your mental health. Overall, the therapeutic literature associates consciousness-raising with failure to individuate, adolescent needs, increased "homophobia", and over-intellectualising of deeply-rooted emotional problems. Presumably things are easier for therapists now that consciousness-raising has almost disappeared!

Several therapists have tried to "take over" consciousness-raising as a therapeutic tool – improving upon it with their own refinements. At the Association for Women in Psychology Annual Conference (1991), Dawn Harris-Parker and Gayle Cummins gave a paper on "Consciousness Raising Groups for Adolescent Women". They set up a "CR curriculum" for young women, and used an "experienced consciousness-raising facilitator" to run sessions at the

local university. "We felt that it would be more appropriate", they say, "to hold the consciousness-raising group
sessions at the university than to have them at the high
school or someone's house. Because it was at the
university, it gave the group an official ceremonious air that
might encourage the participants to attend. . . ." This is a
very long way from the egalitarian spirit of early CR
groups. So, too, is clinical psychologist Jill Masterson's
(1983) concept of "lesbian consciousness-raising discussion groups". These groups had a "leader" who, because
"this was not a group therapy group", was responsible for
stoppping the discussion "if it became intense or deep". If
anyone brought up a difficult problem, the leader would
"say that this problem was deeper (etc) than this group
could handle, or that the problem was not further soluble
within the framework of a CR discussion group, and that
some other group format (eg group therapy) would be
more appropriate if the person wanted to pursue that
problem further". It was also stressed that all participants
were expected to take "a nonjudgmental stance about
other group members' beliefs", and the group leader gave
particular emphasis to "reinforcing nonjudgmentalism".
Participants were "educated" about Gordon Allport's theory
that "many minority group defense mechanisms include
criticism of other group members' lifestyles, sexual mores
and the like, especially defenses involving identification
with the aggressor". So – if you make a judgement about
another lesbian's lifestyle you are accused of behaving like
a man. Complete value neutrality is expected. This is not,
and cannot be, feminist. Feminism involves making value
judgements, and engaging critically with other lesbians.
But, as Linda Strega and Bev Jo (1986) say, therapy teaches
"that one value is as good as another – no values are even
better – and the worst crime is to be 'judging' of another's
behavior".

Support groups are just another manifestation of
therapy, in which we become therapists for each other.

> "Where we once formed CR (Consciousness Raising)
> groups, we now have support groups. The difference
> between the two types of group is striking. The goal of
> the CR group was to raise our awareness of our

oppression so that we could fight it. The goal of the support group is to band women together to take care of one another. Although they may claim differently, one can see that the majority of women in support groups spend most of their time nurturing one another. Perhaps the original intent of the support group was to give women the strength to overcome their specific hardship. However, I see little of the overcoming or moving on to action. Support groups have become self-perpetuating systems of dependency, once again encouraging weakness rather than strength." (Ward, 1988)

Judged in terms of therapeutic goals, consciousness-raising does not rate very well. It does not (necessarily) make us feel better. Sometimes it makes us feel worse, as we realise the full horror of our oppression. But we don't think CR should be assessed as though it were a form of therapy. It isn't. It's a form of politics. Therapy has persuaded us that "feeling bad" has to be got rid of. If we're unhappy there must be something "wrong". It's becoming hard for many lesbians to imagine that unhappiness is just an ordinary part of life. Instead it's seen as a symptom. Misery is now defined as a "problem", and we seek the guidance of "special" lesbians, called therapists, to help us "heal" and grow. This is the North American dream: everyone's right to the pursuit of happiness through therapeutic intervention. But distress, misery, and emotional crisis are part of life. Those emotions do not belong in the specialist preserve of therapy: they are the common experience and responsibility of us all. Lesbians can and should have the resources to help and support ourselves. Without using these resources, without looking after each other, caring about each other, our concepts of "friendship" and "community" become very limited.

The Destruction of Friendship

It is sometimes true that therapists can help individual lesbians to feel better. The undivided attention of a sympathetic lesbian/feminist therapist can be valuable in providing us with an ally in our distress, in helping us sort out our dilemmas, in enabling us to feel better, stronger, more able to cope in an oppressive world.

This used to be one of the functions of friendship. Friendship between lesbians used to mean that "friends were there for us in time of crisis just as they were there in good times and even in boring times" (Ward, 1988). Feminist psychologist Paula Caplan reports that many of her colleagues consider therapy essential for some women, and asks us to think long and hard about why they can't get that support from family and friends:

> "A major reason, of course, is that – especially in North America – there's only so far that friends and family will go, only so much that we can ask. Does anyone want to join me in wondering whether that might mean we should invest *some* energy into unmasking the limited nature of North American friendship. . .?" (Caplan, 1992)

Is lesbian friendship, too, so "limited" and circumscribed that we need to pay therapists to fulfil ordinary human needs for understanding, comfort and support?

What therapists are actually providing for many lesbians is prosthetic friendship – an artifical and unequal friend-ship which is paid for. According to some therapists, that's all therapy really is.

> "Maybe Freud and Co hijacked something ordinary people did all the time anyway. After all, at bottom psychotherapy is simply about talking to someone who 'will not judge you, not lash you down with blame, or top you up with guilt, not tell you to pull yourself together or pull yourself up by your socks, but give you a sympathetic hearing.' " (Mo Ross, paraphrased and quoted by Laws, 1991)

Having someone sympathetic to talk to, someone we can rely on to be there for us, is a good thing. In so far as that is what therapy offers, that's fine. But we used to call that friendship. Listening sympathetically was what our friends did – although they also knew when to tell us to pull ourselves together and stop making such a fuss. What has gone wrong with the lesbian community that we now have to pay experts to listen to us? Are the only lesbians we can trust the ones we *pay* for being there?

We are rapidly approaching a situation where all the bad things that happen to us, all our distress and our negative experiences are taken out of our communities and into therapy. As Anna Lee says:

"We bring the most intimate parts of ourselves to paid friends, while offering the most superficial parts of ourselves to our nonpaid friends. The excuse is that burdening our friends with our pain or anger or sorrow is unacceptable. But if we can only bring our joy to our friends, how can we value them? When we exclude our most intimate selves from our friends, we weaken the bonds between wimmin that are necessary to fuel a social movement." (Lee, 1986)

Even if we consider lesbian therapists to be part of our communities, it is still the case that lesbian distress becomes the special preserve of only a few of us – experts, with the proper training. There are problems, anyway, in pursuing the argument that therapy is "just friendship". It often (usually) purports to be much more than that. According to Laura Brown (1985: 297), "it has only been more recently that we feminist therapists have become publicly comfortable saying that our work goes beyond friendship", but go beyond friendship it does. Most therapists are careful to distinguish between "client" and "friendship" relationships. Laura Brown (1984), for example, describes how she found her "opportunities for socializing reduced because of the high likelihood that the next woman I found attractive would turn up in my therapy office a few days later, before the fantasy had ever had a chance to jell into action". Like many lesbian therapists, she finds that the overlap of "personal" and "professional" raises ethical dilemmas for her.

"Because it is common for lesbian therapists to do business with other lesbians, it is usual for a lesbian therapist to have her health-care providers, house-cleaners, lawyer, the woman who cuts her grass, be all lesbians and all women with whom she will rub elbows on social occasions. It is thus also possible that a client in therapy with a lesbian therapist will become lovers with another lesbian with whom the therapist has a prior business or social relationship. In my own case, I have had a client become lovers with my friend/banker, and had the interesting and ethically very informative experience of wondering when the happy couple would tell my partner, also a friend of my client's new lover." (Brown, 1984)

Lesbian therapist Kristine Falco (1991: 52) similarly describes her dilemma when "a professional colleague of mine with whom I also have a social relationship became a lover of a former client of mine – could I see them socially as a couple? In another example, a client whom I was currently seeing became lovers with my accountant – do I switch accountant?". Despite the wealth and privilege taken for granted in these two examples (many of us cannot afford to employ house-cleaners, gardeners and accountants, lesbian or otherwise), the general principle holds true: the lives of lesbian therapists frequently intersect with those of their clients outside the consulting room, but this does not mean that therapist and client meet as equals in the therapeutic encounter. To make such an assumption would be to ignore the power dynamics of the therapy relationship (see next section).

Nonetheless, much of what goes on in therapy – witnessing another lesbian's pain, listening attentively to her story, acknowledging her struggles – can and should be part of the ordinary business of friendship. In *Against Therapy*, the North American ex-psychotherapist Jeffrey Masson makes the same point: people need friends, not therapists. One British reviewer comments:

"Maybe it is different in America, but most of my patients don't have friends. Maybe that's why they're seeing me. And those who do have friends know that all but a few will run a mile if confronted with a suicidal thought or a panic attack; ordinary friends simply don't know what to do, some do not even want to know." (Robertson, 1989)

Lesbian feminist Jeanette Winterson (1989) sees it as "a condemnation of the broken structures of our society that so few of us, particularly women, have a group of strong, dependable friends whom we can trust".

Lesbians have not always been very good at supporting each other. Sometimes we let each other down. (But then therapists sometimes let their clients down too.) Often, when another lesbian tells us about her unhappiness, we feel overwhelmed by it, terrified that we are not "good enough" to help her, or that we cannot bear the burden of her pain. Talking about "betrayals" in the journal *Lesbian Ethics*, one lesbian says:

> "I knew a lesbian couple and was friendly with both. After they broke up, one told me her lover had battered her. I stopped all contact with both of them because I didn't know what to do." (cited in Evans & Bannister, 1990)

This is a common response to lesbian battering. It comes partly out of a shattering of illusions about lesbian community ("Will we always be angry at lesbian survivors for breaking the silence that supports our dreams and visions of a united, nonviolent, celebratory lesbian community?", [Lobel: 1986]), and partly, as Beverly Brown (1982) points out, in her article on lesbian battering, out of the therapeutically encouraged refusal to make judgements, "the refusal to name any woman more culpable than another . . . the elevation of nonjudgementalism in the lesbian community". It comes too out of fear and a sense of incompetence, of not knowing how to help. Lesbian writer Christian McEwan (1988) describes how, when her brother and sister (both in their twenties) died in the same year, one from suicide, the other from accidental drowning, her friends:

> ". . . saw the tragedies hung like a pair of billboards round my neck, and it embarrassed them. They had no idea what to do. They would have liked to help somehow, to act, to solve the problem, but clearly they could not bring the loved ones back from the dead. Awkwardly they reached for other, more familiar tactics: cups of tea and glasses of whiskey, tired words of religious consolation, none of them quite right or good enough, and all of them weighted, finally, with that same uneasy fear: *Don't break down in front of me. Don't tell me you can't cope. Don't cry, oh please don't cry.*" (her emphasis)

She describes her reaction to this fear and embarrassment in her friends: "appalled by my own neediness, I rationed myself carefully, trying to gauge what could fairly be asked from each." Looking back, she sees that people were basically well-intentioned, but simply didn't know how to help. Except for Leonie:

"She made me welcome, gave me teas and so on, but she did not use her kindness as a way to keep me quiet. When I began to talk about James, she encouraged me and asked me questions. For a long time I walked up and down her kitchen, talking and crying, crying and talking. If the stories and the tears grew too much, or the death itself became too sharply focussed, I would go to her and she would hold me for a while. She knew, as I did not just then, that the desperation and the chaos wouldn't last forever... In the meantime, those hugs, that trust, were of immense importance. They allowed me to go down deep into the grief, into the murky hopeless places where only sobbing lived. And in doing that they gave me clarity and strength, allowed me what I needed to move on."

(McEwen, 1988)

We want lesbian friendship to be able to encompass this kind of care and attention. We want genuine friendships between lesbians, not the prosthetic "friendship" of a professional.

In seeking out the pseudo-friendship of a therapist, we run the risk of destroying our capacity for genuine lesbian friendships. Therapy offers us a let-out clause. With the institutionalisation of therapy, we cease to expect to have to deal with each others' distress: it is consigned to the private realm of therapy. This deprives our communities of a whole realm of experience, deprives us of the strength and ability to support each other, and deprives us of understanding the context and meaning of our distress. Therapy privatises pain and severs connections between us, replacing friendship in community with the private therapist-client relationship. We tell each other that what we really need is therapy. We come to feel that we do not have the skills necessary to cope with each other's distress – these only come through proper training. The distress of those we love, value and care about is not safe in our untrained hands. We should leave it to the experts.

This leads to a vicious circle. The more we see our distress as a private specialist affair, the more we see ourselves and our friends as unable to cope with unhappiness, and so we seek out therapy. We are deskilled by the belief that coping with distress is a specialist job. Lesbian friendships and community become arid places to which we dare not bring our anguish or our pain, in which we cannot rely on other lesbians to accept our suffering and help us survive it.

As lesbian communities, we should be looking at ways of supporting and helping each other, and of dealing with our unhappiness collectively and politically. This does *not* mean mass education of lesbians in the use of psychological or therapeutic methods and concepts. We do not need professional training in how to be friends with each other. Too often, the drive for more supportive lesbian communities has simply led to the wholesale translation of feminist goals into psychological goals – what Janice Raymond (1986: 156) calls the "therapeutising of friendship". For example, the Women's Training Link in London ran a course called "Counselling Skills for Lesbians" the aim of which was to introduce participants to "Person-Centred" counselling skills: "attention giving, listening, communicating empathic understanding, non-critical acceptance and genuineness" so they would become able "to support each other in personal, work and social situations." It seems we now need training in how to be "genuine". Ordinary human activities such as listening and communicating are now specialist skills to be taught in evening classes. And, as always in psychology, "non-critical acceptance" of everything anyone says is slid in as an apparently self-evident goal. As Janice Raymond says:

> "In a confessing society, friendship often becomes reduced to 'sorting myself out' and/or to co-counseling – literally when two women set up this formal arrangement with each other, or figuratively when women make of their relationships with other women a context for constant self-disclosure... [Therapism] takes self-revelation, an important part of any friendship, out of the context of the passionate revelation of a woman's life as truly lived and pretends that such

> revelation can exist only within the context of the actual therapist-client relationship or within the informal therapeutic context of friends who act as sisterly co-counselors. . . . Instead of becoming deep friends, women become 'technicians of human relations'."
> (Raymond, 1986: 158–160)

Friendship between lesbians is not a special psychological technique to be learned, monitored and assessed by diploma. Friendship does not mean constant repetition of verbal formalities like "I hear what you are saying" and "you should do whatever you feel comfortable with," as an alternative to moral and political discussion.

We do *not* want our lesbian/feminist community to become one enormous group therapy exercise or co-counselling network. The relationship between therapist and therapee is not a good model for our lesbian relationships. Instead, lesbian communities should become able to accept misery, distress, anguish (as well as joy, delight and happiness) as normal, non-pathological, ordinary human experience, part of the rich fabric of our lives as lesbians. Dealing with those emotions, in ourselves and others, is part of going about our normal everyday lives: we do not need specialist psychological skills or abilities to do that.

The Problem of Power

Despite all our hopes of equality and egalitarianism, and despite the fact that many lesbians see therapists as fulfilling the role of "pseudo-friend" in their lives, therapists wield an enormous amount of power over their clients. Some lesbian therapists acknowledge this. "The power imbalance in therapy *is* real", says Marny Hall (1985: 127). The therapist, she says, "is the sage professional; the client, the needy seeker." According to Laura Brown

> "Lesbian therapists occupy a special position in the social structure of lesbian communities. . . We are leaders, teachers, oracles. In much the same way that the clergy, who healed the wounds in the Black community, are leaders there, so we, the perceived

healers of the wounds of sexism, misogyny, and homophobia, have become leaders among white lesbians. The power available to any therapist is potentially magnified for lesbian therapists because of this special position in our culture. Consequently, our power to do harm is magnified as well." (Brown, 1989a: 15)

Other lesbian/feminist therapists deny their own power, claiming to adhere to "egalitarian" principles (eg Walker, 1990). (As we saw in Chapter 2, most psychologists and therapists do not have very politically astute understandings of the meaning of "power".) Laura Brown describes how, at a conference for advanced feminist therapists, she spoke of the importance of the responsible use of power, "and encountered women saying to me that they had never thought of themselves as powerful. In a room filled with teachers and leaders, this denial of power was particularly poignant, and also particularly dangerous" (Brown, 1989a). The relationship between therapist and therapee is not an ordinary everyday relationship between two lesbians. It is distanced, circumscribed, and asymmetrical. Most of the time one lesbian talks and the other listens. The client tells the therapist about her problems, not vice versa (or only in limited therapeutically desirable amounts in the form of "self-disclosures"). The client tells of her life, her beliefs, her values: the therapist does not, because she must remain neutral, non-judgemental. "Equality" in such a relationship is not possible. The therapist is the "expert": that is why she is consulted rather than other lesbians within the client's community.

Some lesbians have described their experience of therapy in terms of power differentials, although they usually become fully aware of the power their therapist wields only when things go badly wrong. In "An Open Letter to an Abusive Therapist", Mev Miller describes how, when her therapist started a sexual relationship with her own ex-lover, she became:

> "... overwhelmingly aware of the power imbalance between us. (You knew a lot about me, I really knew little about you. Anything I said could masterfully be twisted by the logic of psychobabble.) I couldn't help

but feel the exploitation of my insecurities and self-consciousness... And while I cried my pain, kicked and screamed my hurt, and vented what little anger I could muster, you sat there calm, rational, and quiet. You crossed the line in pursuing your personal desires and then retreated into the role as therapist while I 'dealt with it'.... It is not friendship when one woman does all the emoting and the other is the objective listener. Though at times you may have shared your perspectives and feelings, the power equation was unbalanced (and therefore not mutual) because I was paying and you were the 'professional', the one with the insight and knowledge.... By investing my trust and confidence in a therapist, I handed my own authority over to someone else.... The handing over of one's self-authority to the perceptions of a therapist continues the woman-as-victim cycle. I felt victimized in this situation. And though many l/f therapists think that therapy helps women to discover and claim their own power, this does not address the real power differential that exists between therapist and client." (Miller, 1985)

Caryatis Cardea (1985) wonders what lesbians get out of being therapists: "The power to change the course of other lesbians' lives, the ego-strokes of clients' dependence on them, the addiction many womyn develop to the therapy sessions: All these things are distasteful at best, and dangerous at worst."

Way back in the seventies, lesbian activist Karla Jay (1975) warned us about the ways in which lesbian/feminist therapists abused their power over their clients. Describing the activities of one therapist who ran a sexual fantasy workshop "which turns out to be her own personal recruiting ground for victims of her sadistic 'games' ", and another who "physically attacked her ex-lover and once even broke down someone's door because she thought her ex-lover was inside", Karla Jay commented that some lesbian therapists are in even worse mental shape than most of us. We have, she says, "a flock of rip-off artists in our very midst".

Ten years later, in her report on lesbian therapy,

Jeannette Silveira (1985) documents some of the abuses perpetrated by lesbian therapists against other lesbians. They include the following:

"A prominent lesbian therapist was counseling a lesbian couple. She counseled Lesbian1 to leave Lesbian2, moved Lesbian1 into her house, and the two became lovers.

A prominent lesbian feminist therapist was counseling a lesbian couple. Without the knowledge of Lesbian1 she had an affair with Lesbian2 while couple counseling was continuing.

A prominent lesbian feminist therapist, who wrote a column for the local lesbian paper, formed a therapy cult. . . . She became lovers with one client and made her a co-therapist. She insisted that her clients engage in marathon counseling sessions with her, moved out of town, and would call them at all hours on the phone to do 'counseling'. Several of her clients filed complaints which resulted in her losing her license. One prominent therapist, after giving a lesbian psychological tests, revealed the test results to the lesbian's friends, asking them to convince the lesbian to enter therapy." (Silveira, 1985: 23–24)

In the same issue of *Lesbian Ethics*, another lesbian, currently suing a lesbian feminist psychiatrist for medical malpractice, writes:

"This 'healer' seduced, betrayed and abandoned me. She shattered my ability to trust. She broke my beliefs. She wrecked a long-term relationship, injuring my lesbian lover too. Years have passed and I remain shocked, distraught, and fragmented by the experience. Meanwhile this therapist continues to treat lesbian patients." (Anonymous, 1985)

More recently still, Paula Caplan (1992) lists a number of abuses including feminist therapists who promote sexual contact between themselves and their patients, and a feminist therapist who sent an incest survivor for electro-convulsive therapy: "every feminist therapist to whom I have spoken in recent years", she says, "knows of similar stories, and they have been discussed at every conference on feminism and therapy that I have attended." In a graphic illustration of the power imbalance, she describes how feminist therapists have told her proudly "how much more they understand about their patients than the patients understand about themselves."

We are not suggesting that lesbian/feminist therapists are any more likely than other therapists to behave unethically. For example, studies have shown that about one in ten therapists admit to having had sex with a patient (Bouhoutsos, 1984), and if you ask therapists to how many of their colleagues they would be willing to refer a close friend or family member, you typically get very low percentages. Therapy beyond, as well as within, the lesbian community is riddled with corruption. Clearly, lesbian therapists who manipulate, control and abuse the trust of their clients are damaging our communities. They should be stopped.

Many lesbian therapists and clients have demanded (and produced) ethical codes to ensure that therapists do not abuse their power with impunity. This is not so different from leaving power in the hands of white ruling-class men, but asking them to use it ethically. We are not calling for better codes of ethics, or for the implementation of lesbian investigatory committees. We don't want to "improve" or reform lesbian therapy. Lesbian therapy is a bad thing, not because some lesbians abuse their role as therapist through unethical behaviour, but rather that lesbian therapy is a fundamentally unethical enterprise.

What abusive therapists illustrate, in a particularly graphic and distressing way, is the enormous power therapists have over their clients. There are many "nice" therapists: lesbians who, with integrity, attempt to alleviate the distress of their sisters. They avoid gross abuses of power, but powerful they remain. Why have so many lesbians handed over power to therapists? Why have we set up certain lesbians as "leaders", "teachers", "oracles" over our lives?

Fraudulent "Expertise"

Many lesbians believe that therapists have specialist knowledge and expert abilities that they and their friends don't have. Therapists encourage this belief. According to

Laura Brown (1985: 298), therapists are "practitioners of a healing art that is neither intuitive nor naturally present in all women". JoAnn Loulan (1990: 74–5) compares the power of the therapist to the power of the car mechanic. The only difference, she says, is that "unlike car repair, which can be learned, one cannot learn to be objective about oneself. . .". So, you can learn to service your own car, but there's no way the responsible owner of a "psychology" should tinker with it herself: it has to be properly checked out by a psychological expert. As Janice Raymond (1986: 155) says:

"women have come to believe that what really counts in their life is their 'psychology.' And since they don't know what their psychology means, they submit to another who purports to know – a psychiatrist, counselor, or analyst."

Yet what is it that therapists (and psychiatrists, counselors, analysts etc) do know? They know how to reframe ethical and political debate in psychological terms. When you talk to a therapist, she listens through a specific theoretical framework derived from psychology which influences what she hears, how she responds, the sorts of questions she asks, and the kinds of interpretations she makes. A therapist is an expert in interpreting the experience of others within a framework her profession has invented. She is an expert in reframing and reinterpreting our beliefs, thoughts and feelings within psychological terms of reference. Therapy is simply a form of translation from one language (the language of politics) to another (the language of psychological health and sickness).

Once, all lesbians were sick simply by virtue of being lesbian. Now, some lesbians are self-actualised and fulfilled while others are, well, not necessarily "sick", but functioning sub-optimally, in need of healing. Definitions of self-actualisation and fulfillment, like definitions of sickness, carry with them a freight of implicit values. Criteria of maturity or optimal functioning represent value claims about the nature of the good life, about the kind of personality that is desirable or preferable. For example, an early analysis of the concept of "adjustment" in textbooks written by (predominantly) white middle-class men of semi-rural Protestant extraction, found that ideal adjustment was defined as conformity with middle-class morality and motives:

"The less abstract the traits and fulfilled 'needs' of 'the adjusted man' (*sic*) are, the more they gravitate toward the norms of independent middle-class persons verbally living out Protestant ideals in the small towns of America." (Mills, 1943)

Similarly, the psychological research on individual differences typically places the professional psychologist in a highly positive light. The more similar the person is to the psychologist in terms of eduction, socio-economic background, religion, race, sex, and personal values, the better "adjusted" or more "self-actualised" she (or he) is said to be (Gergen, 1973). When mental health professionals talk about "adjustment", "maturity" or "self-actualisiation", they are accepted as technical experts, when all they are actually doing is making covert value judgements. The value claims implicit in criteria of lesbian maturity and adjustment, then, represent value claims about the beliefs, feelings and behaviours that are desirable or preferable in lesbians. Claims about what the "self-actualised" and "fulfilled" lesbian thinks, feels and believes represent overt attempts to mould lesbian consciousness. (This is explored in more detail in Kitzinger, 1987a.)

An early and frequently cited model of lesbian (and gay male) identity development was invented by psychologist Vivienne Cass (1979). According to her model, a (soon-to-be) lesbian starts out with "identity confusion", a stage at which she is not sure whether or not she is really a lesbian. After this stage (stage 1, at the bottom of the developmental hierarchy), she reaches the second stage, "identity comparison", where she compares herself with heterosexual people and realises she truly is different. At the third stage, "identity tolerance", she admits to her own lesbianism, comes to an understanding and toleration of who she really is, and seeks out the lesbian community. With the support and validation of other lesbians, she progresses to the fourth stage, "identity acceptance", and from there to "identity pride", the fifth stage, marked by activist and "purposeful confrontation with the establishment". But the sixth and final development stage, representing the height of maturity, is "identity synthesis". At this stage, "the 'them and us' philosophy espoused previously, in which all heterosexuals were viewed negatively and all homosexuals positively, no longer holds true", supportive heterosexuals are trusted and "viewed with greater favor" and the lesbian "comes to see no clear dichotomy between the hetero-sexual and homosexual worlds". In Cass's words ("P" denotes her hypothetical lesbian/gay man):

> "P accepts the possibility of considerable similarity between self and heterosexuals, as well as dissimilarity between self and homosexuals. . . . With this develop-mental process completed, P is now able to integrate P's homosexual identity with all other aspects of self. Instead of being seen as *the* identity, it is now given the status of being merely one aspect of self. This awareness completes the homosexual identity forma-tion process." (Cass, 1979: 234–5)

At the highest developmental level, then, the lesbian believes herself to be essentially the same as heterosexuals, sees her lesbianism as a normal aspect of her "whole self", and is integrated into society, trusting and feeling comfort-able in the heterosexual world.

This is a common definition, shared by many psycho-logists and therapists. The fully-functioning, healthy, self-actualised lesbians (real or hypothetical) quoted in the literature are forever saying things like: "My homosexual identity is one very important aspect of myself but not my total identity. I feel comfortable in both the homosexual and heterosexual worlds" (Anthony, 1982). Most psycho-logical models define lesbian mental health in terms of liberal feminist ideology and the politics of assimilation. These psychologists define away political debates about radical feminist politics and lesbian separatism, by simply assigning them to a lower level of lesbian identity. Politics becomes a question of personal maturity, with the psychologist's own preferred political stance located at the top of the developmental hierarchy.

We are *not* suggesting changing these models so as to put radical lesbian feminism at the top. Some therapists have already done that. In particular, Laura Brown, much of whose politics we share, has gone some way towards placing radical (rather than liberal) feminism at the top of her model of lesbian development. We believe that the ideology assigned the accolade of "most mentally healthy" is to a large extent irrelevant. So long as political positions are discussed from within a mental health framework, then, regardless of whether it is anti-feminism, liberal feminism, or radical feminism that is defined as most "self-actualising" or best adjusted, we are still forced to talk politics in the language of psychology. Lesbians who agree with their therapists' politics are defined as mature and fulfilled. Those who disagree with their therapists are seen as lacking in "insight", and in need of further therapeutic intervention.

Therapy may be construed as one lesbian persuading another that *her* own perspective is the correct one. This is why clients so often end up sounding just like their therapists. We have no objections to lesbians trying to persuade each other of different points of view. But we do believe that this should be an open political debate of different values, perspectives and ways of construing experience. Therapy is *not* this kind of debate. Rather, the therapeutic relationship is a special, privileged one in which a powerful lesbian (the therapist) subtly encourages another in distress (the client) to understand her experience in the therapist's "expert" terms. We think this is a bad thing, *even if the therapists' terms are ones with which we are personally in agreement*. If, as is (occasionally) the case, the (radical feminist) therapist persuades the client to become a radical feminist activist, we still oppose the therapeutic process because we distrust the therapist's use of power in this situation.

For example, radical feminist therapist, Laura Brown, believes that her clients should develop radical feminist politics. The development of such politics is, believes Laura Brown, evidence of "healing". Clients entering therapy with her usually do *not* share her radical politics: as she says, "it is rare in my experience that even the most politically savvy of lesbian feminist clients is likely to see her distress in political terms at the start of therapy". Through therapy, lesbians are brought to share Laura Brown's radical perspective. She gives a case example of a woman, pseudonymously named "Ruth", who entered therapy in the early stages of alcoholism recovery to deal with her experiences as a nurse in Viet Nam.

> "It seemed to me from the start that the only way that this woman had a hope of healing was to reverse this process; to break out of her isolation and see her story and her pain through the eyes of a feminist analysis in which the meaning of being a woman in a man's war, and the terrible distortion of self that this required of her, were made explicit."

As a result of four years of therapy:

> "She had learned that her personal experience was in fact a political one, shared by many women who had been trained to be handmaidens to the warmakers....
> This experience epitomizes a feminist therapy, in which a lesbian who has been taught by the dominant culture to see her problems as a form of personal pathology emerges with the knowledge that she is an essentially sane survivor of patriarchal insanity, whose ultimate healing lies in her participation in cultural, not only personal, change." (Brown, 1982)

We applaud "Ruth's" courage, but we wish she were telling her own story, under her own name. We admire Laura Brown's ability to communicate a feminist analysis to "Ruth", and to enable her to apply it to her own situation, but we wish she had done so through open political dialogue instead of through therapy. While politics involves debate and consideration of conflicting issues of morality, right and wrong and social change, therapy – under the guise of helping lesbians to "explore" their feelings – "nudges", interprets, seeks "true" meaning in terms of the therapist's own framework. Laura Brown is actually engaged in covert political re-education: "day in and out, I ask her how she might see her individual predicament as part of a broader social and political phenomenon of misogyny and devaluation and oppression of women".

Nobody enters therapy to have their politics changed; few lesbians understand that that's what therapy's all about. Yet therapy is *always* a form of political re-education. In fact, some feminist therapists describe their role as "psychoeducators" and there is much talk about how important it is for therapists to "model" the appropriate beliefs and feelings for clients to observe and copy. Usually, as we argue elsewhere in this book, the beliefs modeled, and the value system into which women are reeducated is a liberal feminist or anti-feminist political framework. What concerns us about this, regardless of whether or not we approve of the politics dispensed, is that therapy is an underhand method of political conversion. As psychiatric survivor, Judi Chamberlin (1993), says, feminist therapists "claim the right to speak for us and 'interpret' our experiences, even as they reject the right of the psychiatric establishment to speak for women or their experiences."

Open political debate with a therapist becomes impossible when every belief, opinion or perspective is interpreted in terms of psychological processes. A client's views on separatism, sadomasochism or any other political issue are inspected for their psychological determinants: was it "really" an "ego defence mechanism" at work, or a "negative automatic thought" predicated on a "dysfunctional belief" resulting from "internalised homophobia"? In this way, all political debate has the potential to be psychologised away, and the therapist becomes not only an expert in understanding our experience for us, but in defining our politics, our relationships, and our lives.

Therapy makes political and ethical analysis impossible. It literally deprives us of our moral codes, our ability to make ethical judgements about the world. Therapy replaces the words "right" and "wrong" with the words "health" and "sickness", so concealing the value judgements being made. Debate of these is precluded by the language of health and sickness: those who disagree with the prescriptions are by definition "sick" and in need of therapy.

According to JoAnn Loulan (1990), lesbian attempts to make ourselves acceptable to the heterosexual women's movement meant that we agreed not to be out as lesbians. We tried not to alienate other women by denying our erotic images. This, she argues, was pathological, because it ensured that our homophobia became more entrenched. For her, the "well-adjusted" lesbian is one who embraces and accepts the diversity of lesbian experience – including acceptance of butch/femme and sadomasochism. She is not alone. Susan Hamadock (1988) argues that some radical feminists have unresolved conflicts between our politics and particular forms of sexual expression such as sado-masochism. She recommends participation in a Sexual Attitudes Reassessment Programme to help us "to get in touch with and become more comfortable with our own sexuality" (p 211). By definition, those of us who have political objections to sadomasochism are not "well-adjusted": we are "sick" and need to be "cured". Political and ethical debate about sadomasochism is made impossible if objections to it are defined as sick.

Sex therapist and clinical psychologist, Margaret Nichols (1987b) makes a similar argument. According to her, lesbians are sexually repressed, "erotophobic" – we don't have sex enough. But the good news is that we can be cured, and the "cure" is ... *sadomasochism*. Some of us would argue that the "cure" is worse than the "disease". Margaret Nichols does suggest that S/M isn't of course, for everyone ("not all people are stable enough to use a sexual enhancement tool like S/M in a healthy way" [p 250]) but goes on to recommend wrist and ankle cuffs, leather, rubber, bondage and the use of urine. "In some ways", she says, "lesbian sexuality needs to get more 'male' in its orientation". She continues, "trends in the lesbian com-munity suggest that this is happening and I see these trends as, on the whole, extremely healthy" (p 259). If you do NOT want to engage in sadomasochistic practices, this may be because of "deeply internalised forms of homo-phobia" reinforced by the puritanical and erotophobic lesbian/feminist movement, with its emphasis on political correctness. Moreover, lesbians involved in sadomasochism draw on psychology to justify their practice. Take, for example, the British pornographic lesbian magazine, *Quim*, which is heavily reliant on the traditional por-nographic paraphernalia of whips, chains, studded belts, black leather boots, Nazi-style caps and pierced nipples. In the launch issue, the editors quote sex therapists Margaret Nichols and JoAnn Loulan: "It is more important at this stage in history to support women being sexual, however they are sexual, than to judge which aspects of their sexuality are non-patriarchal and which are male-identified" (Nichols); "Some members of the lesbian community foster homophobia by trying to establish 'politically correct' ways in which lesbians may express their sexuality. . . Our beds are not large enough to hold our families, politicians, society and the lesbian community" (Loulan). We fundamentally disagree with both these therapists. Simply celebrating lesbian sex – by which lesbian therapists mean everything sexual done by a woman who calls herself a lesbian (including sex with men) – is not enough. Our sexuality is not constructed in a patriarchy-free zone: sometimes "pleasure" needs questioning.

We don't want to dwell on the sadomasochism debate (but see Kitzinger and Kitzinger, 1993), but we do want to point out that when lesbian therapists define S/M as "healthy" and opposition to S/M as "erotophobic", or as evidence of "internalised homophobia", they are translating a *political* debate into the individualised language of psychology. This undermines our ability to conceptualise the issue in moral and political terms. In fact, Margaret Nichols is clear about her refusal to engage in political discussion about sexuality with her clients:

> "Given the generally sex-negative attitudes women hold, and given the sexual rigidity of the lesbian community as evidenced by the rhetoric of 'politically correct sex', lesbian sex therapists need to model sex-positive attitudes. I have found this often means giving explicit messages about the inappropriateness of the concept of political correctness as applied to personal sexuality." (Nichols, 1987b: 246)

In their zeal for cataloging lesbian pathologies, lesbian therapists have also invented a disease label to characterise lesbian separatists. They are suffering from "heterophobia": "projection is the defense at work here" (Margolies et al, 1987: 232). The symptoms of heterophobia include the rejection and "denigration" (their word) of all heterosexuals, and the feeling of superiority to heterosexuals. Again, this prevents political discussion. Arguing that separatists are sick, and only think that way because they are suffering from heterophobia, makes analysis of the political differences between separatists and non-separatists impossible.

We criticise these lesbian therapists not just because we oppose sadomasochism (although we do), nor yet because we support separatism, (although we do), but because use of their language and concepts closes off even the possibility of discussing these issues in political terms. In other words, they prevent discussion of these issues *as feminists*, or *as radical lesbians*. We are supposed to do things not because it is ethically or politically right that we do them, but because it is in the interests of our health.

Some lesbian therapists recommend that lesbians become more involved in lesbian groups. We agree – we want many more lesbians to participate in our communities, because we think we need all of us to construct lesbian alternatives to the heterosexist and patriarchal world in which we live. But where we, and other feminists, give political reasons, therapists (of course) give psychological reasons. Involvement in lesbian groups is an important aid to psychological adjustment (Sophie, 1982, 1987; Padesky, 1989). One detailed study of the relationship between participation in the lesbian community and lesbian mental health demonstrates that happiness (as measured on the specially designed "affectometer") is positively correlated with involvement in lesbian groups (Rand et al, 1982).

What we have shown, then, is that therapy systematically translates political goals into the language of "health" and "sickness" – a language with a quite unjustified aura of objectivity and specialised knowledge. Therapy camouflages ethical and political issues beneath a privileged language supposedly removed from the political domain. In this, and this alone, is the therapist an "expert".

"Internalised Homophobia": The Oppressor Within

Nowhere is the psychologisation of oppression more evident than in the therapeutic use of "internalised homophobia". Therapists tell us that, as a direct consequence of our oppression in an anti-lesbian world, we are sick and in need of cure. A therapist can help us to "identify and treat the oppressor within" (Margolies et al,

1987: 229). We no longer have to go to heterosexual therapists to be cured of our lesbianism. Instead we go to lesbian therapists to be cured of our "internalised homophobia".

Therapists have had to educate women and lesbians about what is wrong with us in order to ensure a market for their services. Even so, they are forced to admit that "clients rarely seek therapy to deal with self-labeled internalized homophobia" (Margolies et al, 1987: 234). This means that clients who seek out therapy for help with *other* problems find themselves diagnosed as suffering instead (or additionally) from "internalised homophobia". Lesbian therapist Kristine Falco (1991: 69) advises therapists: "Always plan to spend a period of therapy time assessing with your client the effects of possible internalized homophobia". She illustrates how this might work in practice:

> "if a lesbian client enters the therapist's office pre-
> senting primarily with difficulties relating to an eating
> disorder, an in-depth assessment is in order. . . .
> It will be especially critical to sort out how her
> lesbianism may be interacting with the dynamics of
> the eating disorder, but to do so without implying that
> the lesbianism needs to be altered – although *how* she
> deals with her lesbianism may be a matter for change.
> . . . In my experience, it is ineffective to wait for
> the client to bring up these subjects, as some models
> of therapy recommend; the majority of lesbians with
> whom I have worked (though certainly not all) are not
> fully aware of these issues on the surface and may thus
> not bring them up voluntarily. . . . What is called for
> here is a gentle leading approach. . . . It is fairly
> common to hear me say to a client, 'You know, many
> women who love women experience a sensation of
> suppression, or a painful feeling of never being fully
> accepted by some important people in their lives. Is
> that sensation a familiar one to your inner self?'. . .
> These comments are intended to invite the client to
> examine her own inner experience in a way she may
> not have conceptualised it before, while at the same
> time leaving room for her to say she does not

experience these things if that is so (or if her repression is strong)." (Falco, 1991: 29)

At first reading this may seem a reasonable course of action. But in "inviting" clients to reconceptualise their experience as "internalised homophobia", Kristine Falco is "gently leading" lesbians into a trap. In applying the label "internalised homohobia" to our (possibly very real and very painful) experiences, we pathologise ourselves. Other people's rejection of and hostility to us is translated into our own "sensation of suppression" and located in our "inner self". When important people in our lives find our lesbianism hard to accept that is an effect and example of anti-lesbianism out there in the real world, and, yes, we get hurt by it. But only by an extraordinary sleight of hand can this be translated into "internalised homophobia". The consequences of translating it into "internalised homo-phobia" are politically very serious: not only does this change the definition of what is wrong (from "they hate me" to "I hate myself"), but it also changes the possible solution. According to Kristine Falco, what needs changing is *how a client deals with her lesbianism* (as quoted above: "how she deals with her lesbianism may be a matter for change" p 29). We think the solution is to change how *everybody else* deals with our lesbianism. The label "internalised homophobia" is simply another pathological label lesbians are conned into applying to ourselves.

Some lesbians (ourselves included) are not always "out" about our lesbianism all the time and in every situation. There are negative consequences to being openly lesbian. We may encounter rejection, hatred, violence. We may just feel bored silly with having the same tired old discussions again and again with curious, well-meaning, liberal heterosexuals. But according to some therapists, not being "out" all of the time is a symptom of deep-seated, internalised self-hatred, internalised homophobia, an irrational fear of being lesbian.

Therapists apparently imagine that if you feel good about yourself, nobody will hate you, reject you, or beat you up. If they do, it's because deep down you weren't really happy with being lesbian, and, riddled with guilt and self-hatred, you were trying to punish yourself:

105

"It is also possible for the person who is not comfortable with being gay to use coming out as a weapon to hurt herself as well as those she has chosen to 'come out' to. One aspect of the process of guilt on the part of the lesbian may be to develop a need for self-punishment which can be accomplished by alienating herself from family and friends. The fear of family rejection can become a self-fulfilling prophecy." (Groves, 1985)

As we argued in the preceding chapter, to define fear of lesbians, fear of being lesbian, as an irrational fear, a phobia, is to say the least paradoxical from a lesbian feminist perspective. By refusing to define ourselves in terms of men, by refusing to service men in the expected manner, we as lesbians are a threat to heteropatriarchal social organisation. As such, we are not welcomed with open arms. We experience hatred, fear, aggression, derision, rejection, marginalisation, as a direct consequence of being lesbian. Is it any wonder that at times we don't like being lesbian very much? Are complex intra-psychic explanations really necessary? Like our fear of being run over if we stand in the middle of a busy road, fear of a real threat cannot be phobic or irrational.

The effect of "internalised homophobia" is to patholog-ise the distress experienced by lesbians as a consequence of oppression. Lesbian suffering under heteropatriarchy is translated into poor psychological health. Instead of oppression being understood as a political issue requiring social change, our oppression becomes a private issue requiring individual adjustment.

Therapy is wrong

Therapy is taking over our everyday lives as lesbians. Although we have criticised many individual therapists and therapies in this chapter, our main objective has been to point out that the very *idea* of therapy is wrong. We do not think the situation is substantially improved by "ethical guidelines" for therapists, however efficiently these are enforced, because we think therapy in and of itself is a fundamentally unethical enterprise. Some lesbians have criticised therapy as a white, middle-class preoccupation: sliding scales and other variations are recommended for making therapy more "accessible" to poor lesbians, black lesbians, or severely disturbed lesbians (eg O'Sullivan, 1984; Laws, 1991). We don't think this is the answer either. If something is bad, it doesn't become "good" just because more people have access to it. The fundamental problem is not the abuses some therapists perpetrate, nor the racist, classist and able-minded conditions of access to therapy (though all these things are problems too). The fundamental problem is the nature of therapy itself.

We would like lesbians to know the difference between therapy and feminism (even if they sometimes still choose therapy). We would like lesbians to reclaim the right, and the necessity, for moral and political judgements about our lives. We would like lesbians to believe that most of us, most of the time, are strong and capable human beings who do not need to be "cured" of imaginary addictions and internalised self-hatred. And that on those occasions when we are *not* strong and capable, we are – or should be, could be – able to take care of each other. To the extent that we are not, that is an indictment of our movement.

LOVING OURSELVES, LOVING EACH OTHER:
LESBIANS IN COMMUNITY

Our individual selves, and our relationships with one another – as friends, as lovers, and as a community: these are topics upon which psychology claims special expertise. This chapter looks at psychological notions of selfhood and relationships, and discusses the problems these present for lesbian feminist theory.

Psychologists have invented innumerable models of the healthy, normal, fully-functioning human being – models adapted by lesbian/feminist psychologists to describe the self-actualised lesbian. In all psychological theories, a healthy person develops from a dependent child to become an autonomous and independent adult. In virtually all models, the bonds that unite people cannot be built securely until people have fully individuated themselves – sloughed off the layers of conditioning, the masks and disguises, the self-deceptions and inauthenticities. According to feminist psychologist Judith Bardwick (1979: 128) women should

"... develop a sense of their own selves, because until they do, there is too good a possibility that they will be only the sum of their roles, adapting to others expectations, consensual rather than authentic selves. People cannot or should not live through others. There must be an anchor of *ME*!"

Lesbian therapist Laura Brown (1992) makes the same assumption of "an anchor of *ME*", a core real self when she writes of her client's need to "recover her self from the snares of patriarchy" and to "peel away the layers of patriarchal training which have distorted her abilities to see herself clearly". We suggest that there is no "real" self to be reclaimed and loved – that this very concept is one of psychology's inventions, and that the concept of true selves keeps lesbians locked into perpetual cycles of "self-discovery".

The notion of the "true self", damaged by heteropatriarchy, also means that lesbians construe themselves as wounded. We are sick; and our relationships are necessarily flawed. Psychologists take it upon themselves to offer advice on how to find and keep "the perfect lover", diagnose problems in our relationships such as "merger" or "codependency", and explain our failure to live up to the Superdyke image of lesbian sexuality as due to invented diseases like "erotophobia", "Inhibited Sexual Desire" (ISD), "repression", or "internalised homophobia".

Indeed, most of the things that go wrong in our lives these days can be explained in psychobabble. Pain and suffering is not caused directly by oppression, but by our own pathology – especially our "internalised homophobia". In an article about counselling lesbian and gay couples, Beverly Decker warns that therapists should not "blame society" for their clients' misery, nor should they:

> "encourage politicizing of the issue of sexual preference when it is being used to avoid dealing with issues of intimacy and separation/individuation or the pain engendered by nonrecognition or total rejection by family, co-workers or friends. Same-sex couples need to be helped to distinguish between exogenous and internalised homophobia and to see all the ways in which they may maintain a victim attitude or provoke and perpetuate their social isolation." (Decker, 1984)

So, there you have it! Lesbians deliberately "provoke and perpetuate their social isolation". We oppress ourselves. This "blame the victim" position is a common thread running through much psychology.

Psychologists focus on "the individual" and therefore most commonly make pronouncements about individuals; sometimes this extends to couples; less often to "families". There are no fully developed psychological theories about lesbian communities. The notion of "communities" pushes theory over the border into sociology. Nonetheless, psychologists do make passing comments about lesbian communities, either as "support networks" for individuals or as judgemental and moralistic groups which undermine the therapeutic endeavour. Psychology has a profound impact on lesbian communities through its conception of communities as made up of wounded individuals, each defined by that which hurts her. Lesbian communities, in their psychologised conception, are places where we bind each others wounds and nurture each others recovery from a toxic world. This is a very long way from the vital, creative and politically active idea of "lesbian community" of radical feminism. Those of us who still want to build that political base, to create lesbian/feminist possibilities in the world, have to recognise psychology for the enemy it is.

Loving Your Self

According to psychology, each of us has a very special possession called a "self", and we are all responsible for discovering, affirming, loving and improving that "self". Therapists offer to help us "discover and learn to accept your lost and wounded self" and to "promote nurturing self-care" (advertisers in *A Listing Of Women Owned Businesses in the Bay area*, 1992). The same message is promoted in books with titles like: *Reclaiming Your Self*, *Courage to Be Yourself*, *Accepting Yourself*, *Learning to Love Yourself*, and *Living in Love with Yourself*. Although their authors tend to be North Americans, books like these are easily available from feminist bookstores across the world.

These books share an emphasis on everyone's separate, unique individuality. One of the earliest and most famous founders of humanistic psychology, Fritz Perls, put it this way, in his well-known "prayer": "I do my thing, and you do your thing. I am not in this world to live up to your expectations. And you are not in this world to live up to mine. You are you, and I am I. And if by chance we find each other, it's beautiful. If not, it can't be helped." Heterosexual best-selling author, Virginia Satir (1976), speaker at international seminars on self-esteem and personal growth, wrote an inspirational poem on this theme:

"I am me
In all the world.
there is no one else like me.
There are persons who have some parts like me,
but no one adds up exactly like me.
Therefore everything that comes
out of me
is authentically mine
because I alone chose it."

One self-help book even claims, quite unselfconsciously, that "becoming oneself is one of life's greatest achievements" (Namka, 1989).

Most lesbian psychologists and therapists agree with these sentiments. Psychotherapist Ricki Geiger, in her book of "affirming and loving messages", *Empowerment for Lesbians* (1990) explains (like Virginia Satir and so many others) that we are individuals: "No one looks just like you" (p 3); "Yes, you are unique and different!" (p 18). These platitudes are supposed to represent hard-won insights into the lesbian condition. It's not enough just to *be* individuals: we have to *love* our individual uniqueness: "Be your own cheerleader, hurray for me! Be self be!" (p 85). The rewards of being able to accept and cheer yourself are "internal power" and "recovery": "Internal power is knowing who you are, believing in who you are and being that self in the world" (p 30); "Recovery is a process of individuation: seeing yourself as an 'I'; separate and distinct from a past or present relational context" (p 33).

Psychologists generally are very concerned to point out the importance of knowing and loving yourself: until you do, all relationships are doomed to failure and politics are no more than a manifestation of unrecognised psychic conflicts. Once you *do* truly know and love yourself, perfect bliss will be yours, you will win health, fame and fortune – and heteropatriarchy will crumble overnight!

Then comes the catch. Knowing and loving yourself is very difficult. Especially for women, and still more so for lesbians. According to Ricki Geiger, "All women ... grow up feeling 'less than'" (p 5), have "a negative self-concept" (p 21) and "have internalized the shame we learned about

111

being female which feeds our low self-esteem." (p 25). The question then becomes how to feel better about ourselves, and psychology is the answer: "One of the tenets of sexism reflected in childhood socialization encourages girls to seek others to trust. One of the tenets of recovery reflected in 12 Step programs encourages women to trust in themselves" (Geiger, 1990: 75). Psychology makes itself indispensable to those who would discover and love themselves. Not surprising, as the whole notion of true selves, to be discovered and loved, is a psychological invention in the first place.

What's alarming is how quickly this psychological invention has become common coinage in the middle-class cultures of North America and, increasingly, Britain. We have learned to talk about our "selves" in the language of psychology. Lesbians are forever fussing over issues of "self-development" or "self-realisation", worrying that their "potentials" are being suppressed, that their "personal growth" is not on target, that "self-fulfilment" has eluded them. Many lesbians are perpetually focussed inward, hoping to discover their true selves, to become their own persons, even (in rebirthing and self-parenting therapies) to give birth to themselves. Much of this process is negative. It involves, as the titles of other books in the genre put it, *Breaking Free, Cutting the Ties that Bind, Escape from Intimacy*. The assumption is that once the breaking, cutting, and escaping is complete, the "self" will be revealed in all its nakedness. Stripped bare of the demands of culture, community, family, politics, and morality, the de-contextualised "self", shorn of everything that shapes it and gives it meaning, can be interrogated as to its "real" needs and desires. These and these alone form the basis for "autonomous" action and "free" choice.

We think that this is a ludicrous and nonsensical notion. It relies on a profoundly individualistic, modern liberal Western concept of what it means to be a person – a version of personhood alien to most of the world's people. We are simply unable to believe in this autonomous free-floating "self". For the "self" only comes into existence within a context. Individual and society are not formed and defined apart from one another, "interacting" as though each were external to the other. Rather, "society" constitutes and inhabits the very core of whatever passes for personhood. There is no core "real self" lurking beneath the layers of social experience. There are only stories we tell about who we are, who we have been, and who we might become – stories which are structured by the culture in which we live. Our modern individualism, and the psychobabble through which it is often expressed, is itself one of those cultural stories.

In many cultures there is no concept of an autonomous individual: rather, persons are conceived of as integral to the greater whole – the kinship system, the clan, the tribe, or the local community. The Wintu, Native American people, have no word equivalent to our "self", and the Ilongots (Philippine people) have no conception of an autonomous inner life, in opposition to life-in-the-world. Feminist anthropologist Shelley Rosaldo says of the Ilongots:

> "Accounts of why particular persons acted as they did refer almost exclusively to public and political concerns. . . . There is no necessary gap between 'the presentation' and 'the self'. . . . Nor do Ilongots in their self-reflections speak of personal histories or distinctive psychic drives to account for the peculiarities of deed or dreams. . . . In short, it seems misleading to identify individuality with the Ilongot sense of self, first because Ilongots do not assume a gap between the private self and public person, and second, because the very terms they use in their accounts of how and why they act place emphasis not on the individual who remains outside a social whole, but rather on the ways in which all adults are simultaneously autonomous and equal members of a group." (Rosaldo, 1984)

According to another anthropologist, the same is true in Bali:

> "In Bali there is a persistent and systematic attempt to stylize all aspects of personal expression to the point where anything idiosyncratic, anything characteristic of the individual merely because he [*sic*] is who he is physically, psychologically or biographically, is muted

113

in favour of his assigned place in the continuing and, so it is thought, never-changing pageant that is Balinese life. It is *dramatis personae*, not actors, that endure; indeed, it is *dramatis personae*, not actors, that in the proper sense really exist. Physically men [*sic*] come and go – mere incidents in a happenstance history of no genuine importance, even to themselves. But the masks they wear, the stage they occupy, the parts they play, and most important, the spectacle they mount, remain and constitute not the facade but the substance of things, not least the self." (Geertz, 1984: 128–9)

The concept of the private and innermost "self", to be discovered, affirmed and loved by each individual is a peculiarly Western notion. Yet many Western lesbians are now so saturated by this notion, and psychology, that it has become literally unthinkable that our "selves" could be any other way.

The notion of the "self" has been a problem from the very beginning of second wave feminism. The women's liberation movement, like the lesbian movement, has always been rooted in and heavily influenced by Anglo-American individualism. This makes our theories very vulnerable to psychological appropriation. If we frame the problems for women and lesbians as due to insufficient opportunities for "self-fulfillment", we are setting ourselves up for psychological solutions.

Psychology claims that "loving ourselves" is an essential prerequisite to loving others, and to effective political work. We cannot believe this claim. What it usually means is that lesbians get stuck in therapy, or self-help groups, endlessly "processing" their own psychic products. Loving others, and being effective politically, is not something you magically become able to do once you "truly love yourself". Rather, you learn how to love *in the process of loving*; how to to engage politically *through political engagement*. Like learning to ride a bicycle, there's no substitute for actually doing it: no amount of "self-affirmation", or theory about "internal harmony" will substitute for just getting on and having a go. Lesbians who "succeed", in the sense of building good relationships with others, or in their political work, do not (usually) do so by first learning how to "love themselves": rather, they just get on and do it – and may (or may not) learn to "love themselves" in the process. Joanna Russ tells of a conversation between two lesbians, one of whom was living openly as such, and one of whom was afraid to leave her marriage:

> "The married one said, 'I can't leave my husband because I'm not brave like you'. To which the other (who had left *her* husband only two years before) said, 'Don't give me that. I was just as scared as you when I left my marriage, but I did it anyway. *That's what made me brave*'" (Russ, 1981, emphasis in original).

Adrienne Rich makes a similar point about liars who resist confrontation by admitting to their "cowardice".

> "She may bravely declare herself a coward. This allows her to go on lying, since that is what cowards do. She does not say, *I was afraid*, since this would open the question of other ways of handling her fear. It would open the question of what is actually feared." (Rich, 1977: 192)

Turning the spotlight on the "self", psychology plunges the world out there into darkness. We know ourselves as social selves, as members of a culture, inheritors of a history, participants in a movement. We discover who we are face to face and side by side with others in work, learning, love, friendship, groups and communities. We become who we are in the context of the institutions which structure our experience, and the cultural or countercultural patterns through which we interpret it. What it means to be a person, a woman, a lesbian, cannot be uncovered in a therapist's office, ferretted out through artificial exercises in self-help groups, or revealed by assiduous adherence to guidelines in DIY psychology books. We construct our identities only through vital relationships with other lesbians, and passionate involvement in our communities.

"You Deserve the Perfect Lover"

It is a measure of the extraordinary burden placed on sexuality these days that the word "relationship" has come to mean "sexual relationship", as though only sex makes a relationship real, worth commenting on. As Julia Penelope (1990: 98) points out:

> "Our relationships aren't limited to those that are sexual; sexual intimacy isn't the defining characteristic of a 'relationship'. Our friendships are 'relationships', and our disagreements are relationships, too."

Heterosexual feminist psychologists, like Susie Orbach and Luise Eichenbaum (1987), who are close friends as well as therapists and co-authors, have written extensively on women's (and lesbians') friendships, but lesbian psychologists have (so far) said relatively little about our (nonsexual) friendships. For example, therapist Tina Tessina's book, *Gay Relationships: For Men and Women: How to Find Them, How to Improve Them, How to Make Them Last* is actually only about that subset of "relationships" we have with our lovers. And in their book on *Lesbian Couples*, Merilee Clunis and Dorsey Green describe two women getting to know each other for the first time and label it the "Prerelationship stage": by this they mean that the "real" relationship (ie sex and romance [stage 2]) hasn't yet begun. To use the word "relationship" to mean only "sexual relationship" is to prioritise sex and to downgrade other aspects of relationships between lesbians, and so to damage lesbian community. We are not arguing that lesbian psychologists *should* be analysing our friendships – we're delighted they haven't. But we do think that lesbian psychology damages our friendships in all sorts of indirect ways, one of which is by elevating sex to the position of be-all and end-all of a "relationship".

Psychology also damages us by the way in which it portrays relationships between lesbian lovers. In part, this is our own fault. We left a gap in our politics, failed adequately to theorise our sexual relationships – and psychology rushed in to fill the vaccuum. For centuries, lesbians have found lovers, sustained relationships with them, and – often – seen those relationships disintegrate. There is joy, intimacy, and the sheer thrill of it, yes. There is also loneliness, misunderstanding, suffocation, incompatibility, jealousy, irresolvable conflict, rejection, and betrayal: the misery of unrequited love, the trauma involved when long-term lovers separate. Lesbian fiction and poetry explore these issues, but they are curiously absent from our political theory. In countering hetero-patriarchal stereotypes of the lesbian as a shadowy creature haunting a seedy twilight world and enduring a life of unmitigated misery, we seem sometimes to have painted a totally implausible picture of perpetual lesbian ecstasy. This was certainly true in the early days. In the USA, Radicalesbians (1969) described lesbianism as leading to "liberation of self ... inner peace ... love of self and all women": through lesbianism, they said, "we find, reinforce and validate our real selves". In Britain, the Leeds Revolutionary Feminist Group (1981) argued:

"... yes, it is better to be a lesbian. The advantages include knowing that you are not directly servicing men, living without the strain of a glaring contradiction in your personal life, uniting the personal and the political, loving and putting your energies into those you are fighting alongside rather than those you are fighting against, and the possibility of greater trust, honesty and directness in your communication with women."

Heterosexual feminists were never really convinced: Pat Mainardi (1978: 122) of Redstockings commented that:

"The lesbians portrayed their lives with all the reality of a 1950s movie in which once the lovers find each other, they go off into the sunset to the strains of organ music to live happily ever after, unbeset by the ills that afflict us lesser mortals."

And a lesbian responded to the Leeds Revolutionary Feminist Group piece by asking:

"What's the secret? My 'personal life' (I'm a lesbian) is riddled with glaring contradictions, dubious motives, irrational and compulsive needs and desires. I have very few friends I really trust and none of them is a lover.... If we can no longer express our fears and doubts and needs and conflicts without being accused of rocking the right-on boat we'll be driven back into guilt and self-hatred and isolation, and feminism will collapse into clenched fists and empty slogans." (Rickford, 1981: 11–12)

In failing to theorise our misery – in dismissing all

unhappiness as caused by heteropatriarchy and due to disappear after the revolution – we left the door wide open for psychology.

Take, for example, lesbian sex. In countering stereotypes of bitter, rejected, a-sexual spinsters, deprived of the almighty phallus and limited to the odd cuddle, we reacted by presenting wildly unrealistic images of unalloyed multi-orgasmic bliss. One of the first lesbian sex manuals, *The Joy of Lesbian Sex* states quite categorically that:

> "There is no such thing as a frigid lesbian. Unless they are temporarily incapacitated – stoned, ill, quite preoccupied or the like – lesbians *always* reach orgasm in their lovemaking, and frequently experience the joy of reaching it again and again in the same session." (Sisley and Harris, 1977: 137, emphasis in original)

Many lesbians for whom this wasn't true wondered what was wrong with us, felt failures as lesbians, and some (a third in one study, Kitzinger, 1983) regularly faked orgasm with women lovers. In presenting this idealised version of our sex lives, we left a yawning gap in our political theories which psychology rushed in to fill. Psychologists frequently point to the inadequacy of political theorising of sexuality. Clinical psychologist Nancy Toder (1978) wrote one of the earliest psychological papers on "Sexual Problems of Lesbians"; she says "I find this attitude, that all lesbians have great sex all the time, to be one of the most popular and destructive myths in the lesbian community". Lesbian therapist Laura Brown (1986) makes the same point:

> "The 'lesbian-sex-is-magical' model, which appears positive and sexually harmless at first glance, can, when taken as a standard of performance to be sought after, become a source of self-criticism and performance anxiety and potentially lead to dysfunctions in either the arousal or orgasm phases of sexual activity. In such cases, I have encountered clients who enter therapy questioning their adequacy as lovers, women, and indeed as lesbians because they find themselves unable to measure up to standards set by the heroines of post-liberation lesbian romantic novels."

Notice the language Laura Brown uses: our failure to live up to the superdyke image is translated into "performance anxiety" and "dysfunctions". Defining our responses as disorders, psychology comes to the rescue! As a direct result of our reluctance to come up with *political* theories about our unhappiness, we get lumbered with *psychological* ones instead.

Some of these psychological theories are simply trite, often rather crass "how-to" guides, promising to help us find the true love that has so far eluded us – and quickly too. Sondra Ray, a certified rebirther, spiritual healer and founder of the Loving Relationships Training calls her book: *I Deserve Love: How Affirmations Can Guide You to Personal Fulfilment*. According to the blurb on the back cover:

> "You *deserve* the perfect lover and Sondra Ray tells you how to find and win that person. You need only decide what would make you completely happy in a relationship and you can achieve it, quickly and without struggle."

Therapist Tina Tessina – who uses "we" in writing about lesbian experience, but who describes herself in the preface of her book as "bisexual" – offers a "comprehensive guide to creating healthy, loving relationships". A section on "How (and Where) to Find Relationships" exhorts the reader to complete an "Ideal-Lover Exercise". Answer the following questions:

> "Should your lover be a computer buff? A collector of comic books? A vegetarian? A gun enthusiast or hunter? What hobbies would your ideal mate have? Do you want to have similar or different hobbies?
>
> Would you like your partner to be someone who enjoys dancing? Opera? Poetry readings? Sports? Singing? Reading?" (Tessina, 1989: 39)

Once you have made your decisions you can progress step-by-step to find the person of your dreams (p 41): "before too long they'll be eating out of your hand. . . . Success is guaranteed, if you have a little patience" (p 42). First, you prepare yourself and your home: "the bedroom should . . . be the 'pièce de resistance'. . . . Use warm, exciting color combinations, sensual nude pictures, and lots of mirrors;

119

you can even display your favorite sex toys" (p 45). Then
you go in search of "the right hunting grounds" (p 46). She
recommends joining political groups (the National
Organisation of Women, or the Lambda Democratic Club!)
as places to meet potential lovers, but warns *against*
looking for lovers in therapeutic settings: "By all means, go
to therapeutic groups to improve your relationship with
yourself – but don't confuse your agenda by going there to
find someone else" (Tessina, p 48). (Apparently a "confused agenda" in political groups is okay!) Once you're
there, the knack is to just pick someone – anyone – and
interview her: you need to "screen the person to get some
idea of your compatibility and shared values". An Interview
Exercise follows, and then some instructions on "Evaluat-
ing the Hunt" (p 51). Once you've caught your prey, there
are detailed instructions about moving "from dating to
commitment" (via "precommitment evaluation exercises")
and, finally, she recommends we get married – there's a
section on "Creating Your Own Marriage Vows". The last
chapter is called "Happily Ever After". Merilee Clunis and
Dorsey Green (1988) offer very similar advice to finding
one's own true lesbian love: theirs is a three-step approach:
"define the kind of women who interest you; figure out
where they are likely to spend their time; and then arrange
to be there to meet them" (p 247). In their case histories,
Meja volunteers to do some work at her local Women's
Center, and Fiona joins a volleyball team. Realism
overrides optimism for these authors: *their* last chapter is
called "Beginning Again".

None of this advice is significantly different from the
average Agony Aunty suggestion to "join evening classes".
It's a mixture of commonsense and silliness, which hardly
requires a psychotherapy training. What such advice does
is to offer us particular ways of thinking about our
relationships: as hunting and trapping; as personal achievements; as individual havens. It detaches us from our
political and social context, reducing lesbian political
groups to "happy hunting grounds" for true love.

But there are other psychological approaches to the
problem of finding the "perfect lover" relationship which
sound more sophisticated. Drawing on "systems theory"

and "object relations theory" they purport to be able to diagnose what is wrong with lesbian couple relationships. From these theories, a battery of terms have emerged which pathologise lesbian couples as suffering from problems of "boundary maintenance", "distance regulation", "merger-phobia" and "fusion". Our political theories fall short of adequate explanations of many of the problems in our lesbian couple relationships – often we have minimised them or denied their existence. Psychology rushed in to fill the vacuum.

Merger

Psychology's individualising tendencies, and the anti-political values that inform them, are particularly apparent when psychologists address the problems of lesbian couples. The concept of "merger" has become a catch-all term developed as a pseudo-explanation for virtually everything that can go wrong between lesbian lovers. "Merger" is used to explain why a lesbian wants more (or less) sex than her lover; why she has an "affair" outside of her established couple relationship; why she takes (or refuses) a job in a distant location, or becomes very involved with (or alienated from) her work; why she maintains a close friendship with an ex-lover (or doesn't); why she and her partner have difficulties reconciling themselves to unequal incomes; why they stay together "too long", or why they break up.

"Merger": what does it mean? Psychologists Merilee Clunis and Dorsey Green (1988) provide helpful diagrams: two distinctly separate circles are labelled "Separateness"; two circles barely touching – like a figure of eight – are labelled "Contact"; two circles interlinked – the way we sometimes draw double women's symbols – are labelled "Merging". "Merger" or "fusion" (the terms are used interchangeably) is defined as the blurring of boundaries between two people such that each identifies with the other's interests as much as with her own. "Merger can be defined as a psychological state in which there is a loss of a sense of oneself as individual or separate" (Perlman, 1989: 78). This total involvement in, and identification with, a lover is what many of us expect to happen during the "falling in love" and "honeymoon" stage of a relationship – but psychologists warn that for lesbians the situation often continues until each partner loses any sense of her own individuality, her "ego boundaries".

> "Psychological merger occurs in all relationships at moments of sexual and emotional intimacy – the experience of union which is one of the joys of relating. Merger is a problem only when it is no longer a transient state but an almost permanent one. The merged partners in the relationship find it difficult or undesirable to think, act, or feel separately from each other – such behavior being seen as betrayal or rejection." (Burch, 1982)

The fear of merged union ("merger phobia") co-exists with desire for the intimacy it offers ("merger hunger") (Burch, 1982), so that lesbians are continually pulled in two opposing directions. Each partner is supposed to be concerned about regulating the distance between the couple (neither too close nor too separate), ensuring that each can clearly differentiate herself from her lover: "boundary maintenance". Sometimes, (say psychologists) one partner within a couple assumes responsibility for ensuring intimacy, with the implicit understanding that the other is to resist it by demanding independence: the couple as a unit thus ensures appropriate "distance regulation". (The corollary of this theory is that neither "really" wants the increased intimacy – or independence – which lead the couple into therapy.) The concept of "triangulation" is used to explain why some members of lesbian couples sustain close friendships with other lesbians (often ex-lovers): they do so in order to assert their separateness from their lover, and to avoid "merger" in their primary relationship. (They may also have "affairs" for the same reason). Friendships between lesbians are discussed by these psychologists only in so far as they serve as props for, or dangers to, the primary couple relationship.

The most common explanation for lesbian "merger"

relies on what is known as "object relations theory". Little girls, it is said, fail sufficiently to differentiate themselves from their mothers (Chodorow, 1978).

> "The basic gender differences between mother and son promotes differentiation, while the gender sameness of mothers and daughters promotes a more complex relationship in which differentiation is more difficult. Ego boundaries therefore are less tightly formed.... As a result, women may have more difficulty experiencing themselves as separate, and a greater tendency toward psychological merger in intimate relationships." (Burch, 1982)

Mothers and daughters, unlike mothers and sons, have a special sense of oneness and continuity:

> "Mothers 'hold' daughters in relationship longer. This does not mean mothers provide more support, more nurturing, or in any sense a more positive relationship with daughters than with sons, but simply more psychological relatedness, whether positive or negative. The greater length and strength of this early period also means that separating and individuating are more complicated matters for girls. Daughters generally have a more difficult task in leaving the mother behind, and as adults continue to have issues with ego boundaries...." (Burch 1987: 132–3)

Some writers do describe cases of merger in heterosexual relationships, but merger in lesbian relationships is invariably seen as much more of a problem. Whereas in *heterosexual* relationships, a woman may feel dissatisfied by her male partner's emotional distance and his separateness from her, in *lesbian* relationships there is "a greater pull toward merging and loss of boundaries" (Burch, 1982).

> "When two women couple, the potential for increased intimacy and fusion is indeed multiplied. It follows, therefore, that the intimacy level in a lesbian relationship is likely to be greater than in a heterosexual one. Yet, what can be a source of joy and fulfillment also can create strong difficulties with issues of separation and individuality.... This results in feelings of being stifled, separation anxiety, poor boundary

setting, and difficulty in working out disagreements."
(Sharratt and Bern, 1985: 94)
The outcome of this theory is to pathologise lesbian couple relationships. In lesbian couples, two adults with "ego boundary problems" struggle to balance their desire for intimacy, for "oneness" and merger with each other, with their terror of engulfment and loss of self. According to Luise Eichenbaum and Susie Orbach (1987: 181) "the propensity to implode into a merged attachment is exaggerated" in lesbian relationships, and "intimacy may be problematic because the defenses against a loss of self in the merged attachment are in ascendance". In "object relations"-inspired theories of "merger", the problems we face are placed firmly back onto individual lesbians, who are alleged to be insufficiently individuated, and lesbian couples are diagnosed as pathologically flawed. According to lesbian psychotherapists "this pattern is common among lesbian couples" (Hall, 1987) and "there is little question that merger occurs with characteristic frequency in lesbian couple relationships" (Perlman, 1989: 77). The very concept of merger is predicated upon the psychological invention of the "real self" that risks being lost or compromised, and whose boundaries must be vigorously defended.

The frequency with which "merger" is diagnosed conceals an enormous variability in the types of behaviour that attract this label. A vast array of different lesbian experiences are now described as "merger" and it is often hard to see what they have in common beyond the fact that they are all problematic or painful in some way for the individual lesbians involved. For example, one case study of "merger" (Kaufman et al, 1984), describes two lesbians (referred to as Ms A and Ms B), partners for over twenty years, who entered therapy because they had been having arguments. The therapists elicited information about their lifestyle and found that these two lesbians were completely closeted, had no contact with the lesbian community, and (as far as they knew) no lesbian friends. Reliant almost solely upon each other for social and recreational activities, the burden of togetherness had become too great too bear – hence the arguments. "Merger" was diagnosed – a psychotherapeutic label which conveniently disguises the source of the problem, which lies not in lesbian pathology, but in heteropatriarchal oppression which isolates lesbians and divides us from each other.

Another psychotherapist opens two sections of her chapter with quotes from Rich apparently intended to illustrate "merger": "I will not be divided from her or myself by myths of separation"; "And my incurable anger, my unendable wounds break open further with tears, I am crying helplessly, and they still control the world, and you are not in my arms" (Rich, 1978 cited in Pearlman, 1989). Intimacy between lesbian lovers, and distress at separation and at heteropatriarchal power, becomes "merger".

Another instance of so-called "merger" cited in the literature is utterly different both from the isolation of Ms A and Ms B, and from the agony of longing described by Adrienne Rich.

> "I shall include a personal example of merging. Generally, Bonnie likes to take time deciding what to eat at a restaurant. I am a former waitress and when Bonnie and I were still new in our relationship I tended to identify with the waitress, waiting for Bonnie's decision. I would feel embarrassed and angry that Bonnie was not more decisive. Bonnie, quite appropriately reminded me, 'What's the big deal?' I was taking responsibility for Bonnie and the waitress or waiter as well. Now I am quiet and content when Bonnie orders and let everyone take care of themselves." (Hepburn and Gutierrez, 1988: 99)

Here, concern about others – in particular a busy waitress – is pathologised as "merger", and the decision to "let everyone take care of themselves" (that tenet of liberal capitalism) is elevated to the status of mental health.

We do not think that Adrienne Rich, Cuca Gutierrez or Ms A and Ms B are in need of therapy. Nor do we think, in fact, that their experiences have very much in common. The *differences* between these three accounts of so-called "merger" are much more marked than their similarities. "Merger" (or "fusion") seems to have become a catch-all category into which a whole range of different concerns about our relationships are dumped, apparently obviating

125

the need for further analysis. You feel unhappy because your lover is out of town; angry because she demands too much of your time; embarrassed because she takes too long to order in a restaurant ... it must be "merger"! "Merger" has become so popular as a description of lesbian relationships that some heterosexual women now explain their continued adherence to heterosexuality with reference to it. "One of the fears in lesbian relationships," says Robyn Rowland (1992), "is the anxiety of merging... I think it is one of the reasons I remain heterosexual: the fear of merging is not part of a heterosexual relationship."

The concept of "merger" came initially not out of "object relations theory", but out of "systems theory". Systems theory, as its name suggests, directs our attention away from individual and couple psychopathology and focuses instead on the social "systems" within which lesbian couple relationships are embedded – social systems like heteropatriarchy, or the lesbian community. This "systems" approach to lesbian couples was first developed by two psychotherapists, Jo-Ann Kreston and Claudia Bepko, and published in 1980 in a professional psychology journal called *Family Process*. In some ways this theory can be seen as quite progressive, in that it deflects attention away from the individual and her "pathology" in favour of exploring the wider social networks within which individuals operate. Yet it is precisely that insight which is lost in later "object relations" adaptations of the idea. Moreover, the article itself, despite being favourably cited in virtually every contemporary discussion of the problems of "fusion" or "merger" in lesbian relationships (eg Clunis and Green, 1988; the Boston Lesbian Psychologies Collective, 1987; Loulan, 1984; Hall, 1987; Burch, 1982), is firmly anti-feminist.

Called "The Problem of Fusion in the Lesbian Relationship", it argues that the lesbian community (or, in the authors' terminology, "the gay world") is hostile to the development of monogamous lesbian relationships. Lesbian relationships are vulnerable, they say, in part because "gay women [*sic*] rarely respect the sexual boundaries a couple draws around itself": "any woman, attached or otherwise, is considered 'fair game' sexually by another lesbian". Friendships with other lesbians (particularly ex-lovers) are dangerous because such relationships "tend to be intrusive and involve inappropriate claims". These dangers of the lesbian world, combined with the hostility of the heterosexual world, cause lesbians to cling excessively to their lovers, trying desperately to ward off threats to their relationship by "fusing" or "merging" with each other.

But although they recognise that "society" causes "problems" for lesbians, Krestan and Bepko caution against the "politicizing" of lesbianism, warn of the dangers of riding on a "political bandwagon", and the folly of our "tendency to see villains everywhere". Their stated aim is to accomplish a "cognitive conversion" in their clients. Like all therapists, their goal is to convert their clients to their own theoretical perspective (cf Perkins, 1991a). Unlike most therapists, they say so explicitly!

This "cognitive conversion" is accomplished, first, by teaching clients their own particular brand of psychobabble: "concepts such as boundaries, triangling, distancing, de-selfing, and fusion [are] explained. . .". Then, they "coach" clients in how to deal with threats to their lesbian selves.

> "In many day-to-day situations, clients are coached to use humor to defuse the prejudiced and provocative comments relating to their homosexuality. When Janice's mother next asks where Mary sleeps, Janice can be coached to respond humorously, 'She has chronic insomnia', or 'Didn't you notice the straw mat on the floor?', thus deflecting the question with humor rather than joining the issue and escalating it."

Believing that it is (partly) because of prejudice and discrimination that lesbians "fuse" together, Krestan and Bepko argue that if we find satisfactory ways of dealing with prejudice, so that we don't experience it as threatening our core identities, the dangers of "merger" can be avoided. They suggest deflecting prejudice with careful ambiguity ("for example, 'I have a friend I'd like to bring' is a less provocative statement than 'I'd like to bring my lover' ") and describe how each client is "coached not to politicize the issue of her lesbianism". A prerequisite for successful therapy with lesbians, say Krestan and Bepko, is helping them to "see their own role in maintaining and eliciting the unfortunate kinds of pressure that society exerts on their relationship". Thus, in typical psychological style, heteropatriarchal oppression is converted into an "unfortunate kind of pressure" and lesbians, it is claimed, are responsible for "maintaining" and "eliciting" our own oppression.

In this article, Jo-Ann Krestan and Claudia Bepko write from within a psychological framework commonly used by family therapists ("systems theory") and do not claim to be writing either as feminists or as lesbians. Given that their article is not original, not feminist, and not even explicitly lesbian-authored, one might wonder why it has proved so attractive to lesbians within and beyond psychology. We suspect that the concept of "merger" has become widely accepted by lesbians within and outside psychology simply because it offers one way of acknowledging that lesbian relationships are not always the unalloyed bliss we sometimes pretend to believe. Despite the victim-blaming and pathologising tone of these texts, the "fusion and merger" literature does name real problems in lesbian relationships. How do we balance relationships between friends and lovers? How do we relate to the wider lesbian community *and* sustain a relationship with a lover? How do we handle the rejection and derogation of our relationships by the heterosexual world? We think these problems are better discussed in a way that recognises their full complexity (instead of losing sight of the differences between them by applying an identical label, "merger", to them all), and in a way that is *political* rather than psychological.

Sex

Lesbian sex therapists often talk about the "political" nature of lesbian sex: "When working with lesbians, I believe that one must consider and analyze the sociology of the majority culture. Lesbians live in a homophobic, misogynist world" (Loulan, 1988: 221). "The sex therapy field is . . . biased heterosexually" (Nichols, 1987b: 244); "I write here in the spirit of 'the personal is political' " (Nichols, 1978a: 98). Yet, these same therapists are explicitly hostile to radical lesbian and feminist analysis of sexuality: Margaret Nichols says "I repudiate politically correct lesbian love-making" and JoAnn Loulan argues that "Sex should dwell within the privacy of our own lives" (Loulan, 1984: 24).

Overwhelmingly, the message from the sex therapists is that we should stop judging our sexual behaviour in terms of our political values: sexuality should be a "politics-free zone" of personal pleasure. Sex therapists share with sexual libertarians the notion that there is a "pure" female or lesbian sexuality which can emerge intact once the layers of repression, internalised homophobia and political dogma have been peeled away. This is, as radical lesbian theorist Denise Thompson points out, the familiar libertarian notion that:

"... there exists some kind of 'true' sexuality, an intrinsic property of the individual which is suppressed by 'society' but which will come into its full flowering once social restrictions have been removed. The political strategy which follows from this commitment to the 'repression hypothesis' involves the refusal to take a stand against any form of sexual desire or activity and the pejorative labeling of any such stand as 'moralistic'. . . ." (Thompson, 1991: 10)

Most lesbian sex therapists counsel that politically-motivated prescriptions for "correct" and "incorrect" sex are detrimental to "sexual health". According to JoAnn Loulan:

"Some members of the lesbian community foster homophobia by trying to establish 'politically correct' ways in which lesbians may express their sexuality. . . . Some people think that lesbians have to have sex a particular way to be lesbians. Nonsense! Lesbian sex is anything two lesbians do together. Monitoring your own and other's sexual behavior is in no one's interest but our oppressors." (Loulan, 1984: 24 & 27)

In the name of non-judgementalism, lesbian therapists typically refuse to raise any objections to lesbians' involvement with sadomasochism, pornography, or sex with men. Some therapists find this non-judgementalism difficult to achieve. Susan Hamadock (1988: 208) recogn-ises the contradiction between radical feminist politics and lesbian sex therapy and talks of the way in which "for some, unresolved conflicts between our radical feminist politics and particular forms of sexual expression such as S&M contribute to our reluctance to bring sexuality into our work as feminists." Another lesbian therapist describes how Nancy and Lois consulted her because Lois wanted to have sex with men and says:

> "This presented several difficulties since not only did Lois fear my judgement of her, but I felt vulnerable to siding against her. Considerable restraint was required on my part." (McCandlish, 1982)

For therapists who find sex with men and sadomasochism politically problematic, there is always "a brief but invaluable training process known as Sexual Attitudes Reassessment" which is "designed to help participants get in touch with and become more comfortable with their sexuality" (Hamadock, 1988: 211). But many lesbian therapists are apparently already eager to "reassure" so-called lesbians who engage in voluntary sex with men that this is understandable, and they plead with other lesbians to "celebrate diversity". Therapist SallyAnn Roth (1989: 295) is particularly concerned about the "intolerance" shown by other lesbians to so-called lesbians who have sex with men. "Those many women who experience them-selves as having the potential for significant relationship with women *and* with men often feel lonely and trapped with their feelings", she says; and she asks therapists to help clients to address their "own grief over the loss of . . . sexual relations with men". Lamenting the "rigid lovemak-ing patterns and discomfort with particular sexual acts" amongst lesbians, she concludes that "internalized homo-phobia", along with the "heterophobia" of the lesbian community, "may be operating to reduce sexual freedom" (Roth, 1989: 291). Clinical psychologist, Nancy Toder makes a similar plea on behalf of "lesbians" who have sex with men:

> "In my work with lesbians, I have found that many women have sexual feelings or dreams about men, or engage in sexual contact with men. . . Some women

engage in sexual fantasies about or behaviors with men out of curiosity. For those women who have never had sex with men, it is a new experience; for women who once were actively heterosexual and who have been lesbians for some time, sex with men is an old forgotten experience. Sometimes women who live relatively separatist lives find themselves missing men; a dream may communicate this message to a woman, or quick sex may be an easy way to make limited contact. . . . I bring up this taboo subject in order to reassure women that many lesbians share these feelings and experiences, and to make a plea for recognition and acceptance of *all* parts of ourselves. Until we recognise those parts of ourselves that are disquieting and inconsistent, until we respect our individual differences, the unity we build is false. More fundamentally, when we limit ourselves by imposing rigid and punitive rules for acceptable sexual feelings and behaviors, we are in fact capitulating to the same forces that we struggle against in asserting our lesbianism." (Nancy Toder, 1978: 113)

Psychologists apply this same non-judgementalism to fantasies. JoAnn Loulan (1984: 61–62) acknowledges that "for most of us certain fantasies are not acceptable ... fantasies that involve coercion, force, men, pain or perhaps another woman besides your lover," but goes on to claim that "accepting ourselves and our fantasies can free us up to more fully fulfill ourselves sexually. . . . Instead of rejecting fantasy because you feel it's wrong, try embracing it as a gift that enhances your sex life" (p 62). Similarly, lesbian sex therapist Susan Hamadock (1988: 214–5) reports that some lesbians are:

> "very uncomfortable about the presence of rape fantasies or those which include children or animals. Clients need to be reassured that these fantasies are common (Califia, 1980), that there is a difference between fantasy and reality, and that a sexual fantasy does not represent a wish to act out a particular behaviour."

Most sex therapists recommend the use of pornography or "erotica" (eg Brown, 1986; Loulan, 1984) to overcome

131

"internalised homophobia" and to encourage a rich fantasy life.

Sadomasochism is usually presented by psychologists as an interesting variation to spice up our sex lives. Margaret Nichols (1987b) goes a little further in explicitly recommending the use of wrist and ankle cuffs, paddles, the playful use of leather and rubber, and experiments with S/M, bondage and the use of urine. The bisexual psychotherapist, Tina Tessina (1989: 131), in her book on *Gay Relationships for Men and Women*, claims that:

"the following activities all fall within the range of 'usually normal':
– Using toys (dildos, vibrators, ticklers, and so on)
– Urinating on each other in the shower
– Wearing leather and/or rubber costumes, high heels, and handcuffs
– Role-playing (teacher/student, nurse/patient, and so on)."

Unlike Margaret Nichols, she doesn't approve of S&M which "has an unhealthy emphasis on inflicting or receiving pain"; instead, she recommends B&D (Bondage and Domination) which she says is "a harmless cousin to sadomasochism. . . . B&D is just for fun" (p 129):

"Many people experience a thrill in being dominated or in dominating someone else. . . . B&D games involve lots of costumes and props (usually rubber, leather, and studs). . . Some afficionados have complete 'dungeons' – elaborately decorated rooms with whips, chains, and restraints used for decor. . . . Agree in advance on a word or phrase that can be used to end the game instantly. . . ." (Tessina, 1989: 128–9)

We can't tell the difference between this, and S&M.

Lesbians engaged in S&M now often use therapists to support their activities. The first issue of *Quim* – a British lesbian pornography magazine – used quotations from therapists Margaret Nichols and JoAnn Loulan to attack lesbians who might object on political or ethical grounds. Other lesbians use psychological justifications for sadomasochism:

"For people like myself, who had an unloved childhood, S&M is one way of expressing the trust that

we should have had from our parents. A person who
you give absolute control to but who abides by your
limits as to what is to happen, well, it's a very
comforting situation to be in." (Hibbert, 1990)
Ex-lesbian, Jan Clausen now takes the line: "Do what you
feel like doing – to hell with living by theory".

"My gut reaction was rebellion against the personal/
political equation itself. . . . I felt the need of a zone of
experience off-limits to instant political critique. . . . In
this, I knew I had something in common with the
participants in the feminist sexuality debate who have
talked about the complexity and intractability of desire
. . . the connection helped support my determination
to say yes to what I wanted rather than to what I or
anybody else thought I should want." (Clausen, 1990)
What she wanted, and perpetrated, was repeated sex with a
man in the home she shared with Elly Bulkin, her lover of
twelve years. The rationale for her involvement is the
familiar psychological cry – don't judge me, I must do what
feels right for me, or in her own words, "I don't want to
take a position on my body before I know what position
my body's in". Elly Bulkin (1990: 62) writes of her "loss of
the woman I'd loved and trusted most in the world, my
fury, my grief, my feeling of profound betrayal – not simply
as a lover but as a dyke." If we refuse to "live by theory", if
we simply "do what feels right", we abandon our moral
and political values. Loulan says sexuality is scary for
lesbians partly ". . . because of so much judgement in the
Lesbian community". Linda Strega and Bev Jo, in their
excellent critique of *Lesbian Sex* ask:

"Why doesn't she mention fear caused by the presence
of so much heterosexism among Lesbians, fear caused
by Sado-Masochism, by the presence of Het women,
bisexuals and 'transsexual' men masquerading as
Lesbians, fears caused by racism, classism, ableism,
ageism, anti-Semitism, fat oppression, looksism,
imperialism among Lesbians?" (Strega and Jo, 1986)

Within the psychological framework of lesbian sex
therapy, "pleasure" is a natural, individual and private
phenomenon – a "right" denied us both by heteropatriarchy and, equally, by radical feminists brandishing

prescriptions for "politically correct" sex. Sexual response and orgasm are seen by psychologists as completely unproblematically "good" things. But, as lesbian historian, Sheila Jeffreys (1990b: 22) says:

> "We have got to understand that sexual response for women and orgasm for women is not necessarily pleasurable and positive. It can be a very real problem. It can be an accommodation of our oppression. It can be the eroticizing of our subordination. We need to appreciate that the word pleasure is often used for what we experience as humiliation and betrayal."

Instead of exploring the political framework within which lesbians do not feel sexual, or do not like certain sexual activities, psychologists label us "sexually repressed". If we don't like penetration this can be labelled "vaginismus" (eg Richardson and Hart, 1980), and therapists like JoAnn Loulan devote three full pages to explaining how someone can train herself to accept larger and larger objects in her vagina. If we don't like oral or anal sex this is labelled a "phobia" (Richardson and Hart, 1980), and according to Laura Brown (1986), "lesbians suffer from sexual dysfunctions of similar types and etiologies as do many heterosexual women". In branding particular sexual preferences and dislikes as "dysfunctions" or "phobias", sex therapists are promoting their own definition of "correct" lesbians sex, smuggling in covert value judgements under the banner of non-judgementalism. Their use of psychological terms to make moral and political judgements about lesbian sex simply serves to camouflage the political nature of this exercise. In failing to question the sources of our desires, in refusing to locate them within an explicitly moral and political framework, we comply with our own oppression.

Psychologists do more than simply celebrate the range of different sexual activities in which "lesbians" engage. They also seek to explain them *within a therapeutic framework*. Where lesbians like Sheila Jeffreys (1990a&b) draw on revolutionary feminist explanations of lesbian sadomasochism, therapists draw on a range of therapeutic terms to describe the "need" lesbians have for such activities. Concepts like "internalised homophobia", "erotophobia" and "heterophobia" are used to dismiss some lesbians' distaste for, and political objections to, sadomasochism. The notion of "merger" has also been invoked to provide a spurious psychological "legitimation" for these kinds of activities.

Psychologists have found notions of "fusion" and "merger" very useful in theorising about lesbian sex. In particular, sexual involvement with another woman is supposed to relate to unconscious wishes to recapture the lost mother-daughter union.

> "The intimacy of lesbian relationships, perhaps more than any other kind of relationship, approaches the intensity of the mother-daughter relationship. The parallel between the mother's body and the lover's body, so powerful unconsciously, is capable of evoking deepest childhood experiences." (Burch, 1987: 140)

Lesbian sexual problems are interpreted either as a fear of this merger and the loss of self that it entails *or* as the attainment of merger, and its ensuing difficulties. Everything that could conceivably go wrong in a sexual relationship can then be explained with reference to this concept. Feminist psychotherapists Luise Eichenbaum and Susie Orbach (1983: 122), for example, describe how one of their clients, Gillian, felt initially hurt, and later relieved, when her lover Rose leapt out of bed immediately after sex and spent ages in the shower: it was all due to merger during sex – "their merger touched off fears in both of them that they would be stuck together, lose their own identity and be subsumed by the other!"

In particular, "merger" is used to explain the purported loss of interest in sex between members of long-term lesbian couples. Once "fused", the need for sex is obliterated – the two are already one. According to Marny Hall (1987):

> "There are a number of reasons cited for the plunge in sexual exchanges between lesbians in long term relationships. Primary among them is a dissolution of individual boundaries, a submergence of self in the larger arena of the relationship. In the beginning, such

135

a commingling of souls is intensely erotic. If each partner does not reclaim herself eventually, however, the relationship becomes stultifying, and the spark of difference that ignites eroticism disappears."

Psychotherapist Margaret Nichols describes the same problem:

"Lesbian relationships, in part because they are 'advanced' relationships, sometimes suffer difficulties of overinvolvement, called fusion or merging. To some extent, intimacy involves the lessening of differences between partners; certainly it is more difficult to maintain a purely independent sense of self within a very intimate relationship. As intimacy increases and individual differences decrease, so may the very distance, mystery, and unpredictability necessary to maintain sexual tension." (Nichols, 1987a: 107)

Sustaining sexual interest between two lesbians over the course of their relationship then becomes an exercise in creating and maintaining "differences" between them. Without "difference", sex becomes boring and "Inhibited Sexual Desire" sets in. According to Margaret Nichols, "sexual desire requires a 'barrier': some kind of tension, a taboo, a difference of some sort, a power discrepancy, romance, the excitement of newness or the thrill of the chase – some form of disequilibrium" (Nichols, 1987a: 106). Inhibited sexual desire (ISD) is caused by too much merger, too little difference in power.

Consequently, lesbian therapists concerned to regain, maintain, or enhance lesbian sexuality promote the seeking out of differences. The simplest way to do this is to encourage lesbians to have sex with men. Men, after all, are obviously different from us. Sadomasochism and fantasies of heterosexual or sadomasochistic sex can also be used to enhance desire. As Joanna Ryan (1983: 201) claims (drawing on Ethel Person), "because of the real dependence of a helpless child on a relatively powerful adult, 'it is unlikely that sexuality will ever be completely free of submission-dominance connotations'."

We believe that if it is true that differences in power lie at the root of sexual desire, then this is a problem for lesbian feminism, and something which we would want to change. Yes, we acknowledge and recognise that some women who identify as lesbians sometimes have sex with men. And yes, we acknowledge and recognise that some lesbians find S/M (or B&D) sexually arousing and politically acceptable. But recognition of what is actually happening is not the same as accepting its legitimacy – and certainly does not involve "celebrating" it. Sexual desire does not have to be accepted as a "given"; it can be actively constructed and reconstructed (Kitzinger and Kitzinger, 1993; Kitzinger, 1993a). Sheila Jeffreys (1990a: 4) points out, "When equality is exciting, not just at the level of theory but in love and sex, then the liberation of women becomes a real possibility". We also recognise that in making these statements we are laying ourselves open to being branded "lesbian thought police" (Loulan, 1990) or diagnosed as "erotophobic" (Nichols, 1987a: 122). These are labels used to dismiss, trivialise or pathologise our arguments. They do not constitute debate and cannot advance feminism.

The Wounded Self

Not only does psychology pathologise our relationships, it also pathologises our "selves". We are encouraged to see our individual "selves" as fragile and needy – to organise our identities around our frailties, our inadequacies, our wounds. The bad things that have happened to us in our lives are what define us. To know who we are, look at the wounds we bear. The original Alcoholics Anonymous greeting, "I'm Betty, and I'm an alcoholic", has expanded into an ever-multiplying list of wounded identities. Ask Bonita Swan who she is, and she will tell you:

"I am an adult great-granddaughter of an alcoholic.

I am an adult granddaughter of a foodaholic.

I am an adult granddaughter of a workaholic.

I am an adult granddaughter of a sugarholic.

I am an adult daughter of an alcoholic.

I am an adult daughter of a teetotaler.

I am an adult daughter of a chocoholic.

and

I am an adult mom to some pot users and drug abusers." (Swan, 1989: 8)

Codependency is a North American epidemic, offering a diagnosis and support group to virtually anyone with a problem who can read. As Paula Caplan (1992) says, "Everyone in North America now seems to be a codependent and/or to have a chemical or interpersonal addiction and/or to come from a dysfunctional family", and members of the American Psychological Association's Division for the Psychology of Women report that the second most frequent area of therapist members' work is codependency. Even therapists need a "safe place" to share their wounds. In Berkeley, California, we picked up a leaflet advertising a special group for therapists in recovery: "a drop-in, 12 step-based peer support group for therapists and counselors in recovery from any issue."

Addiction is chic, within and beyond feminist and lesbian communities. Survivorhood is marketed as the only alternative to victimhood. Health Communications Inc., which specializes in paperback codependency books, has well over 100 titles and sales were expected to top three million in 1991 (Kaminer, 1990). An estimated 12–15 million people in the United States are in codependency/addiction programs (Rapping, 1990) and the number of purported addictions and treatments for them is multiplying wildly. It is now possible to see your core self defined by and reflected in "survivor" labels, and to organise your life around your wounds. All of us are "in recovery", "survivors of a dysfunctional society" (therapist advertising in *A Listing of Women Owned Businesses in the Bay area*, 1992):

> "Although the term 'recovery' has come to be associated with addiction, all of us, in a sense, are recovering from something. We may be recovering from not getting what we needed as a child to grow up confident and sure of our specialness and worth. Or we may be recovering from being married. Or we may be recovering from the effects of sexual or physical abuse, or from severe depression and anxiety, or from addiction to food, alcohol or drugs. Individual therapy, Twelve Step Programs such as Alcoholics Anonymous, and self-help reading and groups are

some of the ways women seek help in the recovery process." (Clunis and Green, 1988: 190).

Wendy Kaminer (1992: 83) contrasts twelve-step groups with refuge Cambodian women's groups, pointing out that, unlike twelve-steppers, the Cambodian women don't seem to revel in their victimhood.

"There is more laughter and lightness in these meetings of vulnerable, impoverished survivors of genocide than in any twelve-step group I've attended, where people pursue recovery with deadening earnestness. Twelve-step groups depress me – so many people talking about such relatively trivial problems with such seriousness, in the same nonsensical jargon. The Cambodian women's groups impress and enhearten me – such resilience these women show."

In particular, she emphasises this distinction between the relative triviality of the twelve-steppers' problems and the horrors faced by the Cambodian refugees, who had been persecuted by the Khmer Rouge regime, and survived torture, starvation, multiple rapes, internment in concentration camps, and had witnessed the slaughter of their families. Offering a description of these women's lives as a "reality check", she points out that "victimhood" has gradations:

"In recovery, whether or not you were housed, schooled, clothed, and fed in childhood, you can still claim to be metaphorically homeless. Your inner child is a displaced person, lost and alone. At its worst, the recovery movement's cult of victimization mocks the notion of social justice by denying that there are degrees of injustice. It equalizes all claims of abuse, actual and metaphoric. The personal subsumes the political, with dire consequences for both politics and personality development." (Kaminer, 1992: 156)

We don't want to deny, or to minimise, the fact that lesbians *do* bear the scars of growing up female in this world, that we are victims or survivors of anti-lesbianism, of childhood abuse, rape, violence, alcohol, drugs and abusive relationships. We know (from personal experience) about self-doubt, self-hate, suffering and despair. The

139

two of us have been subjected to the usual range of damage wrought upon lesbians under heteropatriarchy and could easily claim some of these wounded identities as our own. Our decision *not* to define ourselves in these terms is not a denial of our wounds, but a shift of focus. We are saying that we are more than the sum of our wounds. And we are asking whose purposes are served by making our wounds central to our identities. When our suffering is the focus, the root cause of that suffering is obscured. When the onus is on us to become well-adjusted, in spite of oppression, oppression can continue unabated. We are turned into nothing more than a new consumer group for the latest psychological developments. Whether they call us "victims" or "survivors", the emphasis is upon our suffering, our endurance, our pain, our psychic struggles. As "victims"/"survivors" we are defined by that which hurts us.

Louise Armstrong, who wrote one of the first feminist books on child sexual abuse (*Kiss Daddy Goodnight*), has more recently spoken out against its appropriation by psychologists and the subsequent encouragement in victim/survivors of an "incest identity":

"Childhood rape is presented as an opportunity: a challenge to your courage – to heal. . . . [Survivors] have been courted by a cadre of helpers; given codewords and buzz phrases; had an emotional universe custom-designed, their feelings predicted and pre-articulated, their path delineated. In embracing their identity as 'survivors' they are granted belonging in a community which celebrates the primacy of Feelings. . . ." (Armstrong, 1991)

She doesn't blame the victims/survivors of childhood rape for constructing their identities in this way, and "blame" really isn't the issue here. What Louise Armstrong is concerned about is how to reclaim child-rape as a political issue, instead of leaving it in the hands of psychologists and psychologisers. And that is the question we want to raise about *all* the wounded identities currently on offer. Louise Armstrong says she is told by psychologists that "survivors" are too weakened, too emotionally fragile to do anything other than "recover". "Survivors" of the full range of new diagnoses say likewise. We do not know whether this is true. Like Louise Armstrong, we "do not know anymore how much of this fragility is intrinsic and how much is fed by the prevailing wisdom". What is clear, though, is that we live in a world in which "people are volunteering wholesale to identify themselves as addicted to anything-you-name-it, to confess to an illness and subject themselves to a cure." So, when Ricki Geiger (1990: 38) describes all lesbians as "adult survivors of a heterosexist-homophobic world", we cannot say that she is *wrong*, but we can refuse her focus in which we are lesbians in so far as, and by virtue of, our suffering. As lesbians, we used to say that we were strong, and were going to change the world. Now it seems our focus has shifted to our frailties, and the need to "heal" ourselves. Mary Daly has described this as a movement backward among feminists.

> "In the mid-seventies at a women's concert, the performer's 'rap' about alcoholism would have had some power of political analysis. The message would be: 'Don't let the man drive you to drink'. In the early eighties often this was replaced by therapeutic confessional rap sessions, in which the musician proclaimed: 'I have a drinking problem'. In these cases, no agent has been Named, and the ultimate in 'daring' has been to proclaim oneself sick. Since women have always been discouraged by the fathers into such confessional self-descriptions, which hide the agents/causes of their situation, the predictable response elicited is bonding in victimhood. . . ." (Daly, 1984: 205–206)

Acceptance within lesbian communities increasingly appears to depend upon the extent to which we are prepared to define ourselves as victims – scarred by the currently fashionable wounds. Increasingly, we have to conceal or apologise for our strengths. Special anger is directed against those lesbians who do not appear fragile – who do not simply sit and lament their fate or focus on their own healing, but who accept challenges, take risks, and work for social and political change. They do not appear "weak"; they are not "nice". Lesbians who refuse to conform to the prevailing psychologised concepts of

141

lesbian community – lesbians who are determined, obsessed with a lesbian project, sharp with impatience at talk about feelings, irritable at the emphasis on "process", demanding a product – are often subjected to "trashing". Especially those who *achieve* something in the world.

"Write a book, publish an article, appear on TV, be interviewed in the newspapers, start a theatre group dedicated to feminist principles, make a film, be asked to give a lecture and do it well so that you're asked again or referred to other places. Do anything, in short, that every other woman secretly or otherwise feels she could do just as well – and baby, watch out, because you're in for it. . . . [A woman who achieves is] labelled a thrill-seeking opportunist, a ruthless mercenary, out to get her fame and fortune over the dead bodies of selfless sisters who have buried their abilities and sacrificed their ambitions for the greater glory of feminism. Productivity seems to be the major crime – but if you have the misfortune of being outspoken and articulate, you are accused of being power-mad, elitist, fascist, and finally the worst epithet of all: A MALE IDENTIFIER, AAARRGGG!!" (dell'Olio, 1970)

In particular, *dis*agreement between lesbians is seen as incredibly damaging to these wounded selves, and is seen as a personal attack upon selves too fragile to cope with the onslaught. Making judgements about each others ideas or behaviour is seen as something which "takes you down the road to trashing each other" (Loulan, in Hall et al, 1992). Lesbians who publicly criticise other feminists' work find this out very quickly. Julia Penelope, was accused of "trashing" by Shane Phelan whose book on *Identity Politics* she had reviewed in *Women's Review of Books*. She responded:

"I didn't 'trash' you. I criticized what I believe to be serious omissions, conflations and obscurities in your analysis itself. . . . I look forward to a time when disagreements among us are perceived as just that, and not the result of an inherent character flaw, a mean-spirited conspiracy, or a lack of personal integrity." (Penelope, 1990b)

Back in 1981, Joanna Russ wrote an article called "Power and Helplessness in the Women's Movement", which came out of her own experience when, as a relatively well-known author, she wrote a negative review of another feminist's book.

"I violently resent being first elevated to mythological status and then slammed for it. And the insistence on this person's hurt feelings and that one's tremendous vulnerability and the exquisite fragility of everyone (which doesn't prevent some of them kicking up a very nasty fuss when they don't get what they want. . . .)

I believe that trashing, far from being the result of simple envy, arises from a profound ambivalence towards power. . . . The complaint, 'You are so strong and I am so helpless' hides the far worse one, 'I am strong enough that my strength will get me into terrible trouble, and you are too weak to protect me if that happens.'

For all oppressed people strength and success are double-edged: heartbreakingly desirable and very dangerous. But to 'risk winning' . . . is the only way out of oppression.

'Successful' feminists aren't immune to this terror of power; all the women I know feel it. We take the risk anyway." (Russ, 1981)

We cannot attribute this state of affairs solely to psychology. The seeds of "trashing" were incorporated into feminist theory from the beginning with its "anti-leadership" position (see Jo Freeman's discussion in her germinal article, "The Tyranny of Structurelessness"). Reacting against the power concentrations and "star" systems of male-dominated groups, feminists opposed hierarchy, on principle, and were in favour of collectives – which were seen as a means of eliminating "stars", sharing power, and helping all women to develop their own abilities. But, as Charlotte Bunch (1987: 123) says: "this anti-leadership bias often hampered the growth of women by burying female talents within group anonymity, and reinforcing stereotypes of women's weakness".

Psychology offered a resource upon which women and lesbians could draw in order to express and justify their feelings of vulnerability and weakness, and their rage at those whose behaviour suggests otherwise. Psychology enables many lesbians to identify themselves only in terms of that which has hurt them, to forever "process" their feelings about their oppression, to wait to be "healed" before they engage politically with the world which damaged them. As Caryatis Cardea (1985) points out, "what kind of revolution waits until its warriors are happy and fulfilled before confronting the enemy?"

Some writers have suggested that women declare themselves "sick" and "in recovery" in order to find community with other women.

"My hunch is that many women don't truly feel their restlessness and depression result from a co-dependent relationship or from a dysfunctional family (whatever that means), but go to these 12-step groups to find a sympathetic forum where they are accepted, can talk about their problems and meet other women. . . ." (Singer, 1990)

Sadly, even if this is true, we think it is counterproductive. A community of lesbians, each of whom thinks of herself as wounded, is not a place where any one of those lesbians is likely to get the support she so desperately craves. A lesbian who is focused on her own suffering is less able to notice, or to respond to, the suffering of others. Struggling with the intensity of her own "unmet needs", the needs of others appall her. It is not easy to give, when you see yourself as needy; not easy to be generous when you feel you lack inner resources; not easy to reach out to others when you are "getting in touch with" yourself. Wrapped up in "self-development", the development of relationships with others takes a poor second place. Psychology actively encourages us to be *less* available, less giving, less sensitive to others. "What you did is very Nice,..." reads a subheading in Lynne Namka's (1989: 100) book, ". . .But is it Co-Dependency?" Codependency is the obvious outgrowth of the egocentrism encouraged by "wounded self" ideology which teaches us that "it is not my job to take care of anyone but myself" (White, 1991: 13). Refusing to be "codependent" can, as blind lesbian Edwina Franchild (1990: 189) points out in her discussion of ableism amongst lesbians, "lead quite easily, for women who don't want to accept any shared responsibility, to a self-righteous and self-indulgent code of ethics". As Pauline Bart (1989) has pointed out, the concept of "sisterhood" has been replaced with the notion of "co-dependency". We are now criticised for the acts of attention-giving and help which we used to expect from each other in the name of lesbian community. Psychology seeks to allay emotional tensions by reducing the demands lesbians feel able to make on each other – rather than making us better able to meet them.

Defining herself in terms of her suffering, the wounded victim/survivor, is cut off from others by her own self-absorption, obsessed with protecting her "fragile" self. She doesn't take risks in relationships; but weighs and measures the "costs" of each interaction, each personal demand – will this damage or enhance my "self-esteem"? Will this make me feel "good" about myself? Questions like these replace moral and political questions – what is "right" is what enhances a sense of personal well being. Caryatis Cardea (1985) describes how she discussed with another lesbian the various ways in which this lesbian had behaved in class-oppressive ways:

> "Looking utterly unmoved by the pain I had just told her she had inflicted on me, she said that, yes, she could see why I felt this way and she would like to promise to do better. However, she had never felt really good about herself and was trying – with the help, of course, of a feminist therapist – to acquire a better self-image. Therefore, much as she was sorry for my feelings, she would simply be unable to do anything about her classism. To acknowledge her privileged oppression of me would make her feel like a bad person. And her prime motivation at this time of her life was to feel good about herself."

Similarly, Yvon Appleby (1990: 29) quotes a disabled lesbian whose friends told her "that they did not want to go on the gay pride march with her as they felt that they would have to trail her around for 11 hours, which they did not want to do. They agreed that this was selfish on their behalf but this was how they felt, and they were

better to speak their minds". Psychology enables lesbians
to say (with apparent legitimacy) that it is just too painful to
confront our own oppressive behaviour, or to do anything
about it. In a community of wounded lesbians, political
imperatives take second place to the primary aim of
"feeling good". If we act in ways which hurt other lesbians,
it is often difficult to acknowledge their pain. It doesn't
make us "feel good" about ourselves to know that we have
caused that pain. Rather than confront another lesbian's
pain – how can we deal with *her* pain when we are all in
such terrible pain ourselves? – lesbians may refuse to see
it, may, like Caryatis Cardea's acquaintance, be "utterly
unmoved" by it, may deny any responsibility for it. Or they
may lie. As Adrienne Rich (1977: 194) says, the liar "may
say, *I didn't want to cause pain*. What she really did not
want is to have to deal with the other's pain". Lying is
commonplace when pain-avoidance (our own, or someone
else's) is a primary motive. Nancy Berson (1984), writes of
her anger with the dishonesty of her ex-lover, "Jennifer"
(not her real name). Although Nancy and Jennifer had
agreed to be monogamous, and agreed, too, that if either
wished to change the agreement, they would discuss it
with the other *before* taking any action, Jennifer slept with
another woman and only told Nancy a week later. Nancy
understands that Jennifer was under a good deal of stress
at the time – her mother had just died – but says:

> "What I do not understand is the deceit, the
> dishonesty. Jennifer insists that she didn't tell me
> earlier because she didn't want to hurt me.... I am
> aware of the pitfalls of imposing my own moral code
> on others. I realize that we all must have the right to
> live as we wish. But Jennifer and I had an agreement –
> an agreement entered into freely by both of us – and I
> am both hurt and outraged that she broke that
> agreement...."

It is striking that (according to Nancy), Jennifer has no
explanation for her actions: "there was a lapse of morals,
and although she has insisted, many times, that she is sorry,
that she never meant to hurt me, etc., the fact remains that
she has entered the realm of amorality and she finds it
quite comfortable there". Psychology reduces our commit-

ments – in love, in friendship, and in politics – to issues of self-fulfilment and self-protection. They are no longer understood as moral imperatives.

We need to build a lesbian community in which we love and respect each other as more than fellow victims, a community which values individual talents and skills, not incompetence, a community in which disagreements are aired and moral judgements expected. We need to embark upon the difficult task of acknowledging and supporting not just our weaknesses, but also our strengths.

Building Lesbian Community

Lesbian friendships and lesbian communities are now supposed to be places of safety, where we bind each other's wounds, listen to each other's feelings, and help each other to recover from the damage inflicted upon us in a toxic world. They are not, of course, *actually* quite like that. The lesbian friendship networks we know, the communities we are and have been involved in have sometimes been no more than "safe" places for talking about feelings, buffers for tired, hurt lesbians against the outside world. But more often they have been vital and exciting, alive with outward-directed plans and projects, often exhilarating, demanding, exhausting, sometimes riven by conflict, competition, backbiting, exasperation, envy, lovers' disputes and irreconcilable political differences. The lesbian communities and friendships that have excited us, inspired us – even *strengthened* us! – have been forged out of far more than merely our shared experiences as victims/survivors. They have been rooted in shared struggle, shared risk, shared adventure, shared acts of courage. The psychologised notion of "safety" seems, by contrast, a very bland and anodyne notion around which to build our relationships.

"Safety" is one of the many words which has been taken over by psychology and its meaning fundamentally altered. The concept of "safety" has a history in the battered women's movement, in which safety meant escape from her batterer, a shelter. But now:

"Safety has come to be understood not as a real place

where a woman can go to get away from a man's fist, or knife, or gun, or voice, but as anything that is required to make an individual woman *feel* safe (which could be anything). In this context, a woman who plays the sadist role in a sado-masochistic relationship can claim to feel unsafe and vulnerable when she is criticised for using whips and knives and razorblades on other women." (Mann, 1987)

And in the lesbian movement too, the concept of "safety" has a similar history:

"At one time, safe space for Lesbians meant space where we could show affection for each other without fear of heckling or verbal abuse. It meant space where we could dare to look like Dykes without fear of physical assault. . . . As far as I can tell, 'safe space' is now an environment where a woman can express her emotions or feelings without fear of criticism." (Ward, 1988)

As both Bonnie Mann and Joan Ward point out, the focus on "safety" often means that we are not supposed to criticise or make judgements about the things that other lesbians say. Criticisms are felt as "attacks" and disagreements experienced as "hostility". Lesbian relationships, it is thought, are too brittle and precarious to withstand conflict of any kind. Just as therapists are not supposed to be judgemental, angry or critical with us, so we are supposed not to be judgemental, angry or critical with each other. Our "wounded selves" are too fragile to withstand conflict and disagreement. Even professional organisations for women in psychology, like the American Psychological Association's Division for the Psychology of Women (Division 35), apparently now construe themselves as places of retreat and solace. The organisation *could* be a place for vigorous debate both within the Division (with other psychologists specialising in women's issues) and outside it (with more mainstream psychological perspectives, for example). Instead, it is described by its President, Pamela Trotman Reid (1991) as "a safe place . . . a place to share, to grow up professionally and be nurtured by leaders in the discipline". Women and/or lesbians are imagined to be "a mystically loving band of emotional weaklings who make up to each other by our kindness and sweetness for the harshness we have to endure in the outside world" (Russ, 1981), and the assumption is "that hurting another woman's feelings is the worst thing – the very worst thing – the most unutterably awful thing – that a woman can do. In a world where women and men are starved, shot, beaten, bombed, and raped, the above assumption takes some doing...." (Russ, 1981)

Many lesbian groups in the USA have developed sets of formal "rules", often read out at the beginning of meetings, to ensure that lesbian groups are "safe" for their fragile membership. In Britain these rules are less clearly formulated and more often exist at the level of implicit assumptions. In many groups there is a rule that only "I statements" can be made: "I think...", "I feel...", "I experience that as...", "I need..." and so on. This is called "owning your feelings" and "respecting other lesbians' reality". The use of disclaimers ("*I* think ... and of course you might disagree ... this is just my opinion" etc) is supposed to make clear that each lesbian speaks for herself alone. The logic is that each individual lesbian has a uniquely individual set of experiences, and everyone's separate reality is just as valid as everyone else's. "To make a definitive statement about anything other than personal feelings or experience would run the risk of 'invalidating' someone who might have different feelings or experiences" (Mann, 1987). This approach is fraught with political danger. Women have always been expected to hedge our speech around with verbal disclaimers – not to speak strongly, to allow plenty of space for changing our minds. This is especially true for white middle-class gentile women, and Caryatis Cardea describes the imposition of this "ladylike" speech as a form of classism:

"We are not taught in working-class homes to preface everything we say with the phrases: 'I think', 'I feel that', 'In my opinion', 'I could be wrong but'.... We are often attacked for opinions we expressed, because we neglected to provide ourselves and our listeners, in the fashion of feminist process, with those verbal escape clauses. For the emphasis in middle-class language is not on the 'I', but on the doubt-filled

words 'think', 'feel', 'opinion'. . . . The willingness of
working-class lesbians to simply say what we want to
say and take the consequences is an affront to the
devotees of therapy. With such responses as 'Speak for
yourself!', when no one had claimed to be doing
otherwise, middle-class lesbians make clear their
discomfort with, and need to discredit, the fact that
working-class dykes do not negate their own statements." (Cardea, 1985)
Similarly impatient with all these disclaimers, Joan Ward
(1988) retorts that "I've never credited anyone with
infallibility". Yes, of course, each of us speaks out of her
own experience, her own knowledge – how could it be
otherwise? – and each of us can be challenged, and asked
to consider opposing perspectives. That should be so
obvious as to make the disclaimers redundant.

But more than this, through a heavy emphasis on the
inviolability of individual experience, arguing with another
lesbian in a political discussion is now called "attempting
to impose your reality on someone else" or "invalidating
her experience". This throws all lesbian politics back into
individualistic relativism: you have your reality, and I have
mine, and unless they happen to coincide we simply can't
build shared political theory. In fact, of course our
"realities", "experience", and "feelings" are not pure fact:
they are shaped by the values, beliefs and theories through
which we know and understand them. For many women,
for example, the "experience" of wolfwhistle-as-flattery
became the "experience" of wolfwhistle-as-sexual-harrass-
ment, not because anything out there in the world
changed, but because they altered the theories through
which they apprehended the world – often in consciousness-
raising with other women. This is not to say that the
original feelings of flattery weren't "real": often they *were*.
But they were based, as feelings generally are, on a set of
underlying *judgements*: in this case, something along the
lines of "It's important for women to have male admira-
tion". When women challenged that underlying judgement,
in themselves and each other, their *feelings* began to
change. Often we behave as though *feelings* were basic,
but in fact they are supported by an underlying structure of

values. To ask "why do you feel that?" is not just a legitimate, but a very important question. But, according to Bonnie Mann (1987), "Another rule used in some groups is that the question 'Why?' is forbidden. To ask 'Why?' is to question the other woman's experience, and is understood to be almost an act of emotional violence against her". To limit lesbian discussion to the superficial level of "feelings" is to deny us the opportunity to explore our underlying values, and so to develop our politics.

In her book, *Lesbian Ethics*, Sarah Lucia Hoagland uses an example of anger to illustrate how feelings embody value judgements. She describes a case of anger between two white lesbians, one working class, one middle class. When the first is harassed by a man on the street, she gets angry and goes after him. Her lover, in turn, gets angry at her for her lack of control, and claims that her anger is abusive. In therapy, they are expected to work on how the working-class lesbian can better control her anger, and the middle-class lesbian can best cope with it. Sarah Lucia Hoagland offers a different analysis:

"Rather than focusing on the differences in how each lover handles her anger, we can focus on the differences in the political judgment which gives substance to the anger of each. For example, the working-class lesbian has decided that she will claim her space on city streets even at the risk of retaliation. She has decided that the threat of retaliation is less dangerous to her than the damage which would result if she let a man's harassment stand unchallenged, thereby confirming his low opinion of her. Her middle-class lover, on the other hand, has decided that under no condition will she willfully put herself in (more) danger on the streets. She is unwilling to react to every man who irritates her; she would rather use her energy to maintain focus on her own agenda. In considering the implications of their anger, and hence the judgments involved, we become aware not that they approach anger differently so much as that they approach politics differently. And the approaches involve considerations of safety, of identity, of expenditure of energy, and of enacting lesbian value –

elements which affect the meaning and depth of our anger." (Hoagland, 1988: 183)

Feelings, and how we deal with them, imply judgements, values, beliefs, politics. When psychological notions are incorporated into lesbian groups, we are expected to talk about "just feelings" – not to "intellectualise" them, to wallow in sheer sensation without analysing its source, its meaning, its political validity.

Ethical Challenge in Community

It seems that many lesbians have come to believe that they, and other lesbians, are so frail and wounded, that any criticism, disagreement or challenge, will damage or destroy us. The disclaimers and the psychobabble serve to sugar the pill of criticism, making it harder to detect, less explicit, but – as many lesbians have pointed out – no less critical, and often more manipulative. Caryatis Cardea (1985) points out how some lesbians use self-effacing language to dominate meetings and get their own way: "A woman skilled in the manner of speech can still hold the floor for a long, long time by using this verbal trick: talk about yourself but sound modest". Another lesbian points out that "believe it or not, when you say, 'I feel you don't understand,' some of us hear you call us 'stupid' anyway". In the British journal of lesbian ethics, *Gossip*, Joyce Cunningham exposes how the term "you are negating my experience" can be, when properly employed, "the verbal equivalent of an Exocet missile across the bows". Writing in a section of the journal entitled, "Bad Language", she says the term is:

"Best employed just after you have made a tricky flying leap from the particular to the general and you are beginning to sense impending group opposition to the way you have landed. With its subtle echos of 'the personal is political' and the veiled accusation of personal rejection (or even thought policing), this term neatly evades demands for any tedious inter-pretations or analysis of experience. Your opposition is left with the delicate task of trying not to question the self-evident validity of your right as a woman to put any interpretation you like on your experience (after all, it is yours).

This approach is much more forceful than the frankly feeble 'you are disagreeing with me and I don't like it'. Can be combined with 'silencing' for extra impact, as in 'you are silencing me by negating my experience'. For use when expressing sentiments prefaced with 'desire'." (Cunningham, 1986, reprinted 1993)

But despite the dishonest use of psychological language to manipulate, control and get our own way, the explicit agenda is that lesbians are damaged, fragile, and in need of special protection from anything that might further hurt us. Many lesbians are concerned to guard themselves (and other lesbians) against any possible criticism. Lesbians – or "real" lesbians – are mythologised as empathetic, intuitive, "connected", warm, and sensitive, and our relationships with them are supposed to "heal", "nurture" and "support" us. This mythology makes it hard to deal with the realities of lesbian life.

One of those realities is that lesbian communities are *not* always the "safe" and nurturant places we sometimes pretend or wish them to be. Janice Raymond (1986: 223) criticises "a certain sentimentalizing of female bonding which expected too much and then backed away when it was not delivered... Nihilistic disaffection is the easy way out". Another reality is that "safety" does not require consensus: it isn't necessary always to "agree" with each other to have a community. Marilyn Frye (1990b) points out that lesbians in her community don't agree about *anything*, from the importance of recycling jars and paper, through to whether it's okay to go to weddings. "But lesbians in our community *survive* in droves." Disagreeing with each other, challenging and criticising each other's perspectives is an essential part of building not only lesbian community but also lesbian politics. A warm syrup of "acceptance" of fifty-seven different and conflicting viewpoints, a bland acknowledgement of "diversity" and of everyone's "right" to her own opinion, does not advance our critical thinking or sharpen our political analysis. Of course there is diversity, and we could not (even if we so wished) prevent other lesbians from having opinions different from our own. But we can (and we think, *should*) argue about those opinions. Argument, disagreement, challenge is *not* necessarily "trashing", and should not be "psychologised" away as the result of personality flaws or individual psychopathology. Julia Penelope points to the importance of *dis*agreement and criticism in building a strong community.

"When we disagree, when we criticise other Lesbians, we're sharing ourselves and our own ideas and opinions. Disagreement isn't only a way of affirming ourselves; we also affirm the significance of the individuals we criticize. Arguing and disagreeing are ways of paying attention to the ideas and beliefs of others. When we argue we're implying that the ideas we disagree with are important and merit attention. Silence often signals indifference. What we don't find worth responding to, we ignore." (Penelope, 1990: 98)

We know that relationships (of all kinds) can be painful. Lesbians do not always behave towards each other respectfully and honestly. We do not believe that the solution is mass psychology. As Anne and Vera (1987) say in their "cynical look at lesbian relationships":

"While it's true that individually we usually recover eventually (more or less – don't we?), the sum total of pain in our community does not diminish and time is not healing our collective hurt... There has to be a collective answer, individual solutions are not enough. You may have sorted out your problems and to you they are past history, but it's not the movement's past history. The same dramas keep repeating themselves and meanwhile our good feelings about one another and our politics risk going down the drain."

If we want lesbian community and lesbian politics which are vital, sustaining and creative, we need more than the individual solutions implied by therapy. We need open and explicit ("judgemental" and "moralistic") discussion of the ethics and politics of our relationships. Psychology has encouraged us to see our selves as too wounded for such discussions. Our relationships with friends, lovers and the rest of our lesbian communities are then seen as no more than supportive structures, propping up wounded selves.

154

In this chapter we have showed the damaging consequences of these psychologised notions for lesbian
community and lesbian politics.

WORLDS APART: MAD LESBIANS

Most of us can think of lesbians whose behaviour is distressing and/or incomprehensible to us: lesbians who abuse drugs or alcohol, starve themselves, or cut their own bodies with knives; lesbians who are severely depressed, suicidal, or who suffer extreme anxiety such that they are unable to go out of their homes alone, or feel compelled to spend many hours each day performing cleaning or checking rituals. These are all serious and debilitating problems, destructive of lesbian lives, friendships and communities.

For lesbians who experience problems such as these, therapy is often seen as providing the answer. In this chapter we argue that it does not. Not only is lesbian therapy unavailable or inappropriate to meet the needs of such lesbians, but these difficulties are not private and personal; they are problems for us all. We propose that severe difficulties like those described above are best thought of as 'social disabilities'. Whether temporarily or permanently, they present problems in negotiating our able-minded social world in much the same way as physical disabilities present problems in negotiating the able-bodied physical world. It is vital that we extend our theories and communities to accommodate us all, to enable all of us to function and contribute to the best of our abilities, no matter how disabled we are. As lesbians and feminists, we need to think about what access to our culture and politics might mean for lesbians who are socially disabled, just as we have begun to think about access for lesbians who are physically disabled.

Serious disabilities of thought and feeling often attract

labels like "madness" or "mental illness". Lesbian communities often find madness hard to deal with. When confronted with it, many of us feel helpless, unable to understand and unsure how to respond. When our efforts to help fail, or are rebuffed, we sometimes resort to exclusion. One of us (RP) gives an example:

> "An old school friend of mine came into a lesbian bar where I was drinking with friends. We hadn't seen each other for over a decade. She sat down and we talked. After a short while, she asked if I watched the television news. I said I did. She said, 'Oh well, you know then.' 'Know what?' I asked, a little puzzled. She explained in elaborate detail how the newsreader sent out special messages to her, told her to do things she thought were wrong, told her about people who were trying to kill her. . . . My friends helpfully suggested that this was not true, that she must have been mistaken, that she shouldn't worry. She became angry and suspicious, accused them of not understanding (which they didn't), of being 'one of them'. It was not long before she and I were the only ones left. The friends I was with simply drifted away, and spent time afterwards laughing about it, saying the woman was crazy, that she shouldn't have been allowed in ... asking why I had bothered to talk to her."

When Lesley (to use her own words) "went crackers" she was "very disappointed" with the response of other lesbians: "I think that we are seen as 'other' and apart" (quoted in Appleby, 1990: 2). Nancy, hospitalised after a painful break-up with her lover when she was jobless, moneyless and "hearing voices", describes how:

> "Women in the women's movement, in the lesbian movement, women I had known for a long time and worked with, started treating me differently after I had been in the hospital. . . . They had been my friends, but now they would look at me as if I was crazy. When I tried to talk about it, I was afraid I was being paranoid." (quoted in Chamberlin, 1977: 75)

In an article called "Deprivatising Pain", Ruth Elizabeth (1982) describes a similar experience when she tried to discuss her clinical depression in a radical feminist group, and was met with "silences, accompanied by looks of incomprehension":

"... women pretend that my depression doesn't exist. So they never ask me about it and somehow communicate that it's not the sort of thing they're interested in talking about. ... It makes me feel split, as if I lead a double life. An important part of me remains hidden, privatized, a personal problem I have to deal with on my own'." (Elizabeth, 1982: 15–16)

She describes her terror of parties, her anxiety at being away from home for any length of time unless she is "psychologically well prepared and feeling exceptionally strong". Other people, she says, sometimes see her as "unreliable" or "erratic", failing to appreciate the amount of time and energy she puts into doing very basic daily things:

"I'm fed up with feeling always on the fringe of women's things, a sort of emotional cripple who cannot fully take part – I want my struggle to be seen as important too, as something which affects all of us in a fundamental way, something which is an integral part of the building of our movement." (Elizabeth, 1982: 15–16)

As Elana Dykewomon says (1988), "a radical analysis of what is called madness has to be a major cornerstone of lesbian theory".

In this chapter we explore lesbian/feminist approaches to madness, both in terms of the available theories and with reference to the realities of lesbian lives. The experience of profound, socially disabling distress in the lives of some lesbians is a reality which must be incorporated into our theories and into our community lives. We begin by looking at the evidence for madness as a heteropatriarchal *invention* designed to marginalise and control those who deviate from male prescriptions of appropriate behaviour. We then look at the ways in which heteropatriarchal oppression can *cause* madness. Finally we argue the case for considering madness as "social disability", and address the need for challenging able-minded assumptions and ensuring socially disabled access to lesbian culture and politics. Throughout this chapter we both draw on our own experiences and use quotations from socially disabled women to whom we have spoken to illustrate our arguments; all have given permission for their words to be used. We are indebted to them for helping us to develop and refine our ideas and we are pleased that they find the concept of "disability" useful in understanding their experiences, and in explaining them to others.

Madness: A Heteropatriarchal Invention

Feminist theory has always pointed out that some of what is conventionally labelled "madness" is in fact ordinary and "normal" behaviour for women. It is labelled "madness" either because it deviates from male behaviour (the male-as-norm argument) or because it deviates from male definitions of appropriate female behaviour. Many feminists have shown how psychology and psychiatry are powerful means of heteropatriarchal control. Back in 1861, Susan B. Anthony and Elizabeth Cady Stanton commented on the use of the "madness" label to control women:

> "Could the dark secrets of those insane asylums be brought to light ... we would be shocked to know the countless number of rebellious wives, sisters and daughters that are thus annually sacrificed to false customs and conventionalisms, and barbarous laws made by men for women." (cited in Spender, 1986)

During the 1870s, there was a period of legal and journalistic agitation over the wrongful confinement of women in lunatic asylums. Protests against the power wielded by vengeful husbands over rebellious or difficult wives were published by Georgiana Weldon (*How I Escaped the Mad Doctor*, 1878) and Rosina Bulwer-Lytton (*A Blighted Life*, 1878) in her book, *The Bastilles of England; or, The Lunacy Laws at Work*, Louisa Lowe went further in developing a feminist critique of the whole structure of Victorian psychiatry (all cited in Showalter, 1985: 126).

These criticisms were renewed with the advent of second wave feminism. In her ground-breaking work

159

Women and Madness, Phyllis Chesler argues that "madness" is a direct result of the male-defined notion of "femininity":

> "There is a double standard of mental health – one for men, the other for women – existing among clinicians. ... For a woman to be healthy, she must 'adjust' to accept the behavioral norms of her sex – passivity, acquiescence, self-sacrifice, and lack of ambition – even though these kinds of 'loser' behaviors are generally regarded as socially undesirable (i.e. non-masculine)." (Chesler, 1972: 68–69)

Phyllis Chesler illustrates her argument with chilling quotations from public records and from her own interviews with women hospitalised for violating hetero-patriarchal definitions of model feminine behaviour: women who bear children outside marriage, are depressed and unable to do housework after the birth of a child, or who express anger at their husbands. Women who contravene heteropatriarchal prescriptions by refusing to do sex with men, or failing to enjoy it, are labelled as suffering from "sexual dysfunction" or "heterophobia". Dissent is represented as pathology.

The pathologisation of lesbianism has been a prime example of this. Up to the 1960s, most psychologists, psychiatrists and psychoanalysts regarded lesbianism as maladaptive, regressive and infantile, whether "the condition" was seen as a consequence of perverted genes or hormones, or a result of disturbed upbringings. Many psychoanalytic theorists continue to view lesbianism as pathological. For example, Kronemeyer, in 1980, described homosexuality as:

> "... a symptom of neurosis and of a grievous personality disorder. It is an outgrowth of deeply rooted emotional deprivations and disturbances that had their origins in infancy. It is manifested, all too often, by compulsive and destructive behaviour that is the very antithesis of fulfilment and happiness. Buried under the 'gay' exterior of the homosexual is the hurt and rage that crippled his or her capacity for true maturation, for healthy growth and love." (Kronemeyer, 1980: 7)

Two of the leading psychoanalytic training institutions in London, UK, will still not train lesbian or gay male analysts.

Lesbianism remains a specific pathology, coded 302.0, in the "Sexual deviations and disorders" section of the Ninth Revision of the *International Classification of Diseases* (ICD9 – World Health Organisation, 1978) – the diagnostic system used in the UK and most other countries in the world. Under pressure from lesbian and gay activists, a diagnosis of homosexuality was removed from the USA's diagnostic system (*The Diagnostic and Statistical Manual* [DSM] III) in 1973 – although you could still be diagnosed as suffering from something called "ego-dystonic homosexuality". In the revised edition of DSM III (DSM III-R, American Psychiatric Association, 1987), the diagnosis of "ego-dystonic homosexuality" no longer appears: instead there is a diagnosis of "Sexual Disorder Not Otherwise Specified", a symptom of which is "persistent and marked distress about one's sexual orientation". This category describes, and classifies as pathological, people who are homosexual but wish they weren't. The index of DSM III-R contains the entry "Homosexuality, Ego-dystonic", but there is no similar entry of "Heterosexuality, Ego-dystonic" for people who are heterosexual but wish they weren't (a fairly common problem for heterosexual feminists cf. Kitzinger, Wilkinson & Perkins, 1992).

Although a primary diagnosis of "lesbianism" is probably now a rarity, lesbianism is still seen as an index of disturbance. When psychologists are given hypothetical case histories and asked to rate subjects for severity of problems, likelihood of recovery etc, people are judged as more severely disturbed when labelled "gay" than if such a label is not present (cf the review in Kitzinger, 1990b). Madness labels are selectively applied to discredit and dismiss women's behaviour when it deviates from male prescriptions.

Louise Pembroke, chair of Survivors Speak Out, a UK self-advocacy organisation for survivors of the mental health system, describes how she "discovered at an early age that a woman's worth is gauged by her appearance; that expressions of anger and assertion are not easily tolerated; that my low place in society's pecking order has nothing to do with me as a person but is connected to the maintenance of a hierarchy based on white male dominance". She comments that this oppression and discrimination are reflected not only in the mental health services but are "actively reinforced by those working in them" (Pembroke, 1991). The wearing of make-up and dresses is sometimes required as evidence of improved mental health in women (Johnstone, 1989); looking "feminine" is a measure of recovery.

"Laura: Fix yourself up, they told me. So every afternoon I spent in the beauty parlor with the other women. Of course, you had to pay for it. . . . You have to hide your feelings, pretend everything is wonderful, if you want to get out." (Chesler, 1972: 169)

"Laverne: I finally figured it out. You weren't supposed to be angry. Oh no. They lock you up, throw away the key, and you're supposed to smile at them, compliment the nurses, shuffle baby – so that's what I did to get out." (Chesler, 1972: 169–70)

In sum, women and, particularly, lesbians who do not conform to heteropatriarchal expectations, who do not define ourselves in terms of men and service them in the expected manner, are labelled insane, sedated with drugs and incarcerated in psychiatric institutions. The label "madness" is used to invalidate deviant words and actions, and to reinforce conventional images of femininity.

Madness: Caused by Heteropatriarchal Oppression

Another common feminist theory of madness emphasises not simply the "invention" of madness as a label applied to dissident women, but also the "causation" of madness in women as a result of heteropatriarchal oppression. When, in 1885, Charlotte Perkins Gilman collapsed with a "nervous disorder", it was, she said, as if "a sort of grey fog [had] drifted across my mind, a cloud that grew and darkened". On consulting the greatest nerve specialist in the USA, Dr Mitchell, this was his prescription:

" 'Live as domestic a life as possible. Have your child

with you all the time' (Be it remarked that if I did but dress the baby it left me shaking and crying – certainly far from healthy companionship for her, to say nothing of the effect on me.) 'Lie down after each meal. Have but two hours intellectual life a day. And never touch pen, brush or pencil as long as you live."

For some months, she attempted to follow these orders, with the result that:

"[I] came perilously close to losing my mind. The mental agony grew so unbearable that I would sit blankly moving my head from side to side. . . . I would crawl into remote closets and under beds – to hide from the grinding pressure of that distress. . . ."

Barbara Ehrenreich and Deidre English (1978: 92) finish the story:

"Finally, in a 'moment of clear vision' Gilman understood the source of her illness: she did not want to be a *wife*; she wanted to be a writer and an activist. So, discarding S. Weir Mitchell's prescription and divorcing her husband, she took off for California with her baby, her pen, her brush and pencil. But she never forgot Mitchell and his near-lethal 'cure'."

A century later, Jane, married for six months, with a three-month old baby had a "nervous breakdown":

"I thought I was the Virgin Mary and that my child was Jesus. I held endless conversations with God, and I remember being fascinated by the moon. . . ." (Jane, 1986: 10)

She was hospitalised for three months and given electro-convulsive therapy. It was only six years later, "after much unhappiness and violence and desperate attempts to make the marriage work that I found the strength to divorce my husband". Like Charlotte Perkins Gilman, she eventually saw the problems as lying not in *her* but in the intolerable situation in which she was placed:

"I went from being someone's daughter to someone's wife and mother without developing any real identity of my own. . . . I was trying to do what was expected of me as a woman, and when I 'failed' I blamed myself. I somehow felt it was my fault when my husband stayed out all night. I even had the feeling he was justified whenever he hit me – after all, I *was* jealous (justifiably, as it later turned out), and always seemed to be moaning. I couldn't seem to keep myself attractive and desirable: I felt so 'inadequate'. We lived in two rooms, and there was very little money. I went mad."

Feminist theories of madness are often derived from stories like these. Women are "mad" – disturbed, unhappy, distressed – as a result of the intolerable pressures put on us by an oppressive male-dominated world. Faced with the stresses of marriage to men, the demands of small children, and lack of identity in the world, women "go mad". According to Jill Johnston (1973: 84), "going crazy has always been a personal solution *in extremis* to the unarticulated conflicts of political realities, a way of transcending these conflicts by going into orbit and settling the world".

But "going into orbit" can be painful and self-destructive. It can, as Ginny Cook (1985) says, be tempting to romanticise madness. If women's madness is a rebellion against traditional forms of femininity, then this "implies that there are millions of women in this country who are at least passively aligned with the feminist cause". But madness is usually far from glamorous. It is mundane, often stereotyped, frustrating, disturbing, anything but an exciting voyage into the recesses of the human mind. "Psychiatric illness is usually a sign of powerlessness, rather than revolutionary strength and activity" (Cook, 1985: 103), and "neither genuinely mad women, nor women who are hospitalised for conditioned female behaviour, are powerful revolutionaries" (Chesler, 1972: 56). Severe and disabling mental distress of this sort is not some romantic revolutionary stand, not an escape from oppression, nor a higher plane of understanding and creativity. It is part of the damage wrought upon us by heteropatriarchal oppression.

The lesbian/feminist therapy industry is directed towards "healing the wounds of patriarchy". Therapy, lesbian/

feminist or otherwise, understands problems as arising from difficulties within the individual and offers individualised solutions.

Madness as "Social Disability"

It is undoubtedly the case that much of what has been labelled "madness" is a product of heteropatriarchal oppression: self-starvation, alcohol abuse, the lasting consequences of child sexual abuse, anxiety, depression can all be understood in these terms. Yet it is difficult to see *all* disturbances of thought and feeling as exclusively products of oppression. It is hard to see how all learning disabilities (mental handicap), senile dementia, brain injury, and the major disturbances of thought and feeling called "schizophrenia" or "manic depressive illness" will be eliminated along with heteropatriarchy. These problems are, of course, exacerbated by oppression, but are more than simply products or inventions of it.

We cannot know how much mental distress and disability of thought and feeling would exist in the absence of heteropatriarchal social organisation. Nevertheless, the reality is that many lesbians today *do* experience severe disabilities of thought and feeling that cause profound ongoing distress, lead them to behave in ways that others think inappropriate and/or unusual, and often render them unable to cope with the demands of life without support. Sometimes these disabilities are always present, sometimes they disappear completely after a time, but more usually they fluctuate. So lesbians with these disabilities are relatively able to cope at some times, extremely distressed and disturbed at others, and seemingly unpredictable and unreliable to those around them. This very variability is seriously problematic for all concerned. As one woman said to us:

"I can be fine for weeks, months sometimes, but I always have to live one day at a time. I plan things for next week, but I never believe that I will do them until the time actually arrives. I never know when they're going to come back – the voices, the ideas. That's the worst part. Knowing that they will come back but never knowing when."

Some of the women who talked to us, as friends, colleagues or clients, describe their experience in their own words:

"Rachel, they're back, THE AIR BUBBLES. At first I always believed they were part of every day, then you didn't seem to know what I meant. I realised I was the only one who had them – bubbles hitting me all the time. Well they're back anyway, hitting me from every side, and my head is empty, empty as a shell, all my thoughts drained out of me while I was asleep. All mixed up, day, night, whispers all around my head, lots of water, shoes don't seem to fit, colours, it's all going on at once – it's killing me."

"The men are dancing about on the left, the voices are shouting at me, it feels like the ceiling is coming down and the walls are closing in. I'm trapped. Trapped in this head and body and there's no way out."

"My world is like having two or more different levels of what is right and what is wrong. Should I be pulling myself out (*when I can*) to face the everyday motions of life there in your world? Having to keep it all up is very difficult. I want to say slow down, have a rest, yet the reality goes on and I feel as if I'm being smothered by life itself. My world hurts. It's scary. Never ending and painful. When I'm in my world I know that I'm going far away, and although I know this, I can't prevent it. To me it's all so real, and I honestly believe it to be true and genuine when I'm there."

We suggest here that lesbians who have these kind of problems should be described as "socially disabled". In the same way that someone who is physically disabled has difficulty, to a greater or lesser extent, in negotiating the able-bodied physical world, so someone who is socially disabled has difficulties in negotiating the able-minded social world. The term "disabled" is sometimes chosen by these women themselves. Defining madness as "one of the more overtly political forms of disability", one group says that "'Insanity' and 'madness' are appropriate terms when used seriously, as is 'psychiatrically disabled' when used in self-definition" (seamoon house, 1981, cited in Kramarae and Treichler, 1985: 271).

The concept of disability is a useful one. There have been arguments that we should use alternative terms with more positive connotations such as physically/socially challenged. We would argue that the use of such terms tends to underplay and deny the extent of such problems. Bev Jo, Linda Strega and Ruston (1990) make a similar point in relation to hidden physical disability:

> "We find that most well and able-bodied Lesbians want to deny hidden disabilities and assume that if we just try hard enough we'll be able to be as physically functional as they are. . . . Some well and able-bodied Lesbians seem to have taken the term 'physically challenged' to mean that disabled Lesbians can overcome any and all physical limitations if we try hard enough to 'meet the challenge'." (Jo et al, 1990)

This argument is particularly important in the area of *social* disability, because serious problems with thoughts and feelings have often been denied or minimised by both the world at large and by feminists – with the assumption that the disabled lesbian could behave "properly" if she really wanted to, that she should "pull herself together". Our use of the term "social disability" is intended to highlight both the involuntary nature of the disability, and the need for social changes within our communities to accommodate it.

One of us (CK) spent several months as an inpatient in a psychiatric hospital following a suicide attempt related to the traumas of coming out as lesbian at the age of seventeen. One of us (RP) has recently experienced a serious depressive illness which rendered her extremely distressed and unable to concentrate, work, read, drive, go out, think properly or do even the simplest chores for over 4 months. Even the most basic choices, like what to wear or eat, left her in a panic of indecision. Admission to a psychiatric hospital was prevented only because friends organised a rota to ensure that she had someone with her at all times. Our experiences brought home to us the extent to which it is "trivialising" of profound distress simply to dismiss it as an extension of the everyday anxiety or misery all of us experience at some time:

> " 'Oh yes, I get off days too, isn't it *awful*.' Or people who have never been with me when I've been depressed tell me that of course we *all* experience these kinds of things." (Elizabeth, 1982: 15–16)

In apparently trying to break down the barriers between lesbians by emphasising the continuities of our experience, this type of response minimises and obscures the problems faced by some lesbians. Although we have both experienced disabilities of thought and feeling that have forced us to use heteropatriarchal psychiatric services, neither of us has believed that a rat was sitting in our brain and looking out of our eyes, that the television broadcasters were putting thoughts into our heads and taking away our own, or that everyone was trying to poison us. For some women and lesbians, including those that one of us (RP) works with as a clinician, these are a daily reality. Between our experiences and theirs is sometimes a huge and unbridgeable gulf. Lesbians (at least sometimes) can find themselves alone in a world that no-one else understands, believes or experiences. We are worlds apart. To assume false equivalence is to deny the reality of difference.

In the rest of this chapter, then, we discuss the problems traditionally labelled "madness" from the perspective of radical lesbian feminists concerned to make our communities accessible to seriously socially disabled lesbians. We ask how, as radical feminists, we can develop political theory and practice which recognises that some lesbians are seriously socially disabled, and how we can build communities which include us all.

Marginalisation and Exclusion

It often seems that lesbians do not want to believe that some of us are socially disabled – have disabilities of thought and feeling. So frightening is the idea of madness that we want to believe that all problems can be put right with enough effort on the part of the person concerned, with the correct therapeutic approach, or whatever. It is little wonder that many lesbians who have social disabilities deny that they have any problems – as with hidden physical disability, the fact is scary, and the consequences all too often involve marginalisation and exclusion.

Writing about hidden physical disabilities, Linda Strega describes similar problems of marginalisation:

" 'You don't look sick.' I've sensed different motives for people saying that. I think some Lesbians are trying to reassure us, hoping we're not as sick as we feel. It always makes me nervous, though, because it usually means they don't believe us. It's not helpful, because facing the fact of being sick is scary, and we often have to struggle against our own tendencies to deny we're sick. . . . We often look particularly unsick when we're doing everything we can to get well – we shouldn't be punished for that by being disbelieved. Besides, when you're chronically ill, you learn to hide it as best you can. It's a way of trying to be more acceptable and also a way to try and forget for a while. Lesbians should also be aware that ... denial and passing as able-bodied are also difficult issues for disabled Lesbians who aren't ill." (Strega, 1990: 298–300)

Many socially disabled women and lesbians to whom we have spoken echo this sentiment – being disbelieved, especially when you are trying as hard as you can, is particularly oppressive:

"I try to be good, I try to keep the rules. My own private hell, what is it with me, do I want a medal or something? Thoughts running riot, feeling like killing myself. It's so hard to remain cool as they say. I truly can't try any harder – if only I could convince the world of these facts. When I try to act normal they say there's nothing wrong with me – when I act odd, they say I'm not trying hard enough, I'm putting it on. I'm attention-seeking. I can't win. They just don't believe me."

It is possible that some lesbians may claim social disabilities for themselves in order to excuse bad behaviour. Differentiating bad behaviour from disability may not always be easy: heteropatriarchal psychiatry often debates distinctions between 'madness' and 'badness'. Such arguments in relation to any form of disability are dangerous.

There are many physical and sensory disabilities that are not obvious to the observer (multiple sclerosis or back pain for example) and women with such disabilities often fight a long battle to have their problems accepted as real (cf Goudsmit, 1993). Similarly, lesbians with social disabilities are often accused of being inconsiderate or attention-seeking. Anyone can lie about almost anything, but to set "tests" for disabled people who experience disabilities is arrogant and oppressive. We all have an obligation to contribute to our communities, whether we are disabled or not. To accept the reality of social disabilities does not imply that we have to accept all disruptive behaviour. Instead it requires us to understand that behaviour and either reduce it or render it non-disruptive so that the disabled lesbian can contribute.

Disbelief is one way in which socially disabled lesbians can be marginalised and excluded, but marginalisation and exclusion can take other forms. It can be quite literal – as when the lesbian who is being disruptive is simply asked to leave. Alternatively, her perspective, her views, are ignored with the "She's crazy, she doesn't know what she is talking about, don't listen to her, you don't have to take her seriously" type of response. Another form of marginalisation comes under the guise of inclusiveness – the "I know what you mean, I feel like that sometimes" response. This is a variant of the kind of "arrogant perception" of which Marilyn Frye (1983) speaks – a perception that seeks always to understand by drawing parallels with our own experience of the world.

At present, it is often impossible to be accepted as a bone fide lesbian if you have long-term social disabilities. If someone behaves in unusual and disruptive ways, if she expresses strange beliefs that no-one else shares, she cannot really be lesbian. If she has severe learning disabilities, then she either "doesn't know what she's doing" or it is just a "stage" because she has the "mental age of a child". Just as the heterosexual feminist movement tries to sanitise its image by dissociating itself from lesbians, so able-minded lesbians all too often withdraw from lesbians who behave in strange and unpredictable ways. Dai Thompson (1985: 83) laments the fact that "individuals with mental disabilities are frequently shunned by those with physical or sensory ones". This is explicable, she says, because:

".... those who begin to develop multiple sclerosis or other hard-to-diagnose disabilities frequently have their problems dismissed as purely psychiatric in nature. Fighting such dismissals and the denials of treatment and financial help because of them can often go on for years, building up enormous resentment. It is not surprising, then, that such people feel a strong desire to clearly separate themselves from those whose disabilities are, indeed, psychiatrically based.

Issues like these are very complex and not easy to solve. But they are also very real and can be extremely anger-provoking when, for example, physically disabled women refuse to even acknowledge their mentally-disabled sisters' existence." (Thompson, 1985: 83–84)

We try to accept obvious physical disabilities of mobility, sight, and hearing without making the oppressive assumption that we know exactly what it is like to be unable to walk, see, hear, and so forth. Yet all too often disabilities of thought and feeling are seen as somehow more basic, and those of us not affected by disabilities in these domains have difficulty in accepting the idea that some people may be unable to "think like us" in the same way that they may be unable to see like "us". The labels like "schizophrenia" and "depressive illness" used to describe thinking and emotional difficulties may be oppressive, but the problems cannot be ignored. There is nothing sacrosanct about the processes of thought and feeling that somehow render them immune to disability.

Accepting that some lesbians are socially disabled, whether or not as a consequence of heteropatriarchal oppression, is considered by some to be condemnatory. But accepting the existence of *physical* disability does not mean condemning the disabled lesbian. Instead we think about how we can provide support and reorganise the physical world (eg mobility aids, lifts, braille, signers) in order to facilitate access to lesbian culture and politics (eg Appleby, 1990, 1992). If we denied the existence of physical disability then we would not attempt to facilitate access. The focus would be on the individual adjusting herself to fit in, rather than on a collective responsibility to accommodate her physical limitations. Yet this is exactly the position too often assumed in relation to social disability. Without a concept of social disability we deny access. For socially disabled lesbians what becomes paramount is social access – access to the ways in which we organise our friendships, our relationships, our communities, our social world.

Challenging Able-minded Assumptions: Socially Disabled Access

While lesbian communities have begun, albeit inadequately, to address issues around access for physically disabled lesbians, scant attention has been paid to similar access for those with disabilities of thought and feeling. Access to lesbian culture and politics for those who are socially disabled by transitory or ongoing problems of thought or feeling essentially means access to relationships with others.

All of us know the temptation to withdraw from those who behave in inappropriate and disruptive ways. How then can we accommodate into our theories and our communities those who behave in ways we don't like? How can we go on treating socially disabled lesbians who behave in disruptive, difficult, aggressive, unacceptable ways as valued members of our communities when we know that they may, at any time, do the same things again? How do we deal with our fear, frustration, feelings of inadequacy, of being used, let down, cheated, wronged, embarrassed? These are the critical things for us to consider as feminists and as lesbians and we need to examine them in political, not psychological, terms. We suggest four kinds of help that may be offered to socially disabled lesbians.

Friends and allies

Probably above all else, someone who is distressed and socially disabled needs friends and allies she can trust. As one woman said to us:

"It's having someone who listens, who understands. It's listening, it's being concerned. My world's different from yours, but you get close. We talk well. You really listen, you really want to know. We've got a relationship. You share something of yourself – you want to know me, almost no-one else does. They think I'm mad or tell me to 'pull myself together' – if I hear those words again I'll go round the twist. I'm not just a patient, or a client – we've got a relationship. Being friendly is very important – you're straight, hard, strong, caring and interested all at the same time. Knowing that you're there helps me to carry on when things get really bad."

For many lesbians with social disabilities, friends and allies are in short supply. Too many of us withdraw and dissociate ourselves from lesbians who are extremely distressed over long periods of time, or who behave in unacceptable ways, or express odd ideas. But the isolation of disabled lesbians is also a result of a reality shared by no-one else. As one woman said:

"Not believing that I really feel, see or hear the things that trouble me – that's what really makes me lonely. People say things like 'don't worry', 'it's your imagination', 'of course no-one is talking inside your head and at your ears', 'it's just not happening'. Well all I can say to that is 'Yes, it is happening, more's the pity' and 'yes it is difficult' – but they don't understand."

Lesbian theorists like Sarah Lucia Hoagland (1988) and Janice Raymond (1986) have offered important theories of friendship and lesbian connection that move beyond the heteropatriarchal ethic of dominance and subordination. Sarah Lucia Hoagland's book, *Lesbian Ethics*, has been particularly influential in building an ethical vision of the world from a lesbian perspective. However, in assuming able-mindedness, such authors tend to exclude from lesbian community those who have disabilities of thought and feeling. Sarah Lucia Hoagland (1988) says that:

"We already have the ingredients we need to interact: our psychic faculty, intuition, attention, dreams, imagination, humor, emotions, playfulness, and reasoning." (Hoagland, 1988: 267)

Janice Raymond argues that:

"Thinking is a necessary condition for female friendship. The thinking I advocate is better described by the word *thoughtfulness*. In my use of it *thoughtfulness* is characterised on the one hand by ability to reason and on the other by considerateness and caring. It is this kind of thoughtfulness that is necessary for Gyn/affection ... a genuine attentiveness and respect for other women ... the word *thoughtfulness* conveys the meaning of a thinking considerateness and considerate thinking." (Raymond, 1986: 218/221)

Both of these theorists are making an able-minded assumption – that everyone has the intact capacity for reason and attention.

Disabled lesbians and feminists have drawn attention to the able-bodied assumptions of theories which presume mobility or intact sensory capacities. Presumptions of an intact capacity for thought and feeling are equally oppressive and dangerous. Socially disabled lesbians frequently show an apparent lack of the "genuine attentiveness and respect for other women" that Janice Raymond (1986) argues is so important.

Sarah Lucia Hoagland argues that withdrawal from lesbians who behave in unacceptable, disruptive ways is an ethical option:

"if a lesbian's pain is so intense and she is so out of touch with it that she simply hurts everyone she cares about, there may be nothing to do but walk away." (Hoagland, 1988: 229)

Severely socially disabled lesbians know well the consequences of withdrawal which Sarah Lucia Hoagland condones and advocates. Friends, initially caring and attentive, often withdraw because of her unpredictability, become angry and frustrated by her behaviour, her abuse, their own inability to make things better. As one said to us:

"I'm alone. My world hurts. It is never ending and

painful. My thoughts running riot. All my friends have gone – they didn't understand, they didn't believe me, they thought I was stupid, mad, silly, they kept saying 'don't worry' – well I do worry. I can't always be like they want me to be. Don't shut me up. Don't shut me out. Listen to me. Don't be so ignorant. Please help me."

If able-minded assumptions are not to result in the exclusion of lesbians who have disabilities of thought and feeling, and who act in ways that make no sense in our understanding of the world, then we badly need to extend and elaborate lesbian feminist theories such as those of Sarah Lucia Hoagland (1988) and Janice Raymond (1986).

If socially disabled lesbians are to have the friends and allies they need, then we have to begin by accepting that we will sometimes experience different realities. If we are to connect with someone whose reality is profoundly different from our own, then we have to travel to her "world". We may never be able to share her reality, but avoidance of our differences "can lead us to patterns of ignoring, those lapses of attending, those separations, which really do undermine relationships" (Sarah Lucia Hoagland, 1988: 235). We have to begin to acknowledge each other's realities as personally real. If we always endeavour to understand the behaviour of others by drawing parallels with our own experience of the world (what we would think, feel, do), if we always expect others to behave in ways that make sense in our understanding of reality, then we will be angry and upset when they do not. If we actually listen and try to understand and accept that some lesbians' reality is profoundly different from our own we can begin to understand their behaviour in the context of their worlds, and their experiences. We have the possibility of connection.

Practical help

One woman we know believes that her nose controls the weather. This means that she will not go out when the weather is good for fear that she will make it rain. Likewise, she becomes distressed when people complain about bad weather because she believes she has caused it. While we cannot agree that she controls the weather, we can understand and sympathise with her distress when it rains, avoid complaining about the weather, accept that she cannot go out when it is fine, and provide her with practical help so that she gets the things she needs when she cannot go out. This kind of practical help in negotiating the world that others know can be very important.

Socially disabled lesbians often have great difficulty in coping with the essentials of day-to-day life: looking after themselves, cleaning, cooking, shopping, going out, working, joining in with activities become impossibly difficult. Appropriate help involves mundane, practical support. Such practical help serves the function of minimising the extent to which a lesbian is constrained by her disabilities. In the same way as the mobility of a lesbian without legs is influenced by the physical environment (the availability of ramps, lifts, mobility aids, doorways that are wide enough), so the thoughts and feelings of someone who is socially disabled are influenced by the social environment in which she functions.

All of us have experienced difficulty at times in knowing what is expected of us. Take, for example, the rather mundane activity of going to a strange cafe: do I sit down and wait to be served, do I go to the counter, order what I want and then sit down and wait for it to appear, or do I wait at the counter until my food is ready? Rarely are such things made explicit, and the absence of clear information can cause us transitory confusion. Similarly, much of our social world is governed by unwritten rules such as "not butting in whilst others are speaking" or "not monopolising the conversation", and a plethora of rules about what it is appropriate to talk about when, and with whom. If someone has difficulty in organising her internal world – if her thoughts are confused, disorganised, elusive – then the provision of a clear external structure, careful and clear exposition of what is expected, what we think, feel, need, like and dislike is essential – and may indeed avoid some of the confusion that arises in many social situations. Cognitive confusion, and attempting to grapple with a profoundly different reality, often mean that a lesbian is relatively insensitive to the ordinary social cues on which everyone relies so heavily: the raise of an eyebrow, a disapproving look, the shrug of a shoulder are simply insufficient to convey our meaning.

A lesbian who attended a discussion group that one of us (RP) organised, experienced periods when her thoughts went out of her control. As she put it, her thoughts ran away with her and she could not work out what was going on. She described her difficulties in attending the group at such times as twofold. She said that she did not trust herself to be able to get there unaided: she had in the past got side tracked, ended up not knowing where she was in places and situations she had never set out to reach. She needed help to actually get to and from the meeting. While at the meeting, she feared carrying on at great length about things that were irrelevant, talking inappropriately, and causing embarrassment to herself and others. In the past, she had felt so embarrassed about having behaved in an inappropriate manner that she had been unable to face the people again. She needed someone to stay with her at the meeting, help her to control her behaviour, and stop her when she went off at lengthy uncontrollable tangents. Someone to accompany her to and from the meeting, and someone to help her at the meeting, were essential to ensure that she had access to it.

With all the acceptance and understanding and help in the world, some behaviours remain unacceptable: violence is one obvious example. However, to understand the reasons behind a lesbian's violence may enable us to reject the particular aspects of her behaviour that we are unable to tolerate rather than reject the lesbian herself. Such partial withdrawal – withdrawing from the act not the person – may be an important aspect of caring.

When someone hits us, we will undoubtedly withdraw, but if we understand why she acted in this way we may be able to continue our friendship. Perhaps, for example, her "voices" told her we intended to kill her. Intelligibility – our understanding of each other's actions – is important and may reduce the likelihood that she will hit us again. There may be particular things we do that, although appearing innocuous to us, are unacceptable within her world. She may be able to warn us when she thinks that we are about to kill her. There may be things that we can notice about her behaviour that indicate to us that it is time for us to go. However, there may be times when the messages are so bad that she needs respite, asylum, a place free from the demands and expectations of our social world.

Asylum

The concept of asylum has a long and undistinguished history within psychiatry. Yet, many people who have experienced severe and disabling distress express a need for a safe, supportive environment in which they can gain relief from the strains of the social world, asylum from heteropatriarchal expectations of behaviour.

At the moment, many distressed lesbians have no option but to turn to heteropatriarchal psychiatric institutions. Only a minority of those who enter such institutions are compulsorily detained – the majority of women and lesbians who go into hospital do so not because they are forced but because they have nowhere else to turn for the asylum and relief from responsibility that they need.

The degradation and abuse occurring in psychiatric hospitals is well documented (e.g. Johnstone, 1991; Breggin, 1991). Despite the fact that the safety, tolerance and security that such hospitals afford is so inadequate, they are positively valued by many who use them. After 14 psychiatric hospital admissions, one woman with whom we spoke said:

> "When I go in I'm angry at needing to go, but I like the hospital when I don't feel safe in my thoughts. Hospital makes me safe. When I just can't cope with all the cooking, cleaning, shopping, getting up, everything, I can leave all that fast running around behind for a while and have a rest."

Another said, with a sigh of relief, as she came into the hospital ward for the eighth time, "I'm safe now. People here understand. Why did I ever leave?"

Heteropatriarchal psychiatry is not the answer for women who are distressed and disturbed, but at the moment it is often the only form of asylum available.

Lesbians and feminists talk only of the degrading, negative effects of hospitals – often making it even more difficult for other lesbians to use them when they badly need the safety they afford. The provision of alternative sanctuary – alternative respite and relief from the demands of everyday life – cannot realistically lie with any one individual. Helping and caring for someone who is very distressed, very disturbed, is not easy. It is often more than any of us can handle alone. Therefore we need to think collectively about how to provide for the needs of such lesbians. At present we are sometimes able to achieve this for short periods, but only in a rather haphazard, and not very safe, way. We know of examples of lesbians who, when distressed and disturbed, have been "handed round" a series of friends for one or two nights at a time. Similarly one of us (RP), during her depressive illness, was looked after and given enormous amounts of practical help and support, on a rota basis by her friends. While such efforts have undoubtedly been helpful, they can hardly be said to provide the degree of safety and security that is really needed. We must provide safe, tolerant environments – asylums that are a genuine alternative to psychiatrists, psychologists, prisons, and mental institutions – and which are within, not apart from, our communities (Quinn, 1985). As a psychiatric survivor, Judi Chamberlin, says, what we need are "true asylums":

> ". . . places to which people can retreat to deal with the pain of their existence. . . . These asylums would not simply be more humane mental hospitals, they would be true alternatives to the present mental health system – voluntary, small, responsive to their own communities and to their residents." (Chamberlin, 1977: 5)

Some women will need such asylum for short periods of time; others who are more disabled, possibly as a result of learning disabilities, dementia, brain injury, or persistent severe disabilities of thoughts and feelings, will require such an environment on an ongoing basis.

Often asylum is seen as a place rather than a concept – the Collins English Dictionary (1979) defines asylum as a shelter, a sanctuary, a safe inviolable place of refuge. It

179

seems to us more useful to consider asylum not as a place, but as relief from ordinary expectations and demands. Such a conceptualisation allows us not only to consider places to which people can retreat, but also the various forms of partial asylum that may be possible. It allows us to consider relief from some day to day activities – someone else shopping, washing, cooking for you. We can also think about providing relief from some social expectations – not being expected to work, do as much as others, or behave in the prescribed manner. These forms of partial asylum may be achieved by practical help in ordinary situations, or by the establishment of places of refuge within ordinary situations: places to retreat to for a few hours to get a little peace and quiet.

Whether or not our problems are a consequence of heteropatriarchal oppression, it is ableist to assume that all of us, all of the time, will be capable of meeting the demands of everyday life. To acknowledge the possibility that at some times some lesbians will need care may seem to abrogate their integrity, or to validate the idea that someone has a right to dominate (Hoagland, 1988: 120). Yet without some concept of respite for those whose distress or cognitive disabilities render them temporarily or permanently unable to cope, can we really say that we have a responsive, attending, caring community?

Not only do some lesbians need a place where they can gain relief from the stresses and strains of everyday life, but they may also need relief from the distressing thoughts and feelings that they are experiencing. Sometimes these can be alleviated by providing help and shelter; sometimes additional assistance in the form of drugs may be valuable.

Drugs

Sometimes disabilities can be reduced by drugs. Many lesbians with physical disabilities such as diabetes, or painful long-term illnesses such as cancer, benefit from drugs. The drugs do not "cure" the problem, but they do allow the lesbian to function more effectively. Similarly, disabilities of thought and feeling can sometimes – but not always – be alleviated by drugs. Both of us have, at different times, gained relief from antidepressant drugs.

The ways in which mind-altering drugs have been used to sedate and control women who contravene hetero-patriarchal imperatives have been widely documented (eg Chesler, 1972) within psychiatry. It is true that drugs are frequently abused and used as an instrument of social control. People are rarely given a real choice about taking medication: all too often taking it is a condition of getting any help at all. Neither are people given a choice about which medication helps them most.

"Four people pinned me to the ground to force me to take the drug. I would have taken them anyway if only they had talked to me seriously and explained. I was terrified. I thought this can't be a hospital at all. I thought I'd never wake up."

"I was told that I could not have psychotherapy until I was treated with medication. They said the psycho-therapist would not treat me unless I took my drugs. I asked if I could think it over but they did not let me. They said, you have to be quick, you will have to make your mind up by tomorrow morning" (Good Practices in Mental Health & Camden Consortium, 1988)

Drugs may also be used to enable women and lesbians to fit in to an oppressive world – to make it more tolerable and thus distract attention from the need to change that world.

"The psychiatrist I saw on the NHS told me that I was suffering from depression and immediately prescribed anti-depressants. The emphasis seemed to be on getting me 'back to normal' as he put it – never mind the fact that I was actually desperate to change my life and didn't want to go back to just passively accepting things. I was 29, married with two small children. My husband was extremely successful and I was supposed to reflect his glory. The psychiatrist seemed very concerned about the inconvenience of my 'illness' to my husband and showed no interest in exploring what it meant to me. I'd become frightened of meeting people and I remember the psychiatrist commenting 'It's O.K. to be shy – you're just a young girl' – a well meaning but patronizing attitude which I found infuriating. I was an educated, intelligent, articulate, responsible person and I didn't want to spend the rest of my life existing in somebody else's shadow." (cited in Gorman, 1992)

Any form of help for someone who is distressed has the potential for abuse. Sometimes the negative side-effects can outweigh the benefits both for physical disabilities and disability of thought and feeling. The British National Formulary (1991) lists the possible side-effects of drugs used to control epilepsy. Such side-effects include gastro-intestinal disturbances, dizziness, drowsiness, headache, confusion and agitation, nausea and vomiting, and, for a few people, potentially fatal blood disorders such as agranulocytosis: a deficiency in certain blood cells caused by damage to the bone marrow, this disease is characterised by fever, ulceration of the mouth and throat and rapidly leads to prostration and death.

The recently hailed new "wonder-drug" in the treatment of schizophrenia, Clozapine, has been helpful in controlling the symptoms of schizophrenia in people who have not been helped by the other medication available. One of us (RP) knows two women who no longer needed long-term hospitalisation since taking this drug – but it too has several unpleasant side effects: not only things like drowsiness, tachycardia, fatigue, but for the unlucky few, potentially fatal agranulocytosis. Nonetheless, the consequences of thinking and feeling disturbances can be much worse. For some lesbians and women, drugs are quite literally a life-saver when distress becomes too great to tolerate.

One lesbian who believed that someone was coming into her room every night and drinking her blood described the medication she received:

"They made me sleepy and that helped. It's good to sleep. It stops the strain on the brain. Without them I couldn't sleep."

Another said:

"I don't like knowing that I can't manage without the drugs. No-one would. But that stellazine's very good. It stops the visions. It helps to stabilise me – or maybe that's the lithium. The modecate injection takes away the agitation. They make me feel sick sometimes, they make my mouth dry, they make my hand shake sometimes, but it's worth it. Without them I'm out of control – out of control of everything – thoughts, feelings – and that's much worse."

Often lesbians and feminists regard drugs as evil per se. This again is an able-minded perspective that actively oppresses those of us who gain benefit from medication, and whose functioning and coping are enhanced by such medications. If everyone around you condemns drugs then it is very difficult to believe it is all right to take them, even if you know that they help you. Drugs are not good or bad per se. If drugs help you to think more clearly, if they help to alleviate your distress when it reaches a point where you cannot tolerate it any more, they can be a good thing. If they dull your senses, or make you feel so bad that you cope less well, then they are a bad thing.

Toward a Politics of Social Disability

"Psychiatric illness is not an individual problem – it is the responsibility of us all. Its prevention and care is neither physiological or psychological – it is political" (Cook, 1985: 105). It is vital that we extend our theories and communities to accommodate us all – that we help, encourage and enable us all to function and contribute to the best of our abilities, no matter how disabled we are.

For socially disabled lesbians, therapy sometimes provides a supportive environment. In this environment, problems may be reduced, or even disappear entirely. However, there are many dangers in calling this "therapy", and in understanding what is being provided in psychological rather than political or social terms. In "therapy", disability and distress are privatised as individual problems, divorced from our communities, and the onus is on the lesbian to change rather than on the community to accommodate and support all of its members. Trust, friendship, practical help, encouragement and asylum are important for us all, yet so many of these ordinary activities have now been framed as "treatment" or "therapy".

Listening, understanding, learning, encouraging, helping – all of these have been translated into therapeutic exercises and have become the province of experts:

"Because psychiatric ideology mystifies people's difficulties into an 'illness' that only experts are thought capable of treating, we are all rendered a little less human. By turning our friends, our relatives, and ourselves over to psychiatry, we abandon and isolate people when they most need love and nurturance. The continual redefining of various kinds of problems as psychiatric in nature, requiring expert intervention, continually limits the extent to which people reach out to one another and increases the isolation in which we twentieth-century Americans more and more find ourselves. Rather than caring for one another, we turn to remote authority figures and experts, reinforcing the notion that one needs professional degrees and credentials in order to avoid doing irreparable harm to troubled people. . . ."
(Chamberlin, 1977: 237–238)

Socially disabled lesbians do not need a psychiatry, or a lesbian feminist therapy, that individualises and privatises their problems and attempts to enable them to "fit-in" to an able-minded world. We need a politics of social disability to parallel that which we have begun to construct around physical disability. As psychiatric survivor, Judi Chamberlin, argues:

"We must begin to turn toward the people we now isolate – the troubled (and troubling) relatives and friends we both love and fear. It will not be easy. The mental hospital system has developed precisely because this is a job we would rather leave to others."
(1977: 239)

The tasks may not be easy, but they are essential. Consideration, understanding and acceptance of distress and disabilities of thought and feeling are not only important to lesbians who are disabled, they are also of central importance to those of us who are not so disabled. Our communities will be a poorer place if we withdraw from, exclude, marginalise and render invisible socially disabled lesbians.

"I used to feel very angry about my own and other women's banishment from true and complete participation in lesbian life. Nowadays, though, I am weary of anger, and I mostly feel sad. . . . But I do not intend to let nondisabled lesbians off the hook. . . . If we can learn to have real, whole communities, then it will not be only the disabled women amongst us who must live with and come to terms with disability and its consequences in an ableist society. More and more abled lesbians could learn, as few already have, that disabled lesbians are as worthwhile as they and their abled friends are, and they could work with us, both inside and outside the lesbian community. . . ." (Franchild, 1990: 191)

We have much to gain from our connections with severely distressed and disabled lesbians. As Sarah Lucia Hoagland says:

"... as we increase our responsiveness with each other we contribute to the context in which our lesbian values gain sense, and so we develop the means to really be able to respond to [each others'] needs." (Hoagland, 1988: 289)

We also have much to gain in understanding everyday distress. Whilst able-minded lesbians' distress in no way parallels that of severely socially disabled lesbians, we all have insights to offer each other. Socially disabled lesbians are central to the building of our communities.

LESBIAN ETHICS, LESBIAN POLITICS

One of the great insights of second wave feminism was the recognition that "the personal is political" – a phrase first coined by Carol Hanisch in 1971. We meant by this that all our small, personal, day-to-day activities had political meaning, whether intended or not. Aspects of our lives that had previously been seen as purely "personal" – housework, sex, relationships with sons and fathers, mothers, sisters and lovers – were shaped by, and influential upon, their broader social context. A feminist understanding of "politics" meant challenging the male definition of the political as something external (to do with governments, laws, banner-waving, and protest marches) and moving towards an understanding of politics as central to our very beings, affecting our thoughts, emotions, and the apparently trivial everyday choices we make about how we live. Feminism meant treating what had been perceived as merely "personal" issues as political concerns.

There was a time, then, when feminists were clear that "the personal is political". The "personal" details of our lives were topics of political discussion and debate. Today, this situation is reversed. Political concerns, national and international politics, and major social, economic and ecological disasters are now reduced to individual psychological matters. The problem today is to prevent the last residues of political life from being treated as merely personal issues.

This wholesale translation of the political into the personal is characteristic, not just of lesbian/feminist psychology, but of psychology generally. In the USA, a group of 22 professionals spent three years and $735,000

(£448,000) in coming to the conclusion that lack of self-esteem is the root cause of "many of the major social ills that plague us today" (*The Guardian*, April 13, 1990). Gloria Steinem (1992) would agree: low self-esteem, she says, afflicts not only her, but also Hitler, Saddam Hussein, Ronald Reagan and George Bush, along with entire nations (Haiti and Argentina). Sexual violence against women is addressed by setting up social skills training and anger management sessions for rapists (now available in 60 jails in England and Wales, *The Guardian*, May 21, 1991), and racism becomes something to get off your chest in a counselling workshop (Green, 1987). Even environmental disaster can be translated from a major ecological concern to a psychological problem: in 1989, in the first week after the Exxon Valduz oil spill, Alaska hired a disaster psychologist, Dr Richard Geist of Kansas University, paying him $600 a day for his "expertise in attending to the special needs of communities struck by tragedy" (*The Guardian*, 15 April, 1989). Many people now think of major social and political issues in psychological terms.

In fact, the whole of life is seen as one great psychological exercise. Back in 1977, Judi Chamberlin (1977: 131) pointed out that mental hospitals tend to use the term "therapy" to describe absolutely everything that goes on inside them: "making the beds and sweeping the floor can be called 'industrial therapy', going to a dance or movie 'recreational therapy', stupefying patients with drugs 'chemotherapy', and so forth. Custodial mental hospitals, which offer very little treatment, frequently make reference to 'milieu therapy', as if the very hospital air were somehow curative". A decade or so later, with psychology's major clientele not in mental hospitals but in the community, everything in our lives is translated into "therapy". Reading books becomes "bibliotherapy"; writing (Wenz, 1988), journalkeeping (Hagan, 1988) and art (cf Chaplin, 1988: 17) are all ascribed therapeutic functions. Even taking photographs is now a psychological technique: phototherapist Jo Spence, drawing on the psychoanalytic theories of Alice Miller, heals (among other "wounds") "the wound of class shame" through photography. And although reading, writing and taking photographs are ordinary activities, in their therapeutic manifestation they require expert guidance: "I don't think people can do this with friends or by themselves ... they'll never have the safety working alone that they'll get working with a therapist because they will encounter their own blockages and be unable to get past them" (Spence, 1990).

We are not denying that reading, writing, art, photography and so on might make some people feel better about themselves. We are, however, disturbed that such activities are assessed in purely psychological terms. As feminists, we used to read in order to learn more about feminist history and culture; we used to write and paint to communicate with others. These were *social* activities, directed outwards; now they are treated as explorations of the self. The success of what we do is evaluated in terms of how it makes us feel. Social conditions are assessed in terms of how the inner life of individuals responds to them. Political and ethical commitments are judged by the degree to which they enhance or detract from our individual sense of well being.

Our relationships, too, are considered in terms of their therapeutic functions. Therapy used to name what happened between a therapist and a client. Now, as Bonnie Mann (1987) points out, it accurately describes what happens between many women in daily interactions: "any activity organized by women is boxed into a therapeutic framework. Its value is determined on the basis of whether or not it is 'healing' ":

"I have often seen an honest conversation turn into a therapeutic interaction before my eyes. For instance: I mention something that has bothered, hurt, or been difficult for me in some way. Something shifts. I see the woman I am with take on The Role of the Supportive Friend. It is as if a tape clicks into her brain, her voice changes, I can see her begin to see me differently, as a victim. She begins to recite the lines, 'That must have been very difficult for you,' or 'That must have felt so invalidating' or 'What do you think you need to feel better about that?' I know very well the corresponding tape that is supposed to click into my own brain: 'I think I just needed to let you

know what was going on for me', or 'It helps to hear you say that, it feels very validating,' or 'I guess I just need to go off alone and nurture myself a little'."
Psychological ways of thinking have spilled out of the therapist's office, the Alcoholics Anonymous groups and self-help books, the experiential workshops and rebirthing sessions, to invade all aspects of our lives.

We have shown, in this book, how thoroughly and how profoundly psychology translates the political into the personal. In lesbian/feminist psychology, "oppression" has been replaced by "homophobia"; "power", "liberation" and "revolution" have been redefined as internal phenomena. The feminist goal of changing the world is displaced by the therapeutic goal of changing ourselves; and our lesbian relationships are psychologised and pathologised with terms like "merger" and "codependency". Political goals and moral commitments are dismissed as secondary to individual self-development. The personalising of the political is rife both within and beyond lesbian/feminist psychology. In this chapter we ask *why* and how this has happened, and what we can do about it.

The Personal and the Political

Many lesbian/feminist psychologists state explicitly their belief that "the personal is political": according to some (eg Gilbert, 1980), this principle has "prevailed as [a] cornerstone of feminist therapy". Yet we have shown throughout this book with what insistence lesbian/feminist psychologists keep the "personal" personal, and render the "political" personal as well. Clearly, then, their understanding of the meaning of "the personal is political" must be very different from our own.

One common lesbian/feminist psychologising of "the personal is political" goes something like this:

> The supposedly "personal" activity of therapy is deeply political because learning to feel better about ourselves, raising our self-esteem, accepting our sexualities and coming to terms with who we really are – all these are political acts in a heteropatriarchal world. With woman-hating all around us, it is revolutionary to

189

love ourselves, to heal the wounds of patriarchy, and to overcome self-oppression. If everyone loved and accepted themselves, so that women (and men) no longer projected on to each other their own repressed self-hatreds, we would have real social change.

This is a very common argument, most recently rehearsed in Gloria Steinem's *Revolution from Within*. As Carol Sternhell (1992) points out in a critical review, "The point of all this trendy, tie-dyed shrinkery isn't simply feeling better about yourself – or rather, it is, because feeling better about all our selves is now the key to worldwide revolution".

In this model, the "self" is naturally good, but has to be uncovered from beneath the layers of internalised oppression, and healed from the wounds inflicted on it by a heteropatriarchal society. Despite her manifest differences from Gloria Steinem in other areas, lesbian feminist therapist Laura Brown (1992) shares Steinem's notion of the "true self". She writes, for example, of a client's "struggle to recover her self from the snares of patriarchy", by "peel[ing] away the layers of patriarchal training" and "heal[ing] the wounds of ... childhood"; in therapy with Laura Brown (1992), a woman is helped to "know herself", to move beyond her "accommodated self" to discover her "true self" (or "shamed inner self"), and live "at harmony with herself". In most lesbian/feminist psychology, this inner self is characterised as a beautiful, spontaneous little girl. Getting in touch with and nurturing her is a first step in creating social change: it is "revolution from within".

This set of ideas has its roots in the "growth movement" of the 1960s, which emphasised personal liberation and "human potential". Back then, the central image was of a vaguely defined "sick society".

"'The System' was poisoned by its materialism, consumerism and lack of concern for the individual. These things were internalised by people; but underneath the layers of 'shit' in each person lay an essential 'natural self' which could be reached through various therapeutic techniques. What this suggests is that revolutionary change is not something that has to be built, created or invented with other people, but that it is somehow natural, dormant in each of us individually and only has to be released." (Scott and Payne, 1984) The absurdity of taking this "revolution from within" argument to its logical conclusion is illustrated by one project, the offspring of a popular therapeutic program, which proposes to end starvation. Not, as might seem sensible, by organising soup kitchens, distributing food parcels to the hungry, campaigning for impoverished countries to be released from their national debts, or sponsoring farming cooperatives. Instead, the project offers the simple expedient of getting individuals to sign cards saying that they are "willing to be responsible for making the end of starvation an idea whose time has come". When an undisclosed number of people have signed such cards, a "context" will have been created in which hunger will somehow end (cited in Zilbergeld, 1983: 5–6). We recognise that Laura Brown (along with many other lesbian/feminist therapists) would join us in challenging the obscenity of this project. Yet the logic of her own arguments permits precisely this kind of interpretation.

Such approaches are a very long way from *our* understanding of "the personal is political". We don't think social change happens from the inside out. We don't think people have inner children somewhere inside waiting to be nurtured, re-parented, and their natural goodness released into the world. On the contrary, as we argued in Chapter 4, our inner selves are constructed by the social and political contexts in which we live, and if we want to alter people's behaviour it is far more effective to change the environment than to psychologise individuals. Yet, as Sarah Scott and Tracey Payne (1984) point out, "when it comes to doing therapy it is essential to each and every technique that women see their 'real' selves and their 'social' selves as distinct". This means that the process of making ethical and political decisions about our lives is reduced to the supposed "discovery" of our true selves, the honouring of our "hearts desires". Political understanding of our thoughts and feelings is occluded, and our ethical choices are cast within a therapeutic rather than a political framework. A set of repressive social conditions has made life hard for women and lesbians. Yet the "revolution from within" solution is to improve the individuals, rather than change the conditions.

Psychology suggests that only after healing yourself can you begin to heal the world. We disagree. People do *not* have to be perfectly functioning, self-actualised human beings in order to create social change. Think of the lesbians and feminists you know who have been influential in the world, and who have worked hard and effectively for social justice: have they all loved and accepted themselves? The vast majority of those *we* admire for their political work go on struggling for change not because they have achieved self-fulfilment (nor in order to attain it), but because of their ethical and political commitments, and often *in spite of* their own fears, self-doubts, personal angsts and self-hatreds. Those who work for "revolution without" are often no more "in touch with their real selves" than those fixated on inner change: this observation should not be used (as it sometimes is) to discredit their activism, but rather to demonstrate that political action is an option for all of us, whatever our state of psychological well-being. Wait until your inner world is sorted out before shifting your attention to the outer, and you are, indeed, "waiting for the revolution" (cf Brown, 1992). And in fact, as Carol Sternhell (1992) points out, Gloria Steinem, despite her current preoccupation with "revolution from within", is herself a good example of someone who was effective as a social campaigner although she suffered, she now tells us, from chronic lack of self-esteem. Our response is the same as that of Carol Sternhell (1992), who says:

> "When I first heard . . . that Gloria Steinem didn't have self-esteem, my reaction was: 'Who cares? Look what she's done with her life! It's the *life* that matters in the end'."

A second psychological version of "the personal is political" as applied to therapy goes something like this:

> Politics develops out of personal experience. Feminism is derived from women's own life stories, and must reflect and validate those. Women's realities have always been ignored, denied or invalidated under heteropatriarchy; therapy serves to witness, affirm, and

validate women's experience. As such, it makes the personal, political.

The politics of therapy, according to this approach, involves no more than "validating", "respecting", "honouring", "celebrating", "affirming", "attending to" or "witnessing" (these buzz words are generally used interchangeably) another lesbian's (or woman's) "experience" or "reality". According to feminist therapist Marcia Hill (1990):

". . . we know what is true not by the 'givens' of society, but by listening to our inner experience and that of others. The fundamental political act is the same as the fundamental therapeutic act: it is the process of joining another person's experience in a way which enables that person to make explicit her internal knowledge of what is real. . . ."

This "validation" process is supposed to have enormous implications: "When we honor our clients, they transform themselves" (Hill, 1990).

There is obviously a lot of sense in listening to each other and in being willing to understand the meaning of other lesbians' experience. We used to do this in consciousness-raising groups; now we do it in therapy. Because it has been transformed into a therapeutic activity, it now carries all the risks of abuse of power endemic to the therapeutic enterprise (see Chapter 3). In particular, therapists are selective about which experiences they will or won't validate in therapy. Those of a client's feelings and beliefs which are most similar to those of the therapist are "validated"; the others are more or less subtly "invalidated". In cognitive therapy, this "invalidation" is explicit (it is called "modifying dysfunctional cognitions", cf Perkins, 1991a); in other therapeutic methods it may be less explicit. Few lesbian/feminist therapists, for example, will uncritically validate a survivor of child sexual abuse who talks of being to blame for her childhood rape because of her seductive behaviour: instead, she is likely to be offered an analysis of the way in which victim-blaming operates under heteropatriarchy. Similarly, few lesbian/feminist therapists will validate the experience of a woman who says she is sick and perverted for being lesbian: instead, as Laura Brown (1992) herself argues, her "dysfunctional attitude" will be challenged and therapy will be geared towards enabling the woman to understand that " 'patriarchy teaches that lesbianism is evil as a means of socially controlling all women and reserving emotional resources for men and dominant institutions' (an analysis that I have offered, in various forms, to women wondering out loud in my office about why they hate themselves so for being lesbian)" (Brown, 1992). While claiming to "validate" all women's realities, in fact only a subset, consisting of those realities with which the therapist is in agreement, are accepted as "true" reflections of the way things are. The others are "invalidated", whether as "faulty cognitions" (Padesky, 1989), or as "patriarchal distortions" (Brown, 1992). In other words, all this talk about "validating" and "honouring" clients' reality is thin disguise for the therapeutic shaping of lesbian experience in terms of the therapist's own theories.

Therapists, then, are selective about which experiences in their clients they validate. Reading the literature, the two of us sometimes agree with a particular therapist's selection (in particular, we like Laura Brown's choices); more often, we are in disagreement (particularly, for example, with those who "validate" lesbians' experience of dominance and subordination in sex, see Chapter 4). Irrespective of whether we happen to like or dislike the selections made, we are opposed, in principle, to the very idea of covertly shaping lesbians' realities under the guise of value-free, uncritical "validation" of everyone's experience.

In any case, as we argued earlier in this book (Chapter 3), "experience" is always perceived through an (implicit or explicit) theoretical framework within which it gains meaning. Feelings and emotions are not simply immediate, unsocialised, self-authenticating responses. They are socially constructed, and presuppose certain social norms. "Experience" is never "raw"; it is embedded in a social web of interpretation and reinterpretation. In encouraging and perpetuating the notion of pure, unsullied, pre-socialised "experience" and natural emotion welling up from inside, therapists have disguised or obscured the social roots of our "inner selves". Placing "experience" beyond debate in this way is deeply anti-feminist (in our understanding of feminist politics) precisely because it denies the political sources of experience, and renders them purely personal. When psychology simply "validates" particular emotions, it removes them from an ethical and political framework. This lack of ethical consideration is highlighted by Julie Bindel (1988) in her critique of assertiveness training. She poses a dilemma:

"An exhausted lesbian mother asks you to look after her children. Do you say:
a) Yes of course
b) Maybe tomorrow, I'll look in my filofax, or
c) No, I don't want to do that. I don't feel good about doing that. I want to read my book. You are guilt-tripping me.
The answer of course depends on what stage of A[ssertiveness] T[raining] you have reached."

As feminists, we have theorised the ethical and political dimensions of lesbian motherhood, and the respon-sibilities and rights of all lesbians in relation to girl and boy children: this theory is ignored in psychological approaches which simply address our personal pre-ferences, and teach us to make decisions on the basis of what "feels right". If "the personal is political" then we cannot simply "validate" (or, covertly, *in*validate) it; it must be explicitly addressed in ethical and political terms.

Finally, a third psychological interpretation of "the personal is political" relies on the notion of "empower-ment". It goes something like this:

Therapy empowers us to act politically. Raising one's personal awareness through therapy enables individuals to release their psychic energies towards creative social change. Through therapy, lesbians can gain both the feminist consciousness and the self-confidence to engage in political action. Many radical feminist political activists are empowered to continue through their ongoing self-nurturing in therapy.

Those in therapy often use this justification: according to Angela Johnson (1992), therapy (along with rock-climbing) "gives me the energy to continue my activism with renewed excitement". And therapists concur. Laura Brown

(1992), for example, says that many of her clients "have precious little to give to the larger struggle from which many are disengaged when I first see them". Her client "Ruth", was helped to understand that "ultimate healing lies in her participation in cultural, not only personal change" and was shown by Laura Brown "how to move her healing process into a broader sphere": as a result of therapy her "energies" were "freed" and she became a speaker, poet and teacher about women and war, and engaged in public anti-war activism. Similarly, clinical psychologist Sue Holland (1991), in an article entitled "from private symptoms to public action", promotes a model of therapy in which the client moves from "passive 'ill' patient/victim" at the start of treatment, to a "recognition of ... oppression as located in the objective environment" which leads to a "collective desire for change" in which "psychic energies can ... be addressed outward onto structural enemies".

Again, this does not reflect *our* understanding of "the personal is political". The "personal", according to this interpretation, consists of "psychic energies" (never clearly defined) which operate according to a hydraulic model: there is a fixed amount of "energy" which can be blocked, freed, or redirected along other channels. The "political" is simply one of these "channels". Therapy can (and some would say *should*) direct lesbian/feminist energy along "political" channels. Often, of course, it does not, and lesbians remain perpetually focussed within – a problem noted with regret by the more radical lesbian/feminist therapists. But *their* therapy (they say) does result in their clients' becoming politically active.

Far from embodying the notion of "the personal is political", these ideas rely on a radical *separation* of the two. The "personal" business of doing therapy is distinguished from the "political" work of going on marches, and once the two have been severed in this way, the "personal" and "political" are then inspected for degree of correlation. For example, an anonymous feminist psychologist who acted as reader for New York University Press responded to our lesbian/feminist critique of therapy by arguing that "many of my friends who are political activists are also in therapy. Rather than subverting their politics, they credit therapy with enabling them to be more active." One might as well respond to an ethical vegetarian critique of meat-eating by arguing that "many of my friends who are involved in animal rights issues are meat-eaters; they say meat-eating gives them more energy to go on animal rights demonstrations." The "empowerment" argument totally ignores the politics of therapy itself. It is seen simply as a hobby (like rock climbing) or personal activity with no particular ethical or political implications in and of itself. Shorn of intrinsic political meaning, it is assessed only in terms of its presumed consequences for "politics" – defined in terms of the old male left banner-waving variety. If "the personal is political", then the very *process of doing* therapy is political, and this process (not simply its alleged outcomes) must be critically evaluated in political terms.

In conclusion, and despite the frequency with which lesbian/feminist therapists routinely state that "the personal is political", it seems to us entirely wrong to claim that this maxim is a "cornerstone of feminist therapy" (Gilbert, 1980). Certainly the notions of "revolution from within", of the importance of "validating" women's reality, and of "empowering" women for political activism *are* central to the thinking of many lesbian/feminist psychologists. As we have shown, these overlapping and interrelated ideas are braided throughout a great deal of lesbian/feminist psychological theory and practice. But such notions are a long way from the radical feminist insight that "the personal is political", and are often interpreted in direct contradiction to it. They are commonly used to keep women focused on an internal "personal" world at the expense of public engagements; they often foster naive concepts of the mechanisms whereby social change is achieved; involve uncritical acceptance of "true feelings" and/or manipulative "reinterpretations" of women's lives in terms preferred by the psychologist; lead women to revert to "external" definitions of politics in contradistinction to the "personal" business of therapy; and leave us shorn of ethical and political language. Acknowledging that the personal really *is* political means rejecting psychology.

We recognise that some women whose politics we

admire and respect have not rejected psychology: many are "in therapy" or providers of therapy. This observation is sometimes used to counter our arguments. We have been told, for example, that Nancy Johnson whose class action suit against the USA government for condemning the people of Utah to cancer we cite favourably in Chapter 2 now works as a psychic healer in a manner which we are likely to find politically problematic.

Obviously feminist activists are sometimes practitioners or consumers of psychology: many lesbian/feminists clearly find it possible to include both in their lives. But then, health campaigners sometimes smoke cigarettes; ecologists sometimes drop litter; and pacifists sometimes slap their children. The observed co-existence of two views or behaviours in the same person does not render them logically, ethically, or politically compatible.

Argument about the ethical and political compatibility of people's different ideas and behaviour is an important part of what feminist political discussion is all about. Our argument is that feminism and psychology are *not* ethically or politically compatible. It's not, necessarily, that lesbians involved in psychology are a-political or anti-feminist. Many are serious about their feminism, and deeply engaged in political activities. But in so far as they organise their lives with reference to psychological ideas, and in so far as they limit their thoughts and actions to what they learn from psychology, they are denying the fundamental feminist principle that "the personal is political".

Psychology as Backlash

Most discussions of ethics in therapy are contained within a psychological framework: that is, they take for granted that people have problems that are "psychological" in origin, and which can only be solved by "psychology". Ethical and political discussion is then limited to questions such as: the approriateness of each of the different psycho-logical solutions available (therapy versus twelve steps, assertiveness training versus cocounselling); the extent to which they are available to all (sliding scales, accessibility for lesbians of different racial and ethnic origins, and for disabled lesbians); the various abuses which limit the effectiveness of therapy (notably, "boundary violations"); what type of furniture to have in the therapist's office ("class-neutral") and where to hang her qualifying certificates ("in sight without being the piece de resistance of the office walls") (Brown, 1985). On the assumption that therapy is A Good Thing, attention is focussed on providing the best possible quality therapy to as many women as possible.

Rarely do lesbian/feminist psychologists question the basic underlying assumptions of psychology in general. Almost every critique culminates with a proposal for a different form of psychotherapy from the ones it criticises, or concludes with suggestions for reforming or restructuring therapy. Few psychologists have explored what might be wrong with the very idea of therapy itself. In this book we have written both as psychologists, and as lesbian/feminists, to expose some of the problems intrinsic to psychology and to illustrate the dangers for lesbian/feminism of psychological and therapeutic models.

Psychology pervades all our thinking – often without us even knowing it. Lesbian/feminists never sound so alike as when asserting their individual uniqueness. When lesbian/feminists fail to see that these beliefs are part of a pervasive common culture, they run the risk of doing just what they attack in other moral traditions – that is, accepting as literally true what is merely a cultural convention, and then refusing to open their position for discussion. Just as, within a heterosexist moral framework, lesbianism is dismissed as "sick" and "perverted", because it challenges the very foundations of heteropatriarchy, so too, those who challenge the foundations of psychology, are often dismissed. Critics of therapy have been described as "out of touch with their feelings, repressed, joyless, slogging on for the revolution but doing nothing for themselves now" (cf Payne, 1984) – and worse!

Throughout these pages we have made various suggestions as to *why* so many lesbian/feminists have embraced, apparently with such enthusiasm, psychological versions of the world. In part, as we've shown, the psychologising of lesbian/feminism is simply an outcome of the growth of psychology more generally in modern Western cultures. In wealthy individualistic societies such as North America and Britain, psychology is a consumer product like any other. As such societies become wealthier, individuals tend to move from the purchase of tangible objects (food, clothes, toasters, washing machines, computers) to the purchase of services which effect material change in the world (someone to clean your house, service your car, iron your clothes) and then to the purchase of immaterial, intangible psychological services: someone to cherish your uniqueness or help you to discover your true self. Psychology today is a product of wealthy North American individualism. It claims to offer solutions to problems that are luxuries in the first place: the "deprived childhoods" of the average British or North American lesbian/feminist would be hard to explain to a Somalian mother struggling to keep her child alive. This observation does not necessarily mean that therapy is unethical (it isn't unethical to buy a toaster just because someone else somewhere in the world can't afford one); but it does put psychology in context. Most of the world's people, historically and cross-culturally, never enter therapy. Nor do they understand the concepts (of true selves, toxic parents, inner children, or self-esteem) upon which therapeutic interventions are based. One North American writer reflects that "the nervous search for the true self and the extravagant conclusions drawn from that search are probably relatively recent in our society" (Bellah, 1985: 55). We have *learned* to frame our problems in psychological terms, and to expect psychological solutions to them.

In part, then, women (lesbian/feminists included) have turned to psychology because it is one of the dominant culturally available frameworks for thinking about experience. More than this, women have historically been excluded from the public world, and have always been expected to be more concerned with "private" and "personal" issues. We get more sympathy and support if we define our problems in psychological instead of in political terms. Perhaps, too, some women's interest in psychology is an attempt to meet perceived deficits in lesbian/feminist communities, by offering superficial community among "wounded selves". It offers quick gratification for lonely or unhappy lesbians and feminists who want to feel part of something (even if only of a twelve step group). It provides prosthetic friendship from a therapist for those who cannot find the real thing. Certainly lesbian/feminists, like everyone else, sometimes feel sad, baffled, frustrated, and overwhelmed by problems in living: psychology appears to offer answers – at a price.

Most of all, in a right-wing "post-feminist" political climate, it becomes increasingly clear that feminist revolution is not going to happen next week, or even next year. Women turn instead to "personal" cures and private solutions, redefining feminist goals such as "power", "liberation", and "revolution" in terms that seem attainable – revolution from within, individual freedom, and liberation in our personal lives through Brand X therapy. Abandoning old moral and political questions about our lives, lesbian/feminists increasingly supplant them with the new question "what makes me feel good right now?"

Lesbians and feminists must reclaim the right, and the necessity, for making moral judgements about our lives. Most of us are adequate human beings who do not need "safety" so much as "freedom". And on those occasions when we are *not* able to cope on our own, we can take care of each other. We do not need psychology. Psychology is, and always will be, destructive of the lesbian/feminist enterprise. Without psychology, we can, like millions of others, bear the limits, contradictions, vulnerabilities and burdens of our humanity. Without psychology we can build lesbian communities, lesbian ethics, and lesbian politics.

REFERENCES

Alderson, L. & Wistrich, H. (1988) Clause 29: Radical feminist perspectives, *Trouble & Strife*, 13, 3–8

American Psychiatric Association (1987) *Diagnostic and Statistical Manual of Mental Disorders* (Third Edition, Revised: DSMIII – R), Washington, D.C.: American Psychiatric Association

Anne & Vera (1987) Lesbian relationships – A cynical view, *The Bristol Radical Lesbian Feminist Magazine*, 3, 8–10

Anonymous (1985) Malpractice, *Lesbian Ethics*, 1(3), 20–22

Anonymous (1992) Comments from a reader for New York University Press

Anthony, B.D. (1982) Lesbian client – lesbian therapist: Opportunities and challenges in working together IN J.C. Gonsiorek (Ed) *Homosexuality and Psychotherapy*, New York: Haworth Press

Appleby, Y. (1990) *Access Limited*, Unpublished undergraduate dissertation, Staffordshire Polytechnic, UK

—— (1992) Disability and 'Compulsory Heterosexuality' IN C. Kitzinger, S. Wilkinson & R. Perkins (Eds) *Heterosexuality: Special Issue of "Feminism and Psychology"*, 2(3), 502–504

Armstrong, L. (1987) *Kiss Daddy Goodnight*, New York: Pocket Books

Armstrong, L. (1991) Surviving the incest industry, *Trouble & Strife*, 21, 29–32

Bardwick J. (1979) *The Psychology of Women*, New York: Harper Row

Barry, K. (1979) *Female Sexual Slavery*, New York: Avon

Bart P. (1977) The mermaid and the minotaur: A fishy story that's part bull, *Contemporary Psychology*, 22(11), 834–835

—— (1983) Review of Chodorow's *The Reproduction of Mothering* IN J. Trebilcot (Ed) *Mothering: Essays in Feminist Theory*, New York: Rowman and Allanheld

Bart P. (1989) Theory of surplus therapists, *Lesbian Ethics*, 3(3), 58–59

Bellah, R.N. (1985) *Habits of the Heart: Individualism and Commitment in American Life*, Berkeley, CA: University of California Press

Benjamin, S.A. et al (1990) *Ethical Standards and Practice in the Lesbian Therapy Community*, available from Sharon L. Seigel, 8235 Santa Monica Blvd., Suite 303, Los Angeles, CA 90046

Bergin, A.E. (1967) Some implications of psychotherapy research for therapeutic practice, *International Journal of Psychiatry*, 3(3), 136–160

Berson, N. (1984) On lesbian morality, *Common Lives/ Lesbian Lives*, 13, 47–49

Bindel, J. (1988) The state of the movement, *Trouble & Strife*, 13, 50–52

Boston Lesbian Psychologies Collective (1987) *Lesbian Psychologies*, Urbana: University of Illinois Press

Bouhoutsos, J. (1984) Sexual intimacy between psychotherapists and clients: policy implications for the future, IN L.E. Walker (Ed) *Women and Mental Health Policy*, Newbury Park, CA: Sage Publications

Bradford, J.B. & Ryan, C.C. (1987) *National Lesbian Health Care Survey: Mental Health Implications*, Richmond, VA: Survey Research Laboratory, Virginia Commonwealth University

Breggin, P. (1991) *Toxic Psychiatry*, New York: St. Martin's Press

British Medical Association and The Royal Pharmaceutical Society of Great Britain (1991) *British National Formulary Number 21*, London: The Pharmaceutical Press

Brown, B. (1982) Lesbian battery, *Lesbian Inciter*, 8, 3

Brown, L.S. (1984) The lesbian feminist therapist in private practice and her community, *Psychotherapy in Private Practice*, 2(4), 9–16

References

Brown, L.S. (1985) Ethics and business practice in feminist therapy, IN L.B. Rosewater & L.E.A. Walker (Eds) *Handbook of Feminist Therapy: Women's Issues in Psychotherapy*, New York: Springer

—— (1986) Confronting internalised oppression in sex therapy with lesbians, *Journal of Homosexuality*, 12, 99–107

—— (1989a) Beyond thou shalt not: thinking about ethics in the lesbian therapy community, *Women & Therapy*, 8, 13–25

—— (1989b) Fat-oppressive attitudes and the feminist therapist: Directions for change, *Women & Therapy*, 8(3), 19–30

—— (1990a) The meaning of a multicultural perspective for theory building in feminist therapy, IN L. Brown & M. Root (Eds) *Diversity and Complexity in Feminist Therapy Part I: Special Issue of Women & Therapy*, 9(1/2), 1–21

—— (1990b) What's addiction got to do with it? A feminist critique of codependence, *Psychology of Women: Newsletter of Division 35, APA*, 17(1), 1–4

—— (1992) While waiting for the revolution: The case for a lesbian feminist psychotherapy, *Feminism & Psychology*, 2(2), 239–253

Brown, R.M. (1972) Take a lesbian to lunch IN K. Jay & A. Young (Eds) *Out of the Closets: Voices of Gay Liberation*, New York: Harcourt Brace Jovanovich

Brunet, A. & Turcotte, L. (1982) Separatism and radicalism, *Lesbian Ethics*, 2(1), 47. Reprinted in S.L. Hoagland & J. Penelope (Eds) (1988) *For Lesbians Only: A Separatist Anthology*, London: Onlywomen Press

Bulkin, E. (1990) *Enter Password: Recovery*, New York: Turtle Books

Bunch, C. (1987) *Passionate Politics*, New York: St. Martin's Press

Burack, C. (1992) A house divided: Feminism and object relations theory, *Women's Studies International Forum*, 15(4), 499–506

Burch, B. (1982) Psychological merger in lesbian couples: A joint ego psychological and systems approach, *Family Therapy*, 1(3), 201–208

—— (1987) Barriers to intimacy: Conflicts over power, dependency, and nurturing in lesbian relationships IN Boston Lesbian Psychologies Collective (Ed) *Lesbian Psychologies*, Urbana: University of Illinois Press

Califia, P. (1980) *Sapphistry: The Book of Lesbian Sexuality*, Tallahassee: Naiad Press

Caplan, P. (1992) Driving us crazy: How oppression damages women's mental health and what we can do about it, *Women & Therapy*, 12(3), 5–28

Card, C. (1985) Virtues and moral luck, *Institute for Legal Studies #4*, University of Wisconsin, Madison Law School

—— (1990) Pluralist lesbian separatism IN J. Allen (Ed) *Lesbian Philosophies and Cultures*, New York: State University of New York Press

Cardea, C. (1985) The lesbian revolution and the 50 minute hour: A working class look at therapy and the movement, *Lesbian Ethics*, 1(3), 46–68

Cartledge, S. (1983) Duty and desire: Creating a feminist morality IN S. Cartledge & J. Ryan (Eds) *Sex and Love: New Thoughts on Old Contradictions*, London: The Women's Press

Cartwright, S.A. (1981) Report on the diseases and physical peculiarities of the negro race IN A.L. Caplan, H.T. Engelhardt & J.J. McCartney (Eds) *Concepts of Health and Disease: Interdisciplinary Perspectives*, Reading, MA: Addison-Wesley

Cass, V. (1979) Homosexual identity formation: a theoretical model, *Journal of Homosexuality*, 9, 105–126

Castel, R., Castel, F. & Lovell, A. (1982) *The Psychiatric Society*, New York: Columbia University Press (trans, A. Goldhammer)

Chamberlin, J. (1977) *On Our Own*, London: MIND Publications (1988 Edition)

References

Chamberlin, J. (1990) The ex-patients movement: Where we've been and where we're going, *Journal of Mind & Behaviour*, 11(3/4), 323–336

—— (1993) A psychiatric survivor speaks out IN S. Wilkinson (Ed) *Women and Madness*: A reappraisal, *Feminism & Psychology*, 3(3)

Chaplin, J. (1988) *Feminist Counselling in Action*, London: Sage

Chaplin, J. & Noack, A. (1988) Leadership and self help groups IN S. Krowski & P. Land (Eds) *In Our Experience: Workshops at the Women's Therapy Centre*, London: The Women's Press

Chesler, P. (1972) *Women and Madness*, New York: Avon Books

Chodorow, N. (1978) *The Reproduction of Mothering*, Berkeley, CA: University of California Press

Clausen, J. (1990) My interesting condition, *Out/Look*, 2(3), 10–21

Clunis, D.M. & Green, G.D. (1988) *Lesbian Couples*, Seattle, WA: Seal Press

Comely, L., Kitzinger, C., Perkins, R. & Wilkinson, S. (1992) Lesbian psychology in Britain: Back into the closet? *Feminism & Psychology*, 2(2), 265–268

CONNEXXUS Women's Centre/Centro De Mujeres, (1990) Ethics agreement IN S.A. Benjamin et al (Eds) *Ethical Standards and Practice in the Lesbian Therapy Community* (1990) available from Sharon L. Seigel, 8235 Santa Monica Blvd., Suite 303, Los Angeles, CA 90046

Cook, G. (1985) Psychiatry as male violence, IN d. rhodes & S. McNeill (Eds) *Women Against Violence Against Women*, London: Onlywomen Press

Coward, R. (1989) *The Whole Truth. The Myth of Alternative Health*, London: Faber & Faber

—— (1992) *Our Treacherous Hearts: Why Women Let Men Get Their Way*, London: Faber & Faber

Cunningham, J. (1986) Bad Language, *Gossip: A Journal of Lesbian Feminist Ethics*, 2, 97–98 reprinted (1993) IN L. Mohin (Ed) *An Intimacy of Equals: Lesbian Feminist Ethics*, London: Onlywomen Press

Daly, M. (1978) *Gyn/Ecology: The Metaethics of Radical Feminism*, London: The Women's Press

——— (1984) *Pure Lust*, London: The Women's Press

Daly, M. & Caputi, J. (1987) *Websters New Intergalactic Wickedary*, London: The Women's Press

Dannecker, M. (1981) *Theories of Homosexuality*, London: Gay Men's Press

Decker, B. (1984) Counseling gay and lesbian couples, *Journal of Social Work & Human Sexuality*, 2(2/3), 39–52

DeHardt, D. (1992) Feminist therapy and heterosexual problems IN C. Kitzinger, S. Wilkinson & R. Perkins (1992) (Eds) *Heterosexuality: Special issue of "Feminism & Psychology: An International Journal"*, 2(3), 498–501

dell'Olio, A. (1970) Divisiveness and self-destruction in the women's movement: A letter of resignation, leaflet by KNOW, Inc., P.O. Box 86081, Pittsburgh, PA 15223, USA

de Monteflores, C. & Schultz, S.J. (1978) Coming out: similarities and differences for lesbians and gay men, *Journal of Social Issues*, 34, 180–197

Douglas, C.A. (1987) Feminism: Beyond 'choice', *off our backs* May, 9–12

——— (1990) *Love and Politics: Radical Feminist & Lesbian theories*, San Francisco, CA: ism press

Dowling, C. (1981) *The Cinderella Complex: Women's Hidden Fear of Independence*, London: Fontana

Dworkin, A. (1981) *Pornography: Men Possessing Women*, London: The Women's Press and New York: Wideview/Perigree Books

——— (1987) *Intercourse*, London: Arrow Books

References

Dykewomon, E. (1988) On surviving psychiatric assault & creating emotional well-being in communities, *Sinister Wisdom*, 36

Ehrenreich, B. & English, D. (1978) *For Her Own Good: 150 Years of Experts' Advice to Women*, New York: Anchor/Doubleday

Eichenbaum, L. (1987) Separate sisters, interviewed by Helen Birch, *City Limits*, August 6th, 47–48

Eichenbaum, L. & Orbach, S. (1982) *Outside in ... Inside out: Women's Psychology – a Feminist Psychoanalytic Approach*, London: Penguin

——(1983) *What Do Women Want?* London: Fontana/ Collins

——(1987) Separation and intimacy: Crucial practice issues in working with women in therapy IN S. Ernst & M. Maguire (Eds) *Living with the Sphinx: Papers from the Women's Therapy Centre*, London: The Women's Press

Eisenbud, R.J. (1986) Women feminist patients and a feminist woman analyst IN T. Bernay & D.W. Canter (Ed) *The Psychology of Today's Woman: New Psychoanalytic Visions*, Cambridge, MA: Harvard University Press

Elizabeth, R. (1982) Deprivatising pain, *Catcall*, 14, 15–16 reprinted and extended in O'Sullivan, S. (1987) (Ed) *Women's Health*, London: Pandora

Ernst, S. (1987) Can a daughter be a woman? Women's identity and psychological separation IN S. Ernst & M. Maguire (Eds) *Living with the Sphinx: Papers from the Women's Therapy Centre*, London: The Women's Press

Ernst, S. & Goodison, L. (1981) *In Our Own Hands*, London: The Women's Press

Ernst, S. & Maguire, M. (1987a) Introduction IN S. Ernst & M. Maguire (Eds) *Living with the Sphinx: Papers from the Women's Therapy Centre*, London: The Women's Press

——(1987b) (Eds) *Living with the Sphinx: Papers from the Women's Therapy Centre*, London: The Women's Press

Evans, L. & Bannister, S. (1990) Lesbian violence, lesbian victims: How to identify battering in relationships, *Lesbian Ethics*, 4(1), 52–65

Falco, K.L. (1991) *Psychotherapy with Lesbian Clients: Theory into Practice*, New York: Brunner Mazel

Faludi, S. (1991) *Backlash: The Undeclared War Against Women*, London: Chatto & Windus

Feminist Therapy Institute (1987) Feminist therapy ethical code IN S.A. Benjamin et al (Ed) *Ethical Standards and Practice in the Lesbian Therapy Community* (1990) available from Sharon L. Seigel, 8235 Santa Monica Blvd., Suite 303, Los Angeles, CA 90046

Franchild, E. (1990) "You do so well": A blind lesbian responds to her sighted sisters IN J. Allen (Ed) *Lesbian Philosophies and Cultures*, New York: State University of New York Press

Francis, D. (1991) Crystal balls, *Trouble & Strife*, 22(winter), 45–48

Freedman, M. (1978) Towards a gay psychology, IN L. Crew (Ed) *The Gay Academic*, Palm Springs, CA: ETC Publications

Freeman, J. (1975) The tyranny of structurelessness, Reprinted in J. Freeman (1985) *The Politics of Women's Liberation*, New York: David McKay Co.

Fritz, L. (1979) *Dreamers & Dealers: An Intimate Appraisal of the Women's Movement*, Boston: Beacon Press

Frye, M. (1983) *The Politics of Reality: Essays in Feminist Theory*, Trumansburg, NY: Crossing Press

—— (1990a) Do you have to be a lesbian to be a feminist? *off our backs*, December, 1990

—— (1990b) The possibility of lesbian community, *Lesbian Ethics*, 4(1), 84–87

—— (1990c) Lesbian sex, IN J. Allen (Ed) *Lesbian Philosophies and Cultures*, New York: State University of New York Press

References

Gardiner, J.K. (1987) Self-psychology as feminist theory, *Signs*, 12, 761–780

Geertz, C. (1984) From the native's point of view: On the nature of anthropological understanding, IN R.A. Schweder & R.A. Levine (Eds) *Culture Theory: Essays on Mind, Self and Emotion*, Cambridge: Cambridge University Press

Geiger, R. (1990) *Empowerment for Lesbians: Affirming and Loving Messages*, Desktop Publishing Inc., Durham, NC. Available from Ricki Geiger, MSW, ACSW, 2634 Chapel Hill Blvd., Suite 123, Durham NC 27767, USA

Gergen, K.J. (1973) Social psychology as history, *Journal of Personality and Social Psychology*, 26, 309–320

Gilbert, L.A. (1980) Feminist therapy IN A.M. Brodsky & R. Hare-Mustin (Ed) *Women and Psychotherapy: An Assessment of Research and Practice*, New York: Guilford Press

Gilman, C.P. (1879) cited in Ehrenreich, B. & English, D. *For Her Own Good: 150 Years of Experts' Advice to Women*, New York: Anchor Books

Gomberg, E.S.L. (1989) On terms used and abused: The concept of 'codependency', *Drugs and Society*, 3, 113–132

Goudsmit, E.M. (1993) All in the mind! Stereotypic views and the psychologisation of women's illness IN S. Wilkinson & C. Kitzinger (Eds) Topic review, women and health: Feminist perspectives, *Health Psychology Update*, 12, 28–32

Green, D. & Clunis M. (1989) Married lesbians IN E, Rothblum & E. Cole (Eds) *Loving Boldly: Issues Facing Lesbians*, New York: Harrington Park Press

Green, M. (1987) Women in the oppressor role: white racism, IN S. Ernst & M. Maguire (Eds) *Living with the Sphinx: Papers from the Women's Therapy Centre*, London: The Women's Press

Gross, M.L. (1978) *The Psychological Society: A Critical Analysis of Psychiatry, Psychotherapy, Psychoanalysis and the Psychological Revolution*, New York: Random House

Groves, P.A. (1985) Coming out: Issues for the therapist working with women in the process of identity formation, *Women & Therapy*, 4(2), 17–22

Gummer, J.S. (1988) The freedom to choose that makes us human, *The Independent*, 8 October, 15

Hadley, S.W. & Strupp, H.H. (1976) Contemporary view of negative effects in psychotherapy, *Archives of General Psychiatry*, 33, 1291–1302

Hagan, K.L. (1988) *Internal Affairs: A Journalkeeping Workbook for Self Intimacy*, San Francisco: Harper Row

Hall, M. (1985) *The Lavender Couch: A Consumer's Guide to Psychotherapy for Lesbians and Gay Men*, Boston: Alyson Publications

—— (1987) Sex therapy with lesbian couples: A four stage approach, *Journal of Homosexuality*, 14(1/2), 137–156

Hall, M., Kitzinger, C., Loulan, J. & Perkins, R. (1992) The spoken word: Lesbian psychology, lesbian politics, *Feminism & Psychology*, 2(1), 7–25

Hamadock, S. (1988) Lesbian sexuality in the framework of psychotherapy: A practical model for the lesbian therapist, IN E. Cole & E.D. Rothblum (Eds) *Women and Sex Therapy: Closing the Circle of Sexual Knowledge*, New York: Harrington Park Press

Hamer, D. (1990) Significant others: Lesbianism and psychoanalytic theory, *Feminist Review*, 34, 134–151

Hanisch, C. (1971) The personal is political IN J. Agel (Ed) *The Radical Therapist*, New York: Ballantine Books

Hansen, G.L. (1982) Measuring prejudice against homosexuality (homosexism) among college students: A new scale, *Journal of Social Psychology*, 117, 233–236

Harris-Parker, D. & Cummins, G. (1991) *Consciousness Raising Groups for Adolescent Women*. Paper presented at the Association for Women in Psychology Conference, March 1991, Hartford, CT, USA

Hay, L. (1984a) *Heal Your Body: The Mental Causes for Physical Illness and the Metaphysical Way to Overcome Them*, London: Eden Grove Editions

Hay, L. (1984b) *Cancer: Discovering your Healing Power* (audiotape), Santa Monica, CA: Hay House Inc.

Hepburn, C. & Gutierrez, B. (1988) *Alive and Well: A Lesbian Health Guide*, Trumansburg, NY: The Crossing Press

Heriot, J. (1985) The double bind: Healing the split IN J.H. Robbins & R.J. Siegel (Eds) *Women Changing Therapy: New Assessment, New Values and Strategies in Feminist Therapy*, New York: Harrington Park Press

Hibbert, L. (1990) Letter in *Rouge* 3(summer), 5

Hill, M. (1990) On creating a theory of feminist therapy IN L. Brown & M. Root (Eds) *Diversity & Complexity in Feminist Therapy Part 1, Special Issue of Women & Therapy*, 9(1/2), 53–65

Himmelweit, S. (1988) More than "A woman's right to choose"?, *Feminist Review*, 29, 38–56

Hoagland, S.L. (1988) *Lesbian Ethics: Toward New Value*, Palo Alto: Institute of Lesbian Studies

Holland, S. (1991) From private symptoms to public action, *Feminism & Psychology*, 1(1), 58–62

Hooks, B. (1984) *Feminist Theory: From Margin to Centre*, Boston, MA: South End Press

Horney, K. (1942) *Our Inner Conflicts*, London: W.W. Norton

Hudson, W.W. & Ricketts, W.A. (1980) A strategy for the measurement of homophobia, *Journal of Homosexuality*, 5, 357–372

Imes, S. & Clance, P.R. (1984) Treatment of the imposter phenomenon in high achieving women IN C. Brody (Ed) *Women Therapists Working with Women: New Theory and Process in Feminist Therapy*, New York: Springer

Jackson, S. (1983) The desire for Freud: Psychoanalysis and feminism, *Trouble & Strife*, 1 (winter), 32–41

Jane (1986) Going mad IN *Finding our Own Solutions*, London: MIND

Jay, K. (1975) Oppression is big business: Scrutinising gay therapy IN K. Jay & A. Young (Eds) *After You're Out: Personal Experiences of Gay Men and Lesbian Women*, New York: Links

Jay, K. & Young, A. (Eds) *After You're Out: Personal Experiences of Gay Men and Lesbian Women*, New York: Links

Jeffreys, S. (1978) Therapy: Reform or revolution? *Spare Rib*, 69, 21

—— (1990a) *Anticlimax*, London: The Women's Press

—— (1990b) Eroticizing women's subordination IN D. Leidholt & J.G. Raymond (Eds) *The Sexual Liberals and the Attack on Feminism*, New York: Athene Series, Pergamon Press

Jo, B., Strega, L. & Ruston (1990) *Dykes-Loving-Dykes: Dyke Separatist Politics for Lesbians Only*, Oakland, CA: Battleaxe

Johnson, A. (1992) For feminists, talk is cheap: But in therapy it'll cost you $38 an hour (and that's on a sliding scale), *off our backs*, January, 8–9

Johnson, M. (1976) An approach to feminist therapy, *Psychotherapy: Theory, Research and Practice*, 13(1), 72–76

Johnson, N. (1981) The dragon slayer, *off our backs*, 6(5), 8

Johnston, J. (1973) *Lesbian Nation: The Feminist Solution*, New York: Simon & Schuster

Johnstone, L. (1989) *Users and Abusers of Psychiatry: A Critical Look at Traditional Psychiatric Practice*, London: Routledge

Kaminer, W. (1990) Chances are you're co-dependent too, *New York Times* Book Review, 11(Feb), 3, 26, 27

—— (1992) *I'm Dysfunctional, You're Dysfunctional: The Recovery Movement and Other Self-Help Fashions*, Reading, MA: Addison-Wesley

References

Kaufman, P.A., Harrison, E. & Hyde, M.L. (1984) Distancing and intimacy in lesbian relationships, *American Journal of Psychiatry*, 141(4), 530–533

Kitzinger, C. (1983) The politics of orgasm, *Revolutionary & Radical Feminist Newsletter* (Women Only), 12, 15–18

—— (1987a) *The Social Construction of Lesbianism*, London: Sage Publications

—— (1987b) Heteropatriarchal language: The case against homophobia, *Gossip: A Journal of Lesbian Feminist Ethics*, 5, 15–20

—— (1988) Sexuality: Cause, choice and construction, *Lesbian & Gay Socialist*, 15, 18–19

—— (1989a) Liberal humanism as an ideology of social control: The regulation of lesbian identities IN J. Shotter & K. Gergen (Eds) *Texts of Identity*, London: Sage Publications

—— (1989b) The rhetoric of pseudoscience IN I. Parker & J. Shotter (Eds) *Deconstructing Social Psychology*, London: Routledge

—— (1990a) Resisting the discipline IN E. Burman (Ed) *Feminists and Psychological Practice*, London: Sage Publications

—— (1990b) Heterosexism in psychology, *The Psychologist*, September, 391–392

—— (1991a) Feminism, psychology & the paradox of power, *Feminism & Psychology*, 1(1), 111–129

—— (1991b) The great miracle baby business, *New Internationalist*, 217 (March), 18–19

—— (1992a) Problematising pleasure: Radical feminist deconstructions of sexuality and power IN H.L. Radtke & H.J. Stam (Eds) *Gender and Power*, London: Sage Publications

—— (1992b) The 'real' lesbian feminist therapist: Who is she? *Feminism & Psychology*, 2(2), 262–264

214

Kitzinger, C. (1993) Editorial introduction IN C. Kitzinger (Ed) "Psychology constructs the female": A reappraisal, *Feminism & Psychology*, 3(2)

Kitzinger, C. & Wilkinson, S. (1993) A feminist critique of postmodernism, *Women's Studies International Forum* (forthcoming)

Kitzinger, C., Wilkinson, S. & Perkins, R. (1992) (Eds) *Heterosexuality: Special issue of "Feminism & Psychology: An International Journal"*, 2(3)

Kitzinger, J. (1990) Who are you kidding? Children, power and the struggle against child sexual abuse IN A. James & A. Prout (Eds) *Constructing and Reconstructing Childhood: Contemporary Issues in the Sociological Study of Children*, London: The Falmer Press

——— (1992) Sexual violence and compulsory heterosexuality IN C. Kitzinger, S. Wilkinson & R. Perkins (1992) (Eds) *Heterosexuality: Special issue of "Feminism & Psychology: An International Journal"*, 2(3)

Kitzinger, J. & Kitzinger, C. (1993 in press) 'Doing it': Representations of lesbian sex IN G. Griffin (Ed) *Outwrite: Popular/izing Lesbian Texts*, London: Pluto Press

Kitzinger, S. (1992) Heterosexuality: Challenge and opportunity, IN C. Kitzinger, S. Wilkinson & R. Perkins (1992) (Eds) *Heterosexuality: Special issue of "Feminism & Psychology: An International Journal"*, 2(3), 440–441

Kitzinger, S. & Kitzinger, C. (1989) *Talking with Children About Things that Matter*, London: Allen & Unwin – Pandora imprint (Also Munich: Biederstein, 1990; Milan: Bompiani, 1990. Published as *Tough Questions* by Harvard Common Press, 1991)

Koehner, P. (1991) Snap out of it (letter) *off our backs* Aug/Sept 1991, 27

Kramarae, C. & Treichler, P.A. (1985) *A Feminist Dictionary*, London: Pandora Press

Kreston, J. & Bepko, C.S. (1980) The problem of fusion in the lesbian relationship, *Family Process*, 19, 277–289

Kronemeyer, R. (1980) *Overcoming Homosexuality*, Macmillan: New York

Krzowski, S. (1988) Guidelines on running workshops, IN S. Krzowski & P. Land (Ed) *In Our Own Experience: Workshops at the London Women's Therapy Centre*, London: The Women's Press

Larsen, K., Reed, M. & Hoffman, S. (1980) Attitudes of heterosexuals towards homosexuality: A Likert-type scale and construct validity, *Journal of Sex Research*, 16, 245–257

Lauritzen, L. (1987) *The Dykes Digest*, London: Hit and Run Publications

Laws, S. (1991) Women on the verge, *Trouble & Strife*, 20, 8–12

Lee, A. (1986) Therapy: The evil within, *Trivia*, 9(fall), 34–44

Leeds Revolutionary Feminist Group (1981) Political lesbianism: The case against heterosexuality IN Onlywomen Press (Ed) *Love your enemy?: the debate between heterosexual feminism and political lesbianism*, London: Onlywomen Press

Lehne, G.K. (1976) Homophobia among men, IN D. Davis & R. Brannon (Eds) *The Forty-nine Percent Majority: The Male Sex Role*, Reading, MA: Addison-Wesley

Leidholdt, D. & Raymond, J. (1990) (Eds) *The Sexual Liberals and the Attack on Feminism*, New York: Pergamon Press

Leon, B. (1970) Brainwashing and women: The psychological attack, *It Ain't Me Babe*, (August), 10–12 Reprinted in Redstockings (Ed) (1978) *Feminist Revolution*, New York: Random House

Lerner, H. (1990) Problems for profit, *Women's Review of Books*, VII (7), 15–16

Livia, A. (1992) Dick dykes in the granola state, Unpublished short story

Lobel, K. (1986) *Naming the Violence: Speaking Out about Lesbian Battering*, Seattle, WA: The Seal Press

Lorde, A. (1980) *The Cancer Journals*, London: Sheba

Loulan, J. (1984) *Lesbian Sex*, San Francisco: Spinsters Ink

—— (1988) Research on the sex practices of 1566 lesbians and their clinical implications IN E. Cole & E.D. Rothblum (Eds) *Women and Sex Therapy: Closing the Circle of Sexual Knowledge*, New York: Harrington Park Press

—— (1990) *The Lesbian Erotic Dance*, San Francisco: Spinsters Book Company

Lugones, M. (1990) Playfulness, "world" – travelling, and loving perception, IN J. Allen, (Ed) *Lesbian Philosophies and Cultures*, New York: State University of New York Press

Lyn, L. (1991) It's a small world: Lesbian and bisexual women therapists' social interactions. Paper presented at the Association for Women in Psychology Conference, March 1991, Hartford, Connecticut, USA

McDaniel, J. (1982) We were fired: Lesbian experiences in academe, *Sinister Wisdom*, 20, 30–43

MacDonald, A.P. (1976) Homophobia: Its roots and meanings, *Homosexual Counseling Journal*, 3, 23–33

MacDonald. A.P. & Games, R.G. (1974) Some characteristics of those who hold positive and negative attitudes toward homosexuals, *Journal of Homosexuality*, 1, 9–27

McEwan, C. (1988) The colour of the water, the yellow of the field IN C. McEwan & S. O'Sullivan (Eds) *Out the Other Side: Contemporary Lesbian Writing*, London: Virago Press

MacKinnon, C. A. (1987) *Feminism Unmodified: Discourses on Life and Law*, Cambridge, MA: Harvard University Press

McCandlish, B.M. (1982) Therapeutic issues with lesbian couples, *Journal of Homosexuality*, 7, 71–78

Mainardi, P. (1970) The politics of housework IN R. Morgan (Ed) *Sisterhood is Powerful*, New York: Vintage Books

—— (1978) The marriage question IN Redstockings (Ed) *Feminist Revolution*, New York: Random House

Malina, D. (1987) On integrity and integration: Toward a feminist vision of psychology, *Women of Power: A Magazine of Feminism, Spiritualism & Politics*, 5, 14–17

Mann, B. (1987) Validation or liberation? A critical look at therapy and the women's movement, *Trivia*, 10, 41–56

Mara, J. (1985) A lesbian perspective IN J.H. Robbins & R.S. Siegel (Eds) *Women Changing Therapy: New Assessments, Values & Strategies in Feminist Therapy*, New York: Harrington Park Press

Margolies, L., Becker, M. & Jackson-Brewer, K. (1987) Internalised homophobia: Identifying and treating the oppressor within IN Boston Lesbian Psychologies Collective (Ed) *Lesbian Psychologies*, Urbana: University of Illinois Press

Marmor, J. (1980) *Homosexual Behaviour*, New York: Basic Books

Masson, J. (1988) *Against Therapy*, London: Fontana/Collins

Masterson, J. (1983) Lesbian consciousness raising discussion groups, *Journal for Specialists in Group Work*, 8, 24–30

Matazarro, J.D. (1967) Some psychotherapists make patients worse, *International Journal of Psychiatry*, 3(3), 156–157

Miller, M. (1985) An open letter to an abusive therapist, *Lesbian Ethics*, 1(3)

Millham, J., Miguel, C.L.S. & Kellogg, R. (1976) A factor analytic conceptualization of attitudes toward male and female homosexuals, *Journal of Homosexuality*, 2, 3–10

Mills, C.W. (1943) The professional ideology of the social pathologists, *American Journal of Sociology*, 49, 165–180

Miranda, J. & Storms, M. (1989) Psychological adjustment of lesbians and gay men, *Journal of Counseling and Development*, 68, 41–45

Mohin, L. (1987) Letter, *Gossip: A Journal of Lesbian Feminist Ethics*, 6, 19–20

—— (1993) (Ed) *An Intimacy of Equals: Lesbian Feminist Ethics*, London: Onlywomen Press

Morgan, R. (1972) *Monster*, New York: Random House

Morris, M. (1990) Is it within your power? *New Woman* (July), 58–60

Name Withheld (1991) Heterophobia, *off our backs*, 6(5), 8

Namka, L. (1989) *The Doormat Syndrome*, Deerfield Beach, FL: Health Communications Inc.

Nestle, J. (1981) New York lesbians illness support group: What being a lesbian means in the deepest sense, *off our backs*, 6(5), 8

Nichols, M. (1987a) Lesbian sexuality: issues and developing theory, IN Boston Lesbian Psychologies Collective (Ed) *Lesbian Psychologies*, Urbana: University of Illinois Press

—— (1987b) Doing sex therapy with lesbians: Bending a heterosexual paradigm to fit a gay life-style, IN Boston Lesbian Psychologies Collective (Ed) *Lesbian Psychologies*, Urbana: University of Illinois Press

North, M. (1972) *The Secular Priests*, London: Allen & Unwin

O'Donnell, M., Leoffler, V., Kater, P. & Saunders, Z. (1979) *Lesbian Health Matters*, Santa Cruz: Santa Cruz Women's Health Collective

Oliver-Diaz, P. & O'Gorman, P. (1990) *12 Steps to Self-Parenting for Adult Children*, Deerfield Beach, FL: Health Communications Inc.

O'Sullivan, S. (1984) Patients and power, *Trouble & Strife*, 3, 50–53

Padesky, C.A. (1989) Attaining and maintaining positive self-identity: A cognitive therapy approach, *Women & Therapy*, 8, 145–156

Payne, T. (1984) Postscript to S. Scott & T. Payne Underneath we're all lovable: Therapy and feminism, *Trouble & Strife*, 3, 21–24

Pearson, G. (1975) *The Deviant Imagination: Psychiatry, Social Work and Social Change*, London: Macmillan

Pembroke, L. (1991) Surviving psychiatry, *Nursing Times*, 87(49, Dec 4th), 30–32

Penelope, J. (1986) The mystery of lesbians, *Gossip: A Journal of Lesbian Feminist Ethics*, 2, 16–68

—— (1987) Letter, *Gossip: A Journal of Lesbian Feminist Ethics*, 6, 20–22

—— (1990a) The lesbian perspective, IN J. Allen, (Ed) *Lesbian Philosophies and Cultures*, New York: State University of New York Press

—— (1990b) Letter, *Women's Review of Books*, VII(10–11), 10

Perkins, R. (1991a) Therapy for lesbians? The case against, *Feminism & Psychology*, 1(3), 325–338

—— (1991b) Women with long-term mental health problems: Issues of power and powerlessness, *Feminism & Psychology*, 1(1), 131–139

—— (1992a) Catherine is having a baby ..., *Feminism & Psychology*, 2(1), 110–112

—— (1992b) Waiting for the revolution – or working for it? A reply to Laura Brown and Katherine Sender, *Feminism & Psychology*, 2(2), 258–261

—— (1992c) Working with socially disabled clients: A feminist perspective IN J. Ussher & P. Nicholson (Eds) *Gender Issues in Clinical Psychology*, London: Routledge

—— (1992d) Worlds Apart: A lesbian feminist approach to madness and social disability. Paper presented at the Association for Women in Psychology National Feminist Psychology Conference, February, Long Beach, CA

Perkins, R. & Bishop, J. (forthcoming) *Madness and Feminist Communities*

Perkins, R. & Dilks, S. (1992) Worlds apart: Working with severely socially disabled people, *Journal of Mental Health*, 1(1), 3–17

Perkins, R. & Rowland, L. (1990) Sex differences in service usage in long-term psychiatric care: Are women adequately served? *British Journal of Psychiatry*, 158 (suppl. 10), 75–79

Perlman, S.F. (1989) Distancing and connectedness: Impact on couple formation and lesbian relationships, *Women & Therapy*, 8(1), 77–88

Perls, F. (1972) *Gestalt Therapy Verbatim*, New York: Bantam Books

Peslikis I. (1970) Resistence to consciousness, IN S. Firestone (Ed) *Notes from the Third Year*, New York: Random House

Pies, C. (1985) *Considering Parenthood: A Workbook for Lesbians*, San Francisco: Spinsters Ink

Price, J.H. (1972) *Psychiatric Investigations*, London: Butterworth

—— (1982) High school students' attitudes toward homosexuality, *Journal of School Health*, 52, 469–474

Quinn, K. (1985) The killing ground: Police powers and psychiatry IN C.T. Mowbray, S. Lanir & M. Hulce (Eds) *Women and Mental Health*, New York: Harrington Park Press

Raban, J. (1989) *God, Man & Mrs Thatcher: A Critique of Mrs Thatcher's Address to the General Assembly of the Church of Scotland*, London: Chatto & Windus

Radicalesbians (1969) *Woman-Identified Woman*, Somerville, MA: New England Free Press

Rand, C., Graham, D. & Rawlings, E. (1982) Psychological health and factors the court seeks to control in lesbian mother custody trials, *Journal of Homosexuality*, 8, 27–39

Rapping, E. (1990) Hooked on a feeling, *The Nation*, March 5th, 5, 316–319

Ray, S. *I Deserve Love: How Affirmations can Guide You to Personal Fulfilment*, Berkeley, CA: Celestial Arts

Raymond, J. (1986) *A Passion for Friends. Toward a Philosophy of Female Affection*, London: The Women's Press

Reid, P.T. (1991) Presidential message, *Psychology of Women* (Newsletter of Division 35 of the American Psychological Association), 18(4), 1–2

Rich, A. (1977) *Women and Honor: Some Notes on Lying*, Pittsburgh: Motheroot Publications

——— (1978) Disloyal to civilisation: Feminism, racism and gynephobia, *Chrysalis: A Magazine of Women's Culture*, 7, 29–38. Reprinted in A. Rich (1980) *On Lies, Secrets and Silence*, London: Virago

——— (1980) Compulsory heterosexuality and lesbian existence, *Signs: Journal of Women in Culture and Society*, 5(4), 631–660

Richardson, D. & Hart, J. (1980) Gays in therapy: Getting it right, *New Forum: The Journal of the Psychology and Psychotherapy Association*, 6, 58–60

Rickford, F. (1981) Letter to Onlywomen Press IN Onlywomen Press (Eds) *Love Your Enemy?: the debate between heterosexual feminism and political lesbianism*, London: Onlywomen Press

Robertson, I. (1989) Stewed in corruption, *British Medical Journal*, 299, 1046–1047

Rosaldo, M.Z. (1984) Toward an anthropology of self and feeling IN R.A. Schweder & R.A. Levine (Eds) *Culture Theory: Essays on Mind, Self and Emotion*, Cambridge: Cambridge University Press

Rosen, G. (1976) *Don't be Afraid*, Englewood Cliffs, NJ: Prentice Hall

——— (1987) Self-help books and the commercialization of psychology, *American Psychologist*, 42(1), 46–51

Rosen, G.M., Glasgow, R.E. & Barren, M. (1976) A controlled study to assess the clinical efficacy of totally self-administered systematic desensitisation, *Journal of Consulting and Clinical Psychology*, 44, 208–217

Roth, S. (1989) Psychotherapy with lesbian couples: Individual issues, female socialization, and the social context IN M. McGoldrick, C. Anderson & F. Walsh (Eds) *Women in Families: A Framework for Family Therapy*, New York: Norton

Rothman, B.K. (1986) *The Tentative Pregnancy*, New York: Viking Penguin

Rothblum, E.D. & Cole, E. (1989) *Loving Boldly: Issues Facing Lesbians*, New York: Harrington Park Press

Rowland, R. (1982) *The Anatomy of Freedom*, Garden City, New York: Anchor/Doubleday

—— (1992) Radical feminist heterosexuality: The personal and the political, IN C. Kitzinger, S. Wilkinson and R. Perkins (Eds) *Heterosexuality: Special issue of "Feminism & Psychology: An International Journal"*, 2(3), 459–464

Russ, J. (1981) Power and helplessness in the women's movement, *Sinister Wisdom*, 18, 49–56

Ryan, J. (1983) Psychoanalysis and women loving women, IN S. Cartledge & J. Ryan (Eds) *Sex & Love. New Thoughts on Old Contradictions*, London: The Women's Press

—— (1988) (with P. Trevithick) Lesbian workshop IN S. Krzowski & P. Land (Eds) *In Our Experience: Workshops at the Women's Therapy Centre*, London: The Women's Press

Sarachild, K. (1978) Psychological terrorism IN Redstockings (Ed) *Feminist Revolution*, New York: Random House

Satir, V. (1976) *Self-Esteem*, Milbrae, CA: Celestial Arts

Schofield, W. (1964) *Psychotherapy: The Purchase of Friendship*, Englewood Cliffs, NJ: Prentice Hall

References

Scott, S. & Payne, T. (1984) Underneath we're all loveable: Therapy and feminism, *Trouble & Strife*, 3, 21–24

Seamoon House (1981) cited in C. Kramarae & P.A. Treichler, (1985) *A Feminist Dictionary*, London: Pandora Press

Sender, K. (1992) Lesbians, therapy and politics: Inclusion and diversity, *Feminism & Psychology*, 2(2), 255–257

Sethna, C. (1992) Accepting 'total and complete responsibility': New age neo-feminist violence against women, *Feminism & Psychology*, 2(1), 113–119

Sharratt, S. & Bern. L. (1985) Lesbian couples and families: A co-therapeutic approach to counseling IN L.B. Rosewater & L.E.A. Walker (Eds) *Handbook of Feminist Therapy*, New York: Springer

Showalter, E. (1985) *The Female Malady: Women, Madness and English Culture, 1830–1980*, London: Virago

Shulman, S. (1981) Lesbian feminists and the great baby con, *Spinster*, 4, 7–23

Siegel, R.J. (1985) Beyond homophobia: Learning to work with lesbian clients IN L. Rosewater & L.E.A. Walker (Eds) *Handbook of Feminist Therapy*, New York: Springer

Silveira, J. (1985) Lesbian feminist therapy: A report of some thoughts, *Lesbian Ethics*, 1(3), 22–27

Singer, A. (1990) Letter, *Women's Review of Books*, VII (July), 10–11

Sisley, E.L. & Harris, B. (1977) *The Joy of Lesbian Sex*, New York: Simon & Schuster

Sophie, J. (1982) Counseling lesbians, *The Personnel and Guidance Journal*, 6, 341–345

—— (1987) Internalised homophobia and lesbian identity, *Journal of Homosexuality*, 14, 53–65

Spence, J. (1990) Sharing the wounds: Interview with J.Z. Grover, *Women's Review of Books*, VII(July), 38–39

Spender, D. (1980) *Man Made Language*, London: Routledge & Kegan Paul

—— (1984) Untitled IN R. Rowland (Ed), *Women who do and women who don't join the women's movement*, London: RKP

—— (1986) *Women of Ideas and What Men have Done to Them*. London: The Women's Press

Spitzer, T. (1980) *Psychobattery: A Chronical of Psychotherapeutic Abuse*, Clifton, NJ: Humana Press

Steinem, G. (1992) *Revolution From Within: A Book of Self-Esteem*, London: Bloomsbury

Sternhell, C. (1992) Sic transit Gloria, *Women's Review of Books*, IX(9), 5–6

Stone, G.P. & Faberman, H.A. (1981) *Social Psychology through Symbolic Interaction*, 2nd Edn, Chichester, Sussex: Wiley

Storr, A. (1964) *Sexual Deviation*, London: Penguin

Strega, L. (1990) Worker, heal yourself IN B. Jo, L. Strega & Ruston *Dykes-Loving-Dykes: Dyke Separatist Politics for Lesbians Only*, Oakland: Battleaxe

Strega, L. & Jo, B. (1986) Lesbian sex: Is it? *Gossip: A Journal of Lesbian Feminist Ethics*, 3, 65–76

Strupp, H.H. (1973) *Psychotherapy: Clinical Research and Theoretical Issues*, New York: Aronson

Swan, B.L. (1989) *Thirteen Steps: An Empowerment Process for Women*, San Francisco: Spinsters/Aunt Lute Book Company

Tallen, B.S. (1990a) Twelve step programs: A lesbian feminist critique, *National Women's Studies Association Journal*, 2(3), 390–407

—— (1990b) Co-dependency: A feminist critique, *Sojourner*, 15 (January), 20–21

Tavris, C. (1990) In other words, that's life, *Los Angeles Times*, 6.10.1990

Tavris, C. (1992) Has time stood still for women? *Los Angeles Times*, 2.20.1992

Tessina, T. (1989) *Gay Relationships*, Los Angeles: Jeremy P. Tarcher

Thompson, D. (1985) Anger IN S.E. Browne, D. Connors & N. Stern (Eds) *With the Power of Each Breath: A Disabled Women's Anthology*, San Francisco: Cleis Press

—— (1991) *Reading Between the Lines: A Lesbian Feminist Critique of Feminist Accounts of Sexuality*, Sydney, Australia: Gorgons Head Press

Toder, N. (1978) Lesbian sex problems IN G. Vida (Ed) *Our Right to Love: A Lesbian Resource Book*, Englewood Cliffs, NJ: Prentice Hall

Trevithick, P. & Ryan, J. (1988) Lesbian workshop in S. Krzowski & P. Lane (Eds) *In Our Own Experience: Workshops at the Women's Therapy Centre*, London: The Women's Press

Walker, M. (1990) *Women in Therapy and Counselling*, Milton Keynes: Open University Press

Ward, J.M. (1988) Therapism and the taming of the lesbian community, *Sinister Wisdom*, 36, 33–41

Waterhouse, R. (1993) "Wild women don't have the blues": A feminist critique of "person centred" counselling and therapy, *Feminism & Psychology*, 3(1), 54–71

Wegscheider-Cruse, S. (1988) *Choicemaking: For Codependents, Adult Children and Spirituality Seekers*, Deerfield Beach, FL: Health Communications Inc.

Weinberg, G. (1973) *Society and the Healthy Homosexual*, New York: Anchor

Weis, C.B. & Dain, R.N. (1979) Ego development and sex attitudes in heterosexual and homosexual men and women, *Archives of Sexual Behavior*, 8, 341–356

Weisstein, N. (1970) Psychology constructs the female, IN R. Morgan (Ed) *Sisterhood is Powerful*, New York: Vintage Books reprinted in C. Kitzinger (Ed) "Psychology constructs the Female": A reappraisal, *Feminism & Psychology*, 3(2)

Wenz, K. (1988) Women's peace of mind: Possibilities in using the writing process in counselling, Association of Women in Psychology – Arizona Chapter, 1988 Regional Conference, Arizona State University

West, D.J. (1968) *Homosexuality*, Harmondsworth: Penguin

Wetherell, M. & Griffin, C. (1991) (Eds) Feminist psychology and the study of men and masculinity: Part I, Assumptions and perspectives, *Feminism & Psychology*, 1(3), 361–392

—— (1992) Feminist psychology and the study of men and masculinity: Part II, Politics and practices, *Feminism & Psychology*, 2(2), 133–168

White, M. (1991) *The Dyke Daily Companion: Positive Reminders for Lesbians*, Denver: Makaw Press

Wilkinson, S. (1990) Women organizing within psychology IN E.Burman (Ed) *Feminists and Psychological Practice*, London: Sage Publications

Wilkinson, S. & Kitzinger, C. (1993a) Whose breast is it anyway? A feminist consideration of advice and 'treatment' for breast cancer, *Women's Studies International Forum* (in press)

—— (1993b) *Heterosexuality: A "Feminism and Psychology" Reader*, London: Sage Publications

Winterson, J. (1989) Mind your head, *The Guardian*, 27.1.1989

World Health Organisation (1978) *International Classification of Diseases* (ICD – 9) Geneva: World Health Organisation

Zilbergeld, B. (1983) *The Shrinking of America*, Boston: Little, Brown & Co.

Onlywomen Press publishes fiction, poetry and theory to express and illuminate a developing Radical Lesbian Feminism. We have also established the U.K.'s first annual award for Lesbian feminist poetry, the Margot Jane Memorial Poetry Prize.

Some of Onlywomen's non-fiction and poetry titles are listed on the following pages.

VOLCANOES AND PEARL DIVERS: Lesbian Feminist Studies
ed. Suzanne Raitt

This anthology of lesbian literary and cultural criticism is, as the editor remarks, "about the relationship of politics with pleasure". Twelve essays by academics and practitioners (theatre and poetry) detail the work of English language lesbian writers – 17th century verse, 19th century novels, 20th century fiction, poetry and film. Overall, *Volcanoes and Pearl Divers* addresses three centuries of lesbian culture in contemporary feminist terms.

AN INTIMACY OF EQUALS: Lesbian Feminist Ethics
ed. Lilian Mohin

The diverse strands of lesbian ethical strategies in the 1990s make this an intellectually challenging anthology placing well researched theory alongside autobiographical narrative. *An Intimacy of Equals* examines what lesbians gain, if anything, from our connections both within and against the 'mainstream'. Includes work by: Julia Penelope, Celia Kitzinger, Anna Livia, Joyce Cunningham, Sheila Shulman, Patricia Duncker, Rosie Waite, Carole Reeves, Nett Hart, Rachel Perkins and Lis Whitelaw.

FOR LESBIANS ONLY: A Separatist Anthology
ed. Sarah Hoagland & Julia Penelope

An anthology that covers 20 years of radical political work by lesbians. This 600 page collection demands a stepping away from the culture at large in order to analyse – everything – from a lesbian point of view.

BECAUSE OF INDIA: Selected Poems and Fables
Suniti Namjoshi

Work selected from 9 of Suniti's earlier collections are accompanied by prose essays setting the personal and political context of her exemplary poetry. *"blending that which is uncompromisingly Indian with the best of the English satirical tradition."*

LOVE, DEATH AND THE CHANGING OF THE SEASONS
Marilyn Hacker

Elegant sonnets combined to make a verse novel. Formal poetry that tells of the beginning, middle and end of a love affair with a younger woman. *"versatile in the strictest forms, inventive and exuberant in content ... colloquial, lyrical, uncouth, old-fashioned and fun."*

PASSION IS EVERYWHERE APPROPRIATE
Caroline Griffin

First collection from a much anthologised poet. These detail contemporary lesbian life in Britain. Poems with an exhilarating faith in our independent strengths.

THE WORK OF A COMMON WOMAN
Judy Grahn
introduction by **Adrienne Rich**

A collection from the heart of feminism – humour, intensity, realism. As Adrienne Rich says, *"The necessity of poetry has to be stated over and over, but only to those who have reason to fear its power, or those who still believe that language is 'only words' and that an old language is good enough for our descriptions of the world we are trying to transform."*

Our books may be purchased from good bookshops everywhere or by mail-order directly from Onlywomen. For a catalogue detailing all our publications, send S.A.E. to: Onlywomen Press, 71 Great Russell Street, London WC1B 3BN.